Neural Network for Beginners

Build Deep Neural Networks and Develop Strong Fundamentals Using Python's NumPy, and Matplotlib

Sebastian Klaas

www.bpbonline.com

FIRST EDITION 2022

Copyright © BPB Publications, India

ISBN: 978-93-89423-716

LIMITS OF LIABILITY AND DISCLAIMER OF WARRANTY

To View Complete
BPB Publications Catalogue
Scan the QR Code:

Dedicated to

My lovely little daughters: Julie and Rene.
Your endless love and energy charge me every day.
And to my beautiful and patient wife Tifany.
That's all thanks to you.
You are the light of my life.

I love you

About the Author

Sebastian Klaas, data science professional who has great organizational and communication skills. He enjoys solving problems and coming up with unique solutions. I have 10+ year of experience working in data consultancy, customer experience, product analytics, and survey analytics.

He is passionate about Big Data Analysis, Data Driven Decision Making, Data Mining, Data Wrangling, Data Modelling and Predictions, Forecasting the Future, Data Visualization.

Technical statistical and data analysis tools he has grip on includes R, Python, Microsoft Excel, Microsoft SQL.

About the Reviewer

Leonardo Machado is a full stack software engineer and a graduate of General Assembly's Software Engineering Immersive bootcamp. He loves creating mobile friendly applications and designing products that solve problems. He is specialized in JavaScript, React, MERN-stack apps, Python and Django.

Acknowledgement

There are a few people I want to thank for the support they have given me during the writing of this book. First and foremost, I would like to thank my parents for continuously encouraging me to write the book. I could have never completed this book without their support.

My gratitude also goes to the team at BPB Publications for being supportive enough to provide me quite a long time to finish the book and also giving us the opportunity and providing us the necessary support in writing this book.

We would like to thank our family members for the support they have provided for us to focus on the book during our personal time.

Preface

This book deals with profound learning and covers the knowledge needed to comprehend it gradually from the fundamentals, including what it is, what it means, and how the reader may understand the essential technologies as easily as possible.

So what are we gonna do to get deep learning better? Well, one of the greatest methods to do anything is to do practical activities such as creating a programme from scratch that encourages critical thinking when reading a source code. In this sense, "from scratch" means utilizing as few as possible external objects (such libraries and tools). The objective of this book is to use these "black boxes," the content of which is unknown, to start with a minimum level of fundamental information on which you may construct, analyze and execute in order for profound education programmes to be understandable and state-of-the-art. If you compare this book with a handbook for a car, it is not a manual that demonstrates how a car is driven; it is one that is focused on comprehending the concept of a car. It enables you to open the car's hood, to remove and study each part for its shape, function, and position before it is assembled and your model is constructed to its precise proportions and operations. This book is designed to make you feel like you can construct an automobile and familiarize yourself with the technology behind it. We shall utilize Python to carry out profound learning in this book. Python is a most popular and user-friendly programming language. It is ideal for the production of prototypes. You may quickly test your ideas and do different experiments while checking the outcomes. This book outlines the theoretical components of profound knowledge during the course of Python programmes. You may frequently detect, by reading and executing a source code, what you cannot grasp only by a mathematical expression or theoretical description. This book focuses on "engineering" – comprehending profound learning through creating programmes. From a programmer's point of view, you will see much math and also many source codes.

The book consists of eight chapters, in which the reader will learn the following:

Chapter 1 describes how to install and use Python.

Chapter 2 will describe a perceptron and use one to solve easy problems.

Chapter 3 provides an overview of neural networks and focuses on what distinguishes them.

Chapter 4 we will be introduced to the method of using the gradient of a function, called a gradient method, to discover the smallest loss function value.

Chapter 5 covers backpropagation, which is a more efficient way to calculate the gradients of weight parameters.

Chapter 6 describes important ideas in neural network training, including the optimization techniques that are used to search for optimal weight parameters, the initial values of weight parameters, and the method for setting hyperparameters.

Chapter 7 will detail the mechanisms of CNNs and how to implement them in Python.

Chapter 8 will describe the characteristics, problems, and possibilities of deep learning, as well as an overview of current deep learning practices.

Downloading the code bundle and coloured images:

Please follow the link to download the
Code Bundle and the *Coloured Images* of the book:

https://rebrand.ly/848998

Find code in action here:

https://rebrand.ly/0dcf77

Errata

We take immense pride in our work at BPB Publications and follow best practices to ensure the accuracy of our content to provide with an indulging reading experience to our subscribers. Our readers are our mirrors, and we use their inputs to reflect and improve upon human errors, if any, that may have occurred during the publishing processes involved. To let us maintain the quality and help us reach out to any readers who might be having difficulties due to any unforeseen errors, please write to us at :

errata@bpbonline.com

Your support, suggestions and feedbacks are highly appreciated by the BPB Publications' Family.

Did you know that BPB offers eBook versions of every book published, with PDF and ePub files available? You can upgrade to the eBook version at www.bpbonline.com and as a print book customer, you are entitled to a discount on the eBook copy. Get in touch with us at :

business@bpbonline.com for more details.

At **www.bpbonline.com**, you can also read a collection of free technical articles, sign up for a range of free newsletters, and receive exclusive discounts and offers on BPB books and eBooks.

BPB is searching for authors like you

If you're interested in becoming an author for BPB, please visit **www.bpbonline.com** and apply today. We have worked with thousands of developers and tech professionals, just like you, to help them share their insight with the global tech community. You can make a general application, apply for a specific hot topic that we are recruiting an author for, or submit your own idea.

The code bundle for the book is also hosted on GitHub at **https://github.com/bpbpublications/Neural-Network-for-Beginners**. In case there's an update to the code, it will be updated on the existing GitHub repository.

We also have other code bundles from our rich catalog of books and videos available at **https://github.com/bpbpublications**. Check them out!

PIRACY

If you come across any illegal copies of our works in any form on the internet, we would be grateful if you would provide us with the location address or website name. Please contact us at **business@bpbonline.com** with a link to the material.

If you are interested in becoming an author

If there is a topic that you have expertise in, and you are interested in either writing or contributing to a book, please visit **www.bpbonline.com**.

REVIEWS

Please leave a review. Once you have read and used this book, why not leave a review on the site that you purchased it from? Potential readers can then see and use your unbiased opinion to make purchase decisions, we at BPB can understand what you think about our products, and our authors can see your feedback on their book. Thank you!

For more information about BPB, please visit **www.bpbonline.com**.

Table of Contents

1. Python Introduction..1

    Structure...1

    Objective..2

    Know about Python 2

    Python setup...3

        Versions of Python 3

        External libraries 3

    Distribution of Anaconda 4

    Interpreter of Python..4

    Mathematical operations 5

        Data types..5

    Variables...6

    Lists..6

    Dictionaries..7

    Boolean..8

    If statements..8

    For statements..9

    Functions..9

    Python script files 10

    Saving in a file 10

    Classes..10

    NumPy 12

        Importing NumPy 12

        Create an array of numbers 12

        Mathematical operations in NumPy 12

        N-dimensional NumPy arrays 13

        Broadcasting 14

        Accessing elements 15

    Matplotlib 16

        Drawing a simple graph 16

        Features of pyplot..17

Displaying images *18*

Conclusion 19

2. Perceptron in Depth **21**

Structure 21

Objective 22

What is a perceptron? 22

Simple logic circuits 23

    AND gate *23*

    NAND and OR gates *24*

    Implementing perceptron *25*

    Weights and bias introduction *26*

    Implementation with weights and bias *26*

    Limitations of perceptron *28*

    XOR gate *28*

Linear and nonlinear 29

Multilayer perceptron 30

    Combination of gates *30*

    XOR gate implementation *31*

    A computer from NAND *32*

Conclusion 33

3. Neural Networks **35**

Introduction 35

Structure 35

Objective 36

From perceptrons to neural systems 36

    Neural network example *36*

Perceptron review 37

    Presentation of an activation function *39*

Activation function 40

Sigmoid function 40

    Implementation of a step *41*

    Step function graph *42*

        Sigmoid function implementation *43*

Nonlinear function 45

ReLU function 46

    Multidimensional array calculation 47

        Multidimensional arrays 47

        Matrix multiplication 48

        Neural network matrix multiplication 52

Implementation of a network for three layers 53

    Examining the symbols 53

    Transmission of signal in each layer 54

Summary of implementation 57

    The output layer design 59

Softmax identity feature and function 59

    Issues when implementing the Softmax function 61

    Softmax feature characteristics 62

Handwritten digit recognition 64

MNIST dataset 64

Inference for neural network 67

Batch processing 69

Conclusion 72

4. Training Neural Network 73

Structure 73

Objective 74

Learning from data 74

Data-driven 74

Training data and test data 76

Loss function 77

Sum of squared errors 78

Cross-entropy error 79

Mini-batch learning 80

    Implementing cross-entropy error (using batches) 82

    Why configure a loss function? 83

Numerical differentiation 85

    Derivative 85

    Examples of numerical differentiation 87

Partial derivative...89

Gradient 91

    Gradient method 93

    Gradients for a neural network...96

Implementing a training algorithm 99

    Presupposition 99

A two-layer neural network as a class...99

Implementing mini-batch training..103

Using test data for evaluation...105

Conclusion 108

5. Backpropagation...109

Structure..109

Objective..110

Computational graphs 111

    Using computational graphs to solve problems....................111

Local calculation 112

    Why do we use computational graphs? 113

Chain rule 114

Backward propagation in a computational graph....................115

    What is chain rule?...115

Chain rule and computational graphs..116

Backward propagation..117

    Backward propagation in an addition node 117

    Backward propagation in a multiplication node.................119

        Orange example...120

Implementing a simple layer 121

Implementing a multiplication layer 121

    Implementing an addition layer 123

Implementing the activation function layer 125

ReLU layer 125

Sigmoid layer 127

Implementing the affine and softmax layers.............................130

    Affine layer..130

Batch-based affine layer 133

Softmax loss layer 135

Implementing backpropagation 138

Overview of neural network training 138

Presupposition 138

Implementing a neural network that supports backpropagation 139

Gradient check 142

Training using backpropagation 144

Conclusion 145

6. Neural Network Training Techniques **147**

Structure 147

Objective: 148

Updating parameters 148

Story of an adventurer 149

Stochastic Gradient Descent (SGD) 149

Disadvantage of SGD 150

Momentum 152

AdaGrad 154

Adam 155

Which update technique should we use? 156

Using the MNIST dataset to compare the update techniques 157

Initial weight values 158

How to set the initial weight values to zero? 158

Distribution of hidden layers of activation 159

Initial weight values for ReLU 164

Using the MNIST dataset to compare the weight initializers 165

Batch normalization 166

Batch normalization algorithm 166

Evaluating batch normalization 168

Regularization 170

Overfitting 170

Weight decay 172

Dropout 173

Validating hyperparameters 176

    Validation data 176

    Optimizing hyperparameters 177

    Implementing hyperparameter optimization 178

Conclusion 180

7. CNN **183**

Structure 183

Objective 184

Architecture 184

The convolution layer 185

    Demerits with the Affine 185

Processing 186

    Padding 188

    Stride 188

    Performing a convolution operation on three-dimensional data 190

Thinking in blocks 192

Batch processing 193

The pooling layer 194

    Characteristics of a pooling layer 195

It is resilient to a small change in position 195

Implementing the convolution and pooling layers 195

Four-dimensional arrays 196

    Expansion by im2col 196

    Implementing a convolution layer 198

    Implementing a pooling layer 200

Implementing a CNN 202

Visualizing a CNN 207

    Visualizing the weight of the first layer 207

    Using a hierarchical information extraction structure 208

Typical CNNs 208

    LeNet 208

    AlexNet 209

Conclusion 209

8. **Deep Learning**... 211

   Structure... 211

   Objective 212

   Making a network deeper 212

      Deeper networks 212

   Enhanced recognition accuracy.. 214

   Motivation for a deeper network 215

   A brief history of deep learning.. 217

      ImageNet.. 217

      VGG... 218

      GoogLeNet 219

      ResNet.. 220

      Accelerating deep learning 221

      Overcoming challenges.. 221

      Acceleration by using GPUs 222

      Distributed training 223

      Reducing the arithmetic accuracy bit number................... 223

   Practical uses of deep learning 225

      Object detection 225

      Segmentation 225

      Image caption generation.. 226

   The future of deep learning... 227

      Converting image styles 227

      Generating images... 228

      Automated driving 228

      Deep Q-Nets (reinforcement learning).............................. 229

   Conclusion 231

Index 233-238

CHAPTER 1
Python Introduction

It has been almost twenty years since the programming language, Python, was released. It has grown and expanded its user base over this era. Python is the world's most used programming today.

Structure

- Know about Python
- Python setup
  - Versions of Python
  - External Libraries
- Distribution of Anaconda
- Interpreter of Python
- Mathematical operations
  - Data types
- Variables
- Lists
- Dictionaries
- Boolean

- If statements
- For statements
- Functions
- Python script files
  - o Saving in a file
- Classes
- NumPy
  - o Importing NumPy
  - o Create an array of numbers
  - o Mathematical operations in NumPy
  - o N-dimensional NumPy arrays
  - o Broadcasting
  - o Accessing elements
- Matplotlib
  - o Drawing a simple graph
  - o Features of pyplot
  - o Displaying images

Objective

We will use this book to construct a deep learning system in this powerful language. This chapter provides a quick explanation of Python and how it may be used.

Know about Python

Python is an easy-to-read-and-learn language. This language is open source and you can use it as freely as you like. Without time-consuming compilation, you can build a software that employs English grammar. This makes Python easy-to-use so that beginner coders may choose from it. In fact, Python is the first language that is taught at many computer science courses in universities and professional institutions.

Python allows you to build high-performance (quick) and understandable languages. Python will suit your demands if large data processing and high-speed answers are necessary. That is why both beginner and professional Python are favorites.

Python is often used by cutting-edge IT businesses like Google, Microsoft, and Facebook. It is often used in research, especially in machine learning and data science. Python holds an important place in the field of data science, due to its high performance and good libraries for numerical and statistical calculations (for example, NumPy and SciPy). It is commonly used as a backbone to deep learning frameworks like Caffe (Python interface), TensorFlow, and PyTorch. Therefore it is equally useful to understand Python when you want to use a deep learning framework.

In data science in particular, Python is the optimum programming language since it offers many user-friendly and effective functions for novices and specialists alike. For these reasons, deep learning from the basics is the logical choice for fulfilling the purpose of this book.

Python setup

In this section you will find various ways by which Python is installed in your environment (PC).

Versions of Python

Two main versions of Python are available: version 2 and version 3. The two are in active usage at the moment. You need to carefully pick the version you want when installing Python. Some of Python 3's applications cannot be executed in Python 2. Python 3 is used in this book. If Python 2 only is installed, it is suggested to install Python 3.

External libraries

Deep learning from the basics is the aim of this book. So, it's our strategy to utilize external libraries as little as we can, NumPy and Matplotlib being the two exceptions. These two libraries are used to execute deep learning efficiently.

NumPy is a numbering library; it offers numerous practical ways to handle complex arithmetic algorithms and arrays (matrices). We will utilize these easy approaches for efficient implementation of deep learning in this book.

Matplotlib is another external library used as a graphics library. You may view experimental findings using Matplotlib and view the data during profound learning. These libraries are used for deeper study in this book.

The following language and libraries are used for the present book:

- Matplotlib
- Python 3
- NumPy

Now we are going to discuss how Python can be installed on the system for people who require it. You can skip this section if you have previously satisfied these criteria.

Distribution of Anaconda

Although a lot of options for the installation of Python are available, this book suggests using an Anaconda distribution. Distributions contain necessary libraries so the users may collectively install them. Data analysis is the aim of the Anaconda distribution. It also provides libraries that have been mentioned above to be useful for data analysis; for example, NumPy and Matplotlib.

This book uses Python 3, as we said earlier. Therefore, the Anaconda package for Python 3 must be installed. Use the link below to download and install the appropriate distribution for your operating system (OS).

https://docs.anaconda.com/anaconda/install/

Interpreter of Python

Start by checking the version once Python is installed. Open a Terminal (Windows command prompt) and enter the **python —version** command. This command is used to output the installed version of Python:

```
$ python --version
```

```
Python 3.4.1 :: Anaconda 2.1.0 (x86_64)
```

If Python 3.4.1 (depending on the version installed), as seen in the previous command, is displayed, then Python 3 is successfully installed. Now type **python** and start the interpreter for Python:

```
$ python
```

```
Python 3.4.1 |Anaconda 2.1.0 (x86_64)| (default, Sep 10 2014, 17:24:09)
[GCC 4.2.1 (Apple Inc. build 5577)] on Darwin
```

```
Type "help", "copyright", "credits" or "license" for more information.
```

```
>>>
```

The interactive mode through which you may interact with Python to develop languages is also known as the Python interpreter. Interaction implies that when you ask, for example, "What's a 2+3" the Python interpreter responds with "5".

Enter the following:

```
>>> 2 + 3
```

5

This allows you to develop languages interactively with the Python interpreter. In this book, we will deal with simple examples of Python programming using an interactive manner.

Mathematical operations

Mathematical operations like addition and multiplication can be carried out as follows:

```
>>> 5 - 6
-1
>>> 5 * 7
35
>>> 6 / 3
2
>>> 2 ** 3
9
```

From the preceding operation, it is easy to understand that ***** means multiplication, **/** is split, and ****** signifies exponentiation. (**2**3** is 3's second force.) In Python 2, an integer is returned when you divide two entries. The outcome of **6/3**, for instance, is **2**. In Python 3, however, a floating-point value is produced when you divide two integer numbers.

Data types

There are data types in programming. A data type specifies the data character as an integer, a floating-point number, or a string. The **type()** method for checking the data type is provided by Python:

```
>>> type(50)
<class 'int'>
>>> type(3.697)
<class 'float'>
>>> type("hey")
<class 'str'>
```

The preceding output show that **50** is **int** (integer type), **3.697** is **float** (float type), and **hey** is **str** (string type). Sometimes the words "*type*" and "*class*" are employed to the same degree. The result, **<class 'int'>**, might be construed as **50** is an **int** class (type).

Variables

Use alphabetically defined letters like **a** and **b** to define variables. Variables can also be used to compute or assign a different variable value:

```
>>> a = 50 # Initialize
>>> print(a)
50
>>> a = 200 # Assign
>>> print(a)
200
>>> b = 3.14
>>> a * b
314.0
>>> type(a * b)
<class 'float'>
```

Python is a programming language that is dynamically typed. Dynamic means that, based on the scenario, the type of variable is automatically decided. The user does not expressly indicate in the previous example that **a** type is **int** (integer). Python decides that the **a** type is **int** since an integer, **50,** is initialized. The preceding example also illustrates that a decimal is returned by multiplying the integer (automatic type conversion). The **#** symbol indicates characters that Python ignores succeeding characters.

Lists

To assign various integers to a variable, you can use a list (array):

```
>>> x = [5, 6, 8, 7, 9] # Create a list
>>> print(x) # Print the content of the list
[5, 6, 8, 7, 9]
>>> len(x) # Get the length of the list
5
>>> x[0] # Access the first element
5
>>> x[3]
7
```

```
>>> x[4] = 199 # Assign a value
>>> print(x)
[5, 6, 8, 7, 199]
```

For instance, to access an element, **x[0]** can be written. The **[ ]** number is referred to as an index starting at **0**. (The index 0 indicates the first element). Python lists are given with a handy syntax called **slicing**. To access both a single element and a sublist, you can use slicing:

```
>>> print(x)
[5, 6, 8, 7, 199]
>>> x[0:2] # Obtain from the zero index to the second index (the second
one is not included!)
[5, 6]
>>> x[1:] # Obtain from the first index to the last
[6, 8, 7, 199]
>>> x[:3] # Obtain from the zero index to the third index (the third one
is not included!)
[5, 6, 8]
>>> x[:-1] # Obtain from the first element to the second-last element
[5, 6, 8, 7]
>>> x[:-2] # Obtain from the first element to the third-last element
[5, 6, 8]
```

By writing **x[0:2]**, you may divide a list. The elements of **x[0:2]** from the null index to the one before the second index are given by this example. Thus, it shows the zeroth index components and just the first index in this situation. The last element is indicated by an index number of **-1** while the second last element is indicated by **-2**.

Dictionaries

Values with index numbers (0, 1, 2, ...) starting from 0 are kept in a list. Data is stored as a key-value pair in a dictionary. Words connected with their significance:

```
>>> a = {'weight':65} # Create a dictionary
>>> a['weight'] # Access an element
65
>>> a['height'] = 190 # Add a new element
```

```
>>> print(a)
{'weight': 65, 'height': 190}
```

Boolean

Python has a bool type. Its value is **True** or **False**. The operators for the bool type are **AND**, **OR**, and **NOT** (a type determines which operators can be used, such as **+**, **-**, *****, and **/** for numbers):

```
>>> lazy = True # Lazy?
>>> active = False # Active?
>>> type(lazy)
<class 'bool'>
>>> not lazy
False
>>> lazy and active
False
>>> lazy or active
True
```

If statements

You can use **if...else** to switch a process, depending on a condition:

```
>>> lazy = True
>>> if lazy:
...   print("I'm lazy")
...
I'm lazy
>>> lazy = False
>>> if lazy:
...     print("I'm lazy") # Indent with spaces
... else:
...       print("I'm not lazy")
...       print("I'm active")
...
```

```
I'm not lazy
```

```
I'm active
```

Spaces have significance in Python. In the example, the next phrase after **lazy** begins with four spaces. While tab characters for an indent may be used, Python suggests that spaces be used.

Use spaces in Python to show an indicator. For every indent level, four spaces are generally utilized.

For statements

Use a **for** statement for a loop:

```
>>> for i in [4, 9, 13]:
...     print(i)
...
4
9
13
```

This example outputs the elements of a list, **[4, 9, 13]**. When you use a **for…in…:** statement, you can access each element in a dataset, such as a list.

Functions

You can define a group of processes as a function:

```
>>> def hello():
...   print("Hello World!")
...
>>> hello()
Hello World!
```

A function can take an argument:

```
>>> def hello(object):
...   print("Hey " + object + "!")
...
>>> hello("Thomas")
Hey Thomas!
```

Use **+** to combine strings.

To close the Python interpreter, enter *Ctrl + D* (press the *D* key while holding down the *Ctrl* key) for Linux and macOS X. Enter *Ctrl + Z* and press the *Enter* key for Windows.

Python script files

A Python interpreter provides a mode that interacts with Python and that is helpful for small experimentation. But if you want to perform big processing, it is a bit uncomfortable since you must input a language each time. If you are doing this, you can save and run Python as a file (at one time). Examples of Python script files are given in the following section.

Saving in a file

Open your text editor and create a **HelloWorld.py** file. The **HelloWorld.py** file has only one line in it, as shown here:

```
print("Hello World")
```

Then open the terminal and navigate to the place where the **HelloWorld.py** file has been generated. Run the file name parameter Python command, **HelloWorld.py**. Here, **HelloWorld.py** is supposed to be located in the **~/deep-learning-from-zero/chapter01** directory (**HelloWorld.py** is located in the **chapter01** directory of the source code supplied in this book):

```
$ cd ~/deep-learning-from-zero/chapter01 # Move to the directory
$ python HelloWorld.py
Hello World!
```

Thus, you can use the **python HelloWorld.py** command to run the Python language.

Classes

You have learnt about data types, such as **int** and **str** (you can check the object type by using the **type()** method). These sorts of data are referred to as integrated data since they are included in Python. Here, you are defining your data type using a new class. It is also possible to set your own method (**class function**) and attributes.

Python allows you to define a class with a **class** keyword. The following format is followed to do the same:

```
class name:
    def __init__ (self, argument, …): # Constructor
```

```
...

def method name 1 (self, argument, …): # Method 1

...

def method name 2 (self, argument, …): # Method 2

...
```

A particular initialization technique is **__init__**. This initialization function is also termed a builder and is only called once when a class instance is created. In Python, you have a first parameter to describe self explicitly as a method (your instance). This technique may seem odd to individuals who know other languages.

Create a class like the following example and save as **Demo.py**:

```python
class Demo:
    def __init__(self, name):
        self.name = name
        print("Started!")


    def hello(self):
        print("Hey " + self.name + "!")


    def goodbye(self):
        print("Good-bye " + self.name + "!")


a = Demo("Alexa")
a.hello()
a.goodbye()
```

Execute **Demo.py** from the Terminal:

```
$ python Demo.py
Started!
Hey Alexa!
Good-bye Alexa!
```

Here, you defined a new class, **Demo**. In the preceding example, an instance (object), **a**, was created from the **Demo** class. The builders of the **Demo** class (initialization method) utilize name as a parameter and initialize the variable **self.name** instance.

You may use an attribute name in Python to construct and access the instance variable.

NumPy

Arrays and matrices are commonly computed while applying profound learning. The NumPy array (**numpy.array**) class offers several practical techniques for deep learning. A basic description of NumPy is given in this section, which we will use later.

Importing NumPy

It's a library outside of NumPy. Here, the term external implies that the standard Python does not have NumPy. You need to load the NumPy library first (**import**):

```
>>> import numpy as np
```

For the import of a library, an **import** declaration is used in Python. Here, **import numpy as np** indicates **numpy** as **np** is loaded. Thus you may now refer to a NumPy method as **np**.

Create an array of numbers

To construct a NumPy array, the **np.array()** process is used. As an input for creating an array for NumPy, **np.array()** will take a Python list, that is, **numpy.ndarray**:

```
>>> a = np.array([5.0, 15.0, 10.0])
>>> print(a)
[ 5. 15. 10.]
>>> type(a)
<class 'numpy.ndarray'>
```

Mathematical operations in NumPy

The following are a few samples of mathematical operations involving NumPy arrays:

```
>>> a = np.array([5.0, 15.0, 10.0])
>>> b = np.array([20.0, 40.0, 60.0])
>>> a + b # Add arrays
array([25., 55., 70.])
>>> a - b
```

```
array([-15., -25., -50.])
>>> a * b # element-wise product
array([100., 600., 600.])
>>> a / b
array([0.25      , 0.375      , 0.16666667])
```

Note that the arrays **a** and **b** have the same number of items (both are one-dimensional arrays with three elements). For each element, mathematical operations are performed when the element numbers of **a** and **b** are the same. An error occurs if the number of items is different. Therefore, they are the same significant. Element-wise is sometimes referred to as *for every element* and the element-wise product is termed the *product of each element*.

In addition to element-sensitive calculations, there are also a NumPy array mathematical operations and a single number (scalar value). Calculations between each item of the NumPy array and the scalar value are carried out in that scenario.

```
>>> a = np.array([5.0, 15.0, 10.0])
>>> a / 2.0
array([2.5, 7.5, 5. ])
```

N-dimensional NumPy arrays

In NumPy, multi-dimensional and one-dimensional arrays may be created (linear arrays). For instance, a two-dimensional matrix can be created as follows:

```
>>> x = np.array([[5, 6], [1, 2]])
>>> print(x)
[[5 6]
 [1 2]]
>>> x.shape
(2, 2)
>>> x.dtype
dtype('int32')
```

A 2x2 matrix, **x**, has been developed here. The form may be used for checking the shape of the matrix **x** and **dtype** can be used to examine its element type. The mathematical operations of matrices are as follows:

```
>>> y = np.array([[5, 0],[0, 8]])
>>> x + y
```

```
array([[10,  6],
       [ 1, 10]])
>>> x * y
array([[25,  0],
       [ 0, 16]])
```

As with arrays, if they are of the same shape, matrices are computed element by element. There are additional mathematical operations (single number) between an array and a scalar. This is also carried out through radio:

```
>>> print(x)
[[5 6]
 [1 2]]
>>> x * 10
array([[50, 60],
       [10, 20]])
```

An array NumPy (**np.array**) may be an N-dimensional array. Arrays of any sizes, such as one-, two-, three-, ... dimension arrays, can be created. In mathematics, a 1D array is known as a vector, while a 2D array is known as a matrix. A tensor is known as a widespread vector and matrix.

Broadcasting

In NumPy, mathematical operations may also be done across arrays of different forms. A scalar value of s was multiplied by the 2x2 matrix, **x**, in the previous example. The following figure demonstrates what is being done during this process: For this operation, a scalar value of 10 is extended to 2x2 element. This smart feature is called broadcasting:

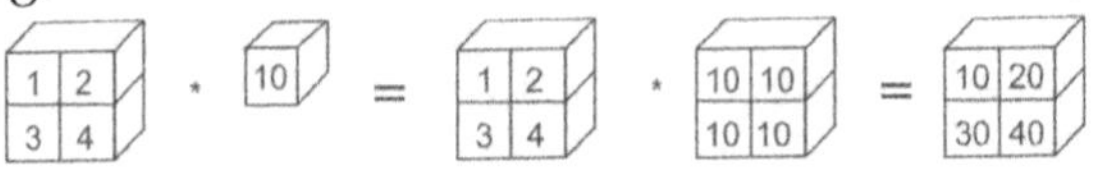

Figure 1.1

Here is a calculation for another broadcasting sample:

```
>>> x = np.array([[1, 2], [3, 4]])
>>> y = np.array([10, 20])
>>> x * y
array([[ 10, 40],
       [ 30, 80]])
```

The one-dimensional array **y** (as seen in *figure 1.2*) is converted to be as shaped and computed element by element as the two-dimensional arrays **x**.

So NumPy may make operations across arrays of different formats by use of broadcasting:

Figure 1.2

Accessing elements

The index of an element starts from 0 (as usual). You can access each element as follows:

```
>>> A = np.array([[21, 25], [54, 59], [0, 4]])
>>> print(A)
[[21 25]
 [54 59]
 [ 0  4]]
>>> A[0]   # 0th row
array([21, 25])
>>> A[0][1] # Element at (0,1)
25
```

Use a **for** loop to access each element:

```
>>> for i in A:
...     print(i)
...
[21 25]
[54 59]
[0 4]
```

In addition to the index operations described so far, NumPy can also use arrays to access each element:

```
>>> A = A.flatten( ) # Convert A into a one-dimensional array
>>> print(A)
[21 25 54 59  0  4]
```

```
>>> A[np.array([0, 2, 4])] # Obtain the elements of the 0th, 2nd, and 4th
indices
array([21, 54,  0])
```

Use this notation to obtain only the elements that meet certain conditions. For example, the following statement extracts values from **A** that are larger than **15**:

```
>>> A > 15
array([ True,   True,   True,   True, False, False])
>>> A[A>15]
array([21, 25, 54, 59])
```

A sign with an array of NumPy (**A > 15**) yields a Boolean array. In this case, the Boolean array is utilized for retrieving elements that are true from the array.

Dynamic languages are believed to be slower than static (compiler) languages such as C and C++ when it comes to processing. In reality, to handle intensive processing, you should build languages in C/C++. If Python requires performance, C/C++ implements the content of a process. Python acts as mediator in this scenario for the calling of C/C++ languages. C and C++ are the key processes of NumPy. So without sacrificing speed, you may utilize easy Python syntax.

Matplotlib

Drawing graphs and data visualization is crucial in deep learning studies. You can quickly make graphs and charts with Matplotlib. This section covers how graphs and pictures are drawn.

Drawing a simple graph

You can use Matplotlib's **pyplot** module to draw graphs. Here is an example of drawing a sine function:

```
import numpy as np
import matplotlib.pyplot as plt
# Create data

x = np.arange(0, 8, 0.2) # Generate from 0 to 8 in increments of 0.2
y = np.sin(x)

plt.plot(x, y, linestyle="-")
plt.show()
```

Here, the technique of changing of NumPy's data is generated and named **x**. For every element of **x**, the sine function **np.sin()**, NumPy and **plt.plot** is used to construct a graph using the data rows of **x** and **y** respectively. Finally, **plt.show** shows a **graph ()**. The image depicted in *figure 1.3* is shown when the previous code is executed:

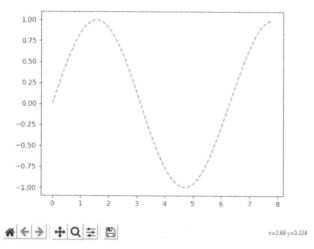

Figure 1.3

Features of pyplot

In addition to the sinus function (**sin**) we studied earlier, we will draw a cosine function (**cos**). We're going to leverage some more **pyplot** capabilities to show the title, the X-axis label name, etc.

```python
import numpy as np
import matplotlib.pyplot as plt


x = np.arange(0, 8, 0.2) # Generate from 0 to 8 in increments of 0.2
y1 = np.sin(x)
y2 = np.cos(x)


plt.plot(x, y1, label="sin")
plt.plot(x, y2, linestyle="-", label="cos") # Draw with a dashed line
plt.xlabel("x")
plt.ylabel("y")
plt.title('sin & cos') # Title
```

```
plt.legend()
```

```
plt.show()
```

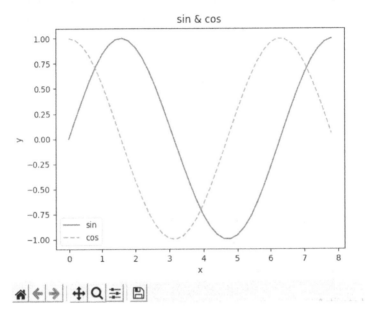

Figure 1.4

Displaying images

The **imshow()** method for displaying images is also provided in **pyplot**. You can use **imread()** in the **matplotlib.image** module to load images, as in the following example:

```
import matplotlib.pyplot as plt
```

```
from matplotlib.image import imread
```

```
img = imread('../dataset/demo.png') # Load an image (specify an appropriate
path!)
```

```
plt.imshow(img)
```

```
plt.show()
```

Figure 1.5

The image, **demo.png**, is presumed to be in the actual directory here. Depending on your environment, you have to adjust the file name and path as needed. The **demo. png** is located underneath the **dataset** directory as an example image in the source code included in this book. For example, in Python interpreter, change the image path from **demo.png** to **../dataset/demo.png** in order to execute the previous **chapter01** code from the directory for proper functioning.

Conclusion

This chapter has provided you with some basic Python language to create deep learning and neural networks. We shall enter the world of profound education in the following chapter and look at a certain Python code.

CHAPTER 2
Perceptron in Depth

This chapter explains the perceptron algorithm. This conventional technique is the reason why neural networks, that is, deep learning, came to be invented by American researcher *Frank Rosenblatt* in 1957, and so represents the first required step in the advanced study of both.

Structure

- Objective
- What is a perceptron?
- Simple logic circuits
    - **AND** gate
    - **NAND** and **OR** gates
- Implementing perceptron
- Weights and bias introduction
    - Implementation with weights and bias
    - Limitations of perceptron
    - **XOR** gate
- Linear and nonlinear

- Multilayer perceptron
  - ○ Combination of gates
  - ○ **XOR** gate implementation
- A computer from **NAND**

Objective

This chapter describes a perceptron and uses it to solve issues easily. You will become acquainted with the mechanisms of perceptron by the end of this chapter.

What is a perceptron?

As one signal inputs and outputs, a perceptron receives many signals. This signal, like an electric current or a river, is *flowing*. Like an electric current flowing through a driver and pushing electrons along, the signal in a perceptron transmits information. In contrast to electrical current, *Flow (1) or Do not flow (0)* in the perceptron is binary. 0 says "*do not flow a signal*" in this book while 1 signifies "*flow a signal*".

Therefore, note that in the interests of accuracy, an artificial neuron or simple perceptron is called, more precisely, the perceptron described in that chapter. We term it as "*perceptron*" here since the fundamental process:

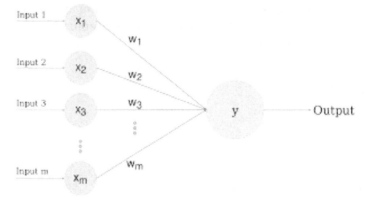

Figure 2.1

Input signals are *x1*, *x2*, *x3* and *xm*, *y* is the output, while weights are *w1*, *w2*, *w3* and *wm* (*w* is the initial letter of "weight"). The circle is termed as "*neuron*" or "*node*" in the above scheme. Each signal is amplified by its own weight when the signal is transmitted to the cell (*w1x1* and *w2x2*). The neuron sums up signals and outputs 1 if the amount goes beyond a specific threshold. Sometimes it is referred to as the "*neuron fire*". This is where the limit value is known as "*threshold*" and the indices is shown.

This is all about the operating principle of a perceptron. The equation *(2.1)* shows what we described:

$$y = \begin{cases} 0 & (w_1x_1 + w_2x_2 \leq \theta) \\ 1 & (w_1x_1 + w_2x_2 > \theta) \end{cases}$$

Equation 2.1

A perceptron has a specific weight for each of the multiple inputs, while the weight controls the importance of each signal. The larger the weight, the more important the signal for the weight. For each of several inserts, a perceptron has a certain weight, whereas the weight determines the significance of each signal. The more the weight, the more the weight signal is significant.

An electrical resistance equals a weight. Resistance is a quantity that evaluates the hardness of electric current transmission. The less the resistance, the greater the stream. In the meantime, the signal that flows is increased as the receiver's weight increases. Weight and resistance operate the same way; thus both manage the difficulty (or ease) of signal transmission.

Simple logic circuits

AND gate

There are some simple difficulties with a perceptron. Here we are going to look at logic circuits. First, let's think of an **AND** door. Two inputs and one output are provided by an **AND** gate. In *figure 2.2*, there is a *truth table* in the table of input and output signals. The **AND** gate is 1 when two inputs are 1. If not, it will release 0:

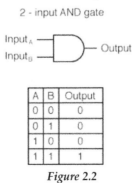

2 - input AND gate

A	B	Output
0	0	0
0	1	0
1	0	0
1	1	1

Figure 2.2

We now utilize a sensor to express this **AND** gate. The values of *w1*, *w2*, and *è* are determined in order to fulfil the truth table in *figure 2.2*. How can we establish a perceptron that meets the requirements of *figure 2.2*?

There are in fact an unlimited number of parameter combinations that meet *figure 2.2*. The perceptron, for example, functions as illustrated in *figure 2.2* when **(w1, w2, è = 0.5, 0.5, 0.7)**. The requirements of the **AND** gate is likewise met: **(0.5, 0.5, 0.8)** and **(1.0, 1.0, 1.0)**. When the weighted signal value is set, the weighted signal value is greater than the indicated threshold, that is, **x1** and **x2**.

NAND and OR gates

Now, look at the gate of **NAND**. The output of the **NAND** gate is opposite to the **AND** gate, and **NAND** denotes **NOT AND**. As demonstrated in *figure 2.3* in the truth table, it produces 0 if both **x1** and **x2** are 1. If not, it will output 1. What are the parameters for a **NAND** gate?

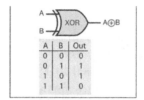

Figure 2.3

A combination of **(w1, w2, è f) = (-0.5, -0.5)** can be the **NAND** portal, and a number of additional possibilities are unlimited. In reality, by reversing all the signs of the parameter values that create **AND** gates, you may make a **NAND** port.

Now, let's look at an **OR** door, as shown in *figure 2.4*. This is a logical circuit which produces 1 if at least one of the input signals is 1. How do you think we can adjust **OR** gate parameters?

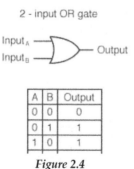

Figure 2.4

We determined the parameters of the perceptron—not a computer. We examined (discovered) the parameter values by **AND** when looking at the training data, also known as a **"truth table"**. We have a computer automatically calculate the parameter values in machine learning issues. The training job is the one that defines the right parameters and we consider the structure (model) of the sensor and provide the computer with training data.

We are able to create **AND**, **NAND**, and **OR** logic loops with a perceptron, as stated above. What is crucial here is that for every **AND**, **NAND**, and **OR** portal, the construction of a perceptron is the same. The three gates differ in the value of the parameter (weights and thresholds). Just as a versatile actor plays many roles, when the parameter values are modified correctly, the perceptron of a similar structure transforms into **AND**, **NAND**, and **OR**.

Implementing perceptron

Let's use Python to implement the previous logic circuits. The **AND** function that accepts **a1** and **a2** as inputs here is defined:

```python
def AND(a1, a2):
    b1, b2, theta = 0.5, 0.5, 0.7
    tmp = a1*b1 + a2*b2
    if tmp <= theta:
        return 0
    elif tmp > theta:
        return 1
```

The parameters **b1**, **b2**, and **theta** are initialized. If the total of the weighted inputs is over the threshold, 1 is returned as 0.

```python
AND(0, 0) # 0 (output)

AND(1, 0) # 0 (output)

AND(0, 1) # 0 (output)

AND(1, 1) # 1 (output)
```

We expect the outputs. You constructed an **AND** door with this. While a similar process may be used to construct a **NAND** or **OR** gate, the implementation is slowly changed.

Weights and bias introduction

Although the previous use of an **AND** gate is basic and easy to grasp, it will be changed to another application for the next sections, which will switch to **-b** (*2.1*) and will reflect the perceptron's behavior in the equation (*2.2*):

$$y = \begin{cases} 0 & (b + w_1 x_1 + w_2 x_2 \le 0) \\ 1 & (b + w_1 x_1 + w_2 x_2 > 0) \end{cases}$$

Equation 2.2

The equations (*2.1*) and equation (2.2) express precisely the same thing; however, the notation of symbols has changed. The *b* is thus referred to as a bias while *w1* and *w2* are referred to as weights. The perceptron illustrates that the input signal values are summed by weight and distortion, multiplied by equation (2.2). It outputs 1 when the sum exceeds 0, otherwise it exceeds 0. Let's use NumPy for the equation (2.2). The Python interpreter will be used to check the results:

```
>>> import numpy as np
>>> a = np.array([0, 5]) # Input
>>> b = np.array([1, 1.5]) # Weight
>>> y = -0.8        # Bias
>>> b*a
array([0. , 7.5])
>>> np.sum(b*a)
7.5
>>> np.sum(b*a) + y
6.7
```

Implementation with weights and bias

You can use weights and bias to implement an **AND** gate, as follows:

```
def AND(a1, a2):
    a = np.array([a1, a2])
    w = np.array([1, 1.5])
    b = -0.7
    tmp = np.sum(w*a) + b
    if tmp <= 0:
        return 0
    else:
        return 1
```

Here, the bias is **b**. Note that the preference functions differently from the weights, **w1**, and **w2**. Specifically, **w1** and **w2** function as input-signal parameters, while the bias works as a parameter to adapt the feed ease—so how likely the output signal is 1. If **b = -0.1**, for example, the neuron will fire if the weighted sum of the signal input is greater than 0.1. If **b = -20.0**, on the other hand, the neuron will only fire if the weighted input signal total is more than **20.0**. Thus, how readily the neuron fires influence the bias value. While the **w1** and the **w2** are referred to as "*weights*", the **b** is sometimes referred to as "*bias*" (that is, **b**, **w1**, and **w2**).

Now, let's implement the **NAND** and **OR** gates:

```
def NAND(a1, a2):
    a = np.array([a1, a2])
    w = np.array([-1.5, -1.5]) # Only the weights and bias are different
from AND!
    b = 0.8
    tmp = np.sum(w*a) + b
    if tmp <= 0:
        return 0
    else:
        return 1


def OR(a1, a2):
    a = np.array([a1, a2])
    w = np.array([1.5, 1.5]) # Only the weights and bias are different
from AND!
    b = -0.4
    tmp = np.sum(w*a) + b
    if tmp <= 0:
        return 0
    else:
        return 1
```

Limitations of perceptron

As already mentioned, **AND**, **NAND**, and **OR** logic gates may be implemented using a perceptron. You will consider an **XOR** gate in this next section.

XOR gate

An **XOR** gate is a gate system also referred to as exclusive **OR**. When both $x1$ and $x2$ are 1, the result is 1 ("*exclusive*" means "*limited to only one person*"). What would the weights be when employing a perceptron to carry out the **XOR** door?

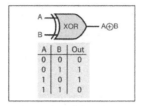

Figure 2.5

Indeed, by just utilizing the perceptron we acquired so much; we cannot create this **XOR** portal. Why can't we construct **XOR** even if **AND** or **OR** gates are built?

Let's first look visually at an **OR** door's behavior. For instance, when weight parameters **(b, w1, w2) = (-0.5, 1,0, 1.0)**, an **OR** gate meets the truth table in *figure 2.5*. The perceptron is expressed in this situation by the equation (2.3):

$$y = \begin{cases} 0 & (-0.5 + x_1 + x_2 \le 0) \\ 1 & (-0.5 + x_1 + x_2 > 0) \end{cases}$$

Equation 2.3

The perceptron equation (2.3) creates two regions split by the line -0.5 + x1 + x2 = 0. One area split by the line 1 is divided, while the other output is 0. This may be seen in *figure 2.6*:

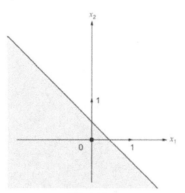

Figure 2.6

An **OR** door produces 0 at *x1, x2* = (0, 0) and the **OR** door outputs 1 at *x1, x2* = (0, 1), and (1, 0) and (1, 1). Here, there is a circle of 0, and a triangle of 1. To build an **OR** door, we have to split a straight line between circles and triangles. In fact, the straight line may appropriately split 4 points.

How about the **XOR** gate example, then? Can we construct regions with a straight line, like with an **OR** door, which splits circles and triangles?

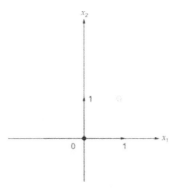

Figure 2.7

You can't split circles and triangles with a straight line, however difficult it may be to solve this. They cannot be divided by a straight line.

Linear and nonlinear

It is impossible to split a straight line from circles to triangles. But if you can eliminate the straight line constraint, you can split them. For example, as illustrated in *figure 2.8*, you may build regions between circles and triangles.

The limit of a perceptron is that the regions split by a straight line can only be represented. As demonstrated in *figure 2.8*, it cannot represent a curve. The *figure 2.8* calls nonlinear areas, whereas regions split into linear zones are referred to as linear zones. In machine learning, linear and nonlinear terms are commonly employed. The *figures 2.6* and *figure 2.8* allow you to visualize them:

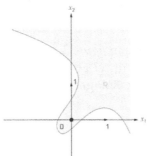

Figure 2.8: *A curve can divide between circles and triangles*

Multilayer perceptron

Regrettably, we cannot utilize an **XOR** gate perceptron. But that's not awful news. The virtue of a sensor is that several layers of perceptron may really be layered (the outline of this section is that multiple layers can represent **XOR**). Later we look at the layers of the stacking. Here we may look from another angle at the difficulty of the **XOR** gate.

Combination of gates

Some approaches to construct an **XOR** gate can be followed. One is to integrate and wire the **AND**, **NAND**, and **OR** doors we have built so far. The symbols displayed in *figure 2.9* are **AND**, **NAND**, and **OR** gates. The *figure 2.9* shows that an output has been inverted from the circle at the top of the **NAND** gate:

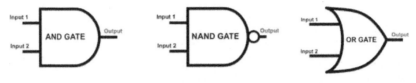

Figure 2.9

Now let's consider wired **AND**, **NAND**, and **OR** for an **XOR** gate. Please note that in *figure 2.10*, the **XOR** gate can be assigned to either of the **AND**, **NAND**, or **OR** symbols:

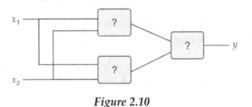

Figure 2.10

In particular, the limits mentioned in the last section of a perceptron are that a single layer cannot be an **XOR** gate and cannot split nonlinear regions. Here, we see that the combination of perceptron may be used as an **XOR** gate (that is, stacking layers).

The cable may create an **XOR** gate in *figure 2.11*. In this case, the input signals are $x1$, $x2$, and y denotes the signal output. $x1$ and $x2$ are the **NAND** and **OR** gate entries, and the **NAND** and **OR** gate exits are the **AND** gate entries:

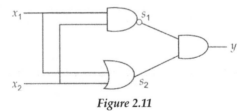

Figure 2.11

A combination of the **AND**, **NAND**, and **OR** gates construct an **XOR** gate

Let's make sure we can actually build an **XOR** gate by wiring in *figure 2.11*. If the output of the **NAND** gate is $s1$ and that of the **OR** gate is $s2$, the truth table will be completed. The findings are shown in *figure 2.12*. If we look at *x1*, *x2*, and *y*, we can see that the outputs of the **XOR** gate are:

x_1	x_2	s_1	s_2	y
0	0	1	0	0
1	0	1	1	1
0	1	1	1	1
1	1	0	1	0

Figure 2.12

XOR gate implementation

We are now using Python to build an **XOR** cable gate in *figure 2.11*. We can implement this as follows with the **AND**, **NAND**, and **OR** functions that we described earlier:

```
def XOR(a1, a2):

    x1 = NAND(a1, a2)

    x2 = OR(a1, a2)

    y = AND(x1, x2)

    return y
```

The **XOR** function outputs the results as expected:

```
XOR(0, 0) # 0 (output)

XOR(1, 0) # 1 (output)

XOR(0, 1) # 1 (output)

XOR(1, 1) # 0 (output)
```

Now, an **XOR** gate may be built. After this, the **XOR** we have built with perceptrons is shown (by showing neurons explicitly). This depiction is seen in *figure 2.13*.

XOR is a network of several layers, as illustrated in *figure 2.13*. Here we are calling Layer 0 to the left, and Layer 1 to its next and Layer 2 to the right.

In *figure 2.13* the perceptron differed in form from those seen by the **AND** and **OR** perceptron (*figure 2.1*). Single-layer **AND** and **OR** perceptron, and **XOR** are two-layer. A multilayer perceptron is occasionally called a multilayer perceived:

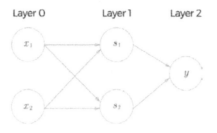

Figure 2.13

While the perceptron in *figure 2.13* comprises of three layers, it will be referred to as "*a two-layer perceptron*", as only the two layers, from 0 to 1 and from 1 to 2, are weighty. In certain literature, *figure 2.13* is called a "*three-layer perceptron*" because it contains three layers.

As *figure 2.13* shows, a two-layer perceptron transmits and gets information between neurons in layers 0 and 1. This behavior is fu her described by the following:

- Two layer 0 neurons receive input and transmit information to the layer 1 neurons.
- Layer 1 neuron transmits signal in layer 2 to the neuron that outputs **y**.

The perceptron's behavior may be compared with an assembly via a pipeline. The first layer worker works on a "*component*" which comes and transfers it to the second layer worker when the task is done. The first layer works on the second layer. In the second layer the worker is working on the component received from the worker in the first tier and ships it (output). Thus the perceptron "*pass components*" between the workers in an **XOR** gate. This layout of two layers allows users to create an **XOR** gate. This might be seen as what *cannot* be accomplished by adding a single layer perceptron.

A computer from NAND

Multilayer perceptrons can be used to create more complex circuits than those we have seen so far. For example, with perceptron, an additional circuit may be built. A perceptron may also be used to represent an encoder that transforms a binary number into a decimal number and a circuit which exits 1 if specific conditions are satisfied (parity-checking circuit). Actually, we can even depict a computer with perceptron.

A computer is a machine that processes information. Once the input is received, a computer somehow processes it and produces the output. Processing in a specific method which both the computer and a perceptron have and calculate the inputs and outputs.

Although a computer appears to be doing highly complex activities, a combination of **NAND** gates may really (surprise) represent how a computer performs. The startling fact that **NAND** doors are necessary for computer creation indicates that perceptron can also be a computer since perceptron can be used to build a **NAND** door itself. Simply said, by combining **NAND** gates, we may likewise represent a computer by just combining multiple perceptron (a combination of perceptron can be represented as one multilayer perceptron).

> You may find it difficult to comprehend that a computer can build a combination of **NAND** gates. *The Elements of Computing Systems: Building a Modern Computer from First* Principles (2008) by Noam Nisan and Shimon Schocken is suggested if you are interested in this subject. This book tries to get a thorough understanding of computers. Under the slogan,NANDs are used to build a PC running Tetris, "From NANDs to Tetris". You will discover that computers from simple elements, i.e., NADNs, may be constructed by reading this book.

Multilayer perceptron can therefore produce a representation as complex as computer production. So, what structure of the perceptron can a computer represent? To construct a computer, how many layers are needed?

The answer is that a computer with a two-layer perceptron can potentially be constructed. It has been demonstrated that any function may be represented in a two-layer perceptron (for specifics, please see the following chapter if the `activation` function is a non-linear `sigmoid` function). However, creating a computer by defining the relevant weights in a two-layer perceptron structure will be a difficult task. It is normal that the needed components (modules) are created step-by-step from low-level components such as **NAND**s, starting with **AND** and **OR** gates and progressing via half adders, full supplements, arithmetical and logical units, and a CPU. The creation of a structure with multiple levels is therefore a logical approach to portray a computer using perceptron.

Although we won't make a computer in this book, remember that multilayer perceptron allows nonlinear representations and can describe what a computer does in principle.

Conclusion

We explored the perceptron in this chapter. The perceptron is a pretty basic algorithm, so you should know how it works fast. The perceptron is the basis for a neural network, to be learned in the following chapter. In the following list, these points may be summarized:

- An algorithm having inputs and outputs is a perceptron. If a specific input is received, a fixed value is generated.

- A perceptron contains parameters of "weight" and "bias".

- Perceptions can be used to depict logical circuits like **AND** and **OR** gates.

- A single layer perceptron cannot be represented on an **XOR** gate.

- The **XOR** gate can be shown using a two-layer perceptron.

- A single-layer perceptron may represent only linear areas, whereas a multi-layer perceptron is nonlinear.

- Multilayers can depict a computer (theoretically).

CHAPTER 3
Neural Networks

Introduction

In the previous chapter, we learnt about perceptrons. The perceptron functions are likely to be complex. The perceptron may represent (theoretically) difficult procedures executed by a computer. The weights need to be manually defined first, in order to match the projected inputs and outputs, before the right weights are established. We utilized the truth table with **AND** and **OR** gates in the previous chapter to manually detect the weights.

To address negative news, there are neural networks. In particular, a neural network's essential characteristic is that it can automatically learn optimal weight parameters from data.

Structure

- From perceptrons to neural systems
  - Neural network example
- Perceptron review
  - Presentation of an activation function
- Activation function

- Sigmoid function
  - o Implementation of a step
  - o Step function graph
- Nonlinear function
- ReLU function
  - o Multidimensional array calculation
- Implementation of a network for three layers
  - o Examining the symbols
  - o Transmission of signal in each layer
- Summary of implementation
  - o The output layer design
- Softmax identity feature and function
  - o Issues when implementing the Softmax function
  - o Softmax feature characteristics
- Handwritten digit recognition
- MNIST dataset
- Inference of neural network
- Batch processing

Objective

This chapter offers an overview of neural networks. You will get a good knowledge of Softmax identity, ReLU function, Batch processing, MNIST dataset.

From perceptrons to neural systems

A neural network is comparable to the perceptron described in a number of ways in the preceding chapter. In this section, we will discuss how the neural network functions and how it varies from a perceptron.

Neural network example

An example of a neural network is shown in *figure 3.1*. The left column is called the input layer; the right column the output layer; and the middle column the middle layer. The middle layer is also known as a concealed layer. "*Concealed*" means that the hidden layer of neurons is unseen (unlike those in the input and output layers).

In this book, we will call the layers layer 0, layer 1, and layer 2 (layer numbers start from layer 0 because doing so is convenient when the layers are implemented in Python later). In *figure 3.1*, the input layer is layer 0, the middle layer is layer 1, and the output layer is layer 2:

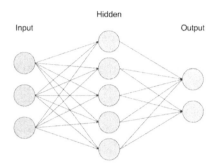

Figure 3.1: *Neural network example*

> Whilst the network is made up of three layers in *figure 3.1*, we term it a "two-layer network" as it has two weight levels. Some publications call it a "network of three layers" based on the number of layers in the network, but the name of the network in this book depends on the weights of the layers (that is, the total number of input, concealed, and output layers, minus 1).

The neural network in *figure 3.1* is similar in form to the perceptron. It is actually no different from the perceptron we saw in the previous chapter, in terms of how the neurons are linked.

Perceptron review

How are neural network signals transmitted? To answer this question, we first need to review the perceptron. Consider a network that has the following structure:

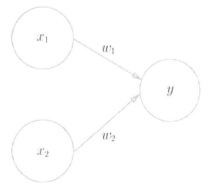

Figure 3.2: *Reviewing the perceptron*

The perceptron receiving two inputs (*x1* and *x2*) and output *y* is shown in the preceding figure. As already explained, equation (*3.1*) is used to depict the perceptron in *figure 3.2*:

$$y = \begin{cases} 0 & (b + w_1 x_1 + w_2 x_2 \leq 0) \\ 1 & (b + w_1 x_1 + w_2 x_2 > 0) \end{cases}$$

Equation 3.1

Here, *b* is the bias parameter and regulates the neuron's firing. *w1* and *w2* are the parameters that regulate the relevance of the "*weights*" of each signal.

You may observe that there is no bias in the network in *figure 3.2*. If we wish, we may express the preference in *figure 3.3*. A signal of weight *b* and input *1* has been introduced in *Figure 3.3*. This perceptron gets the inputs of neuron from three signals (*x1, x2,* and *1*), multiplying the signals by weight before their transmission. The following neuron adds up the weighted signals and then outputs 1 if the total is more than 0.

If it doesn't, it releases 0. The neuron in the following figure is shown in solid grey to separate it from other neurons. The reason for this is that the incoming signal is always 1:

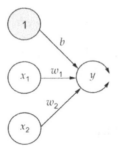

Figure 3.3: *Showing the bias explicitly*

Now, we want to make the equation (*3.1*) easier. To achieve this, we need just one function, where 1 is the output when the total exceeds 0, and 0 is the output if it does not. We shall now provide a new function, *h(x)*, and rewrite equation (*3.1*) to (*3.2*) and (*3.3*) as shown here:

$$y = h(b + w_1 x_1 + w_2 x_2)$$

Equation 3.2

$$h(x) = \begin{cases} 0 & (x \leq 0) \\ 1 & (x > 0) \end{cases}$$

Equation 3.3

The equation (3.2) shows that the *h(x)* function converts input signal sums to *y*. If the input exceeds 0, the function *h(x)* represented in equation (3.3) returns 1; if not, it returns 0. The equations (3.2) and (3.3) thus function in accordance with equations (3.1).

Presentation of an activation function

The *h(x)* function shown below is typically called an activation function. Here, the total input signals are converted into power output. As the word "*activation*" suggests, the activation function defines how the total of the input signals activates (that is, how it fires).

Now, again we may rewrite equation (3.2). The equation conducts two processes: the sum of the weighted input signals, and the sum of the activation function are transformed. Thus, equation (3.2) may be divided into two equations:

$$a = b + w_1 x_1 + w_2 x_2$$

Equation 3.4

$$y = h(a)$$

Equation 3.5

The sum of the weighted input signals and biases in equation (3.4) is *a*. It is converted to *h(a)* in equation (3.5) and *y* is the result. A neuron as one circle has so far been depicted. Equations (3.4) and (3.5) are shown in *figure 3.4*:

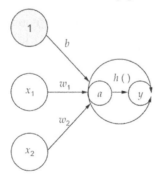

Figure 3.4

The procedure done using the activation function in the neurons circle is explicitly shown in *figure 3.4*. We see clearly that the weighted signals total up to node *a* and by the activation function *h()*, it is transformed to node *y*. In the book you can use the words "*neuron*" and "*node*" interchangeably. Here, circles *a* and *y* are referred to as nodes, used in the same meaning as neurons used previously.

As seen in *figure 3.5*, we shall continue showing a neuron as one circle. The activation process (on the right side of *figure 3.5*) will be shown in this book if the neural network behavior can be clarified:

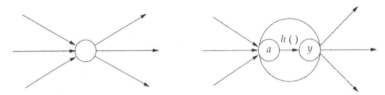

Figure 3.5

The image on the left is an image normal neuron, but on the right, the activation process in a neuron is expressed (*a* is the sum of input signals; *h()* is the activation feature; *y* is the output). Let us now focus on the activation function, which acts as the bridge between a neural network and a perceptron.

This book does not properly specify the algorithm implied by the word *"perceptron"*. A simple perceptron is often a single level network in which an activation function is employed as a step function to alter the output values of a threshold.

Activation function

The activation function of equation (3.3) alters the output values at a threshold and is known as a **step function**. We may thus say, *a perceptron employs an activation function as a step function*. In other words, a perceptron picks a *step role* from a large number of candidate functions for activation. If a perceptron employs a step function as an activation function, what happens if a function is used as activation function other than a step function? Well, we can go into the world of a neural network by altering the activation function from one step function to another.

Sigmoid function

The sigmoid function, given by equation (3.6), is one of the most commonly used activation functions in neural networks:

$$h(x) = \frac{1}{1 + \exp(-x)}$$

Equation 3.6

The equation (3.6) shows *exp(-x)* as e-x. Napier's constant, *e*, is 2.7182... The equation (3.6) appears to be a complex sigmoid function, but is merely a *function*. A converter is the function that returns the input. If for example, the sigmoid function is supplied with a value like 1.0 and 2.0, it gives back values like *h(1.0)* = 0.731... and *h(2.0)* = 0.880...

In a neural network, a sigmoid function is frequently used to transform signals and send the signals to the next neuron. Indeed, the primary distinction from the neural network presented here is the activation function between the perceptron defined in the previous chapter. Other features are virtually the same as the perceptron, such as the structure in which neurons are interconnected in several layers and how signals are conveyed. Let us now examine a sigmoid function (used as an activation feature) more closely by comparing it to a step feature.

Implementation of a step

Here, Python will be used to display the step graph. The step function outputs 1 in equation (3.3) when the input exceeds 0 and outputs 0 if it does not. Following is an illustration of an easy implementation of the step function:

```python
def step_function(a):
    if a > 0:
        return 1
    else:
        return 0
```

It is basic and straightforward to comprehend, but only a true number (a floating-point number) is required as input **a**. Therefore, **step_function(3.0)** is permitted. The function cannot, however, take the argument with a NumPy array. Therefore, it is not permitted to use **step_function(np.array([1.0, 2.0]))**. We want to alter the future implementation here so that the NumPy array may be used.

```python
def step_function(a):
    b = a > 0
    return b.astype(np.int)
```

While just two lines in the previous code are present, it may be somewhat tough to grasp since it employs a handy NumPy *trick*. In this example you will define the type of technique that Python interpreter uses to illustrate. The NumPy **a** array is presented in this example. A comparison operation is performed for the NumPy array:

```python
>>> import numpy as np
>>> a = np.array([-1.0, 1.0, 2.0])
>>> a
array([-1., 1., 2.])
>>> b = a > 0
>>> b
```

```
array([False, True, True], dtype=bool)
```

Each element in the array is compared to a Boolean array when a comparison is made for a NumPy array. Each **a** array entry is changed to **True** if it exceeds **0**, or **False** if it does not. The new range, **b**, is then created.

The **b** array is Boolean and the function must return **0** or **1 int** type. Therefore, from Boolean we change the array elements type to **int**:

```
>>> b = b.astype(np.int)
```

```
>>> b
```

```
array([0, 1, 1])
```

The **astype()** function is used to transform the NumPy array type as seen earlier. The **astype()** process uses the type of argument you want (**np.int**, in our case). In Python, **True** is transformed to **1**, and by transforming the Boolean type into the **int** type, **False** is turned to **0**. The preceding code shows the trick used to implement the step function by NumPy.

Step function graph

Now, let's draw the step function graph that we defined before. To achieve this, we must utilize the library of Matplotlib:

```
import numpy as np

import matplotlib.pylab as plt

def step_function(x):
    return np.array(x > 0, dtype=np.int)

X = np.arange(-6.0, 6.0, 0.2)

Y = step_function(x)

plt.plot(X, Y, linestyle='--')

plt.ylim(-0.1, 1.2) # Specify the range of the y-axis

plt.show()
```

The **np.arange(-6.0, 6.0, 0.2)** function creates a NumPy array (**[-6.0, -5.9,..., 5.9]**) with values ranging from **-6.0** to **6.0** in **0.2** increments. The parameter to **step_function()** is a NumPy array. It calls the step function for each element in the array and returns an array. The graph presented in the following screenshot is generated by plotting these **X** and **Y** arrays:

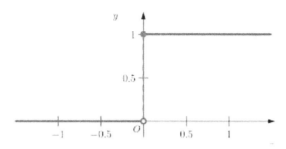

Figure 3.6: Step function graph

At the threshold of 0, the step function's output changes from 0 to 1 (or 1 to 0), as seen in the figure earlier. Because the output of a step function resembles the steps of a staircase, it is frequently referred to as a "*staircase function*".

Sigmoid function implementation

Let us now create a sigmoid function. The sigmoid function of equation (3.6) may be written in Python as follows:

```
def sigmoid(a):
    return 1 / (1 + np.exp(-a))
```

In the equation, **np.exp(-a)** equates to **exp(a)**. It is not difficult to put this system in place. Even if the **a** parameter is a NumPy array, the proper results are delivered. When given a NumPy array, this sigmoid function calculates appropriately, as demonstrated here:

```
>>> a = np.array([-5.0, 5.0, 1.0])
>>> sigmoid(a)
array([0.00669285, 0.99330715, 0.73105858])
```

Because of NumPy's broadcasting, the sigmoid function now supports a NumPy array (refer to the *Broadcasting* section in *Chapter 1: Python Introduction* for details). The broadcast ensures that when an operation is done on a scalar and a NumPy array, the operation is performed between the scalar and each member of the NumPy array:

```
>>> b = np.array([2.0, 4.0, 6.0])
>>> 5.0 + b
array([ 7.,  9., 11.])
>>> 3.0 / b
array([1.5 , 0.75, 0.5 ])
```

Arithmetic operations (such as **+** and **/**) are performed between the scalar value (1.0 in this case) and the NumPy array in the prior example. As a result, the operations employ the scalar value and each element of the NumPy array, and the results are produced as a NumPy array. Because **np.exp(-a)** creates a NumPy array, **3 / (1 + np.exp(-a))** utilizes each member of the NumPy array for the operation in this implementation of the sigmoid function.

Let's draw the sigmoid function's graph now. The drawing code is nearly identical to the step function code. The only difference is that the sigmoid function replaces the function that produces **y**:

```
x = np.arange(-6.0, 6.0, 0.2)

y = sigmoid(X)

plt.plot(X, Y, linestyle='--')

plt.ylim(-0.2, 1.2) # Specify the range of the y-axis

plt.show()
```

The preceding code, when executed, creates the graph shown in the following screenshot:

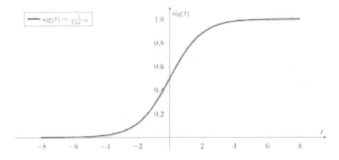

Figure 3.7: Graph of the sigmoid function

Let's examine and contrast the sigmoid and step functions. The sigmoid function and the step function are shown in *figure 3.8*. What are the differences between the two functions? What do they have in common?

You'll notice a change in smoothness when you look at *figure 3.8*. The sigmoid function is a smooth curve whose output varies continuously as the input changes. The output of the step function, on the other hand, abruptly changes at 0. When it comes to training neural networks, the smoothness of the sigmoid function is critical.

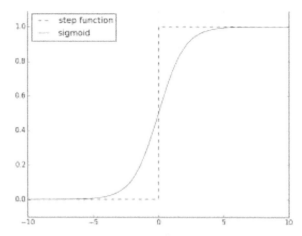

Figure 3.8: *Step function and sigmoid function*

They vary in that the step function only returns 0 or 1, whereas the sigmoid function returns real numbers such as 0.731... and 0.880... They are also distinct in that the step function only returns 0 or 1, whereas the sigmoid function returns real numbers such as 0.731... and 0.880... In a perceptron, binary signals of 0 and 1 flow across neurons, but in a neural network, signals of continuous real numbers flow.

The step function may be compared to a *shishi-odoshi* (a bamboo tube that clacks on a stone when water runs out of it) and the sigmoid function to a waterwheel when we use water to explain the behaviors of these two functions. The step function has two functions: It drains or stores water (0 or 1), and it regulates the flow of water like a waterwheel dependent on the quantity of water that reaches it.

Consider the similarities between the step and sigmoid functions. They differ in *smoothness*, yet when you look at the preceding figure from a different angle, you'll find that they have a similar form. Actually, while the input is tiny, both of them output a value near/of 0, and as the input is larger, the output approaches/reaches 1. When the input signal includes essential information, the step and sigmoid functions output a big value, and when it does not, they output a small value. They are also same in that they output a number between 0 and 1, regardless of how tiny or huge the incoming signal's value is.

Nonlinear function

In another manner, the step and sigmoid functions are comparable. They are both nonlinear functions, which is a significant resemblance. A curve represents the sigmoid function, whereas straight lines that resemble steps indicate the step function. Nonlinear functions are what they are both categorized as.

When an activation function is employed, the phrases, *"nonlinear function"* and *"linear function"* are frequently used. A function is a type of converter that returns a value when given a value. A linear function (expressed by the equation $h(x) = cx$, where c is a constant) is a function that outputs the input values multiplied by a constant.

As a result, a linear function's graph is a straight line. A nonlinear function's graph, on the other hand, is not a simple straight line, as its name implies.

The activation function in a neural network must be a nonlinear function. A linear function, in other words, cannot be utilized as the activation function. Why can't you use a linear function? The reason behind this is that if a linear function is employed, increasing the number of layers in a neural network becomes pointless.

The difficulty with a linear function is that no matter how many layers are added, a *"network without a hidden layer"* that performs the same task always exists. Consider a short example to better comprehend this (and to get a sense of it). The activation function is $h(x) = cx$, and the computation of $y(x) = h(h(x))$ is conducted in the same way as in a three-layer network. It contains $y(x) = cccx$ multiplications, and the identical operation may be expressed by one $y(x) = axe$ (where $a = c3$) multiplication. As a result, a network without a hidden layer may be used to represent it.

Using a linear function offsets the advantage of many layers, as seen in this example. As a result, a nonlinear function must be employed as the activation function to take use of several layers.

ReLU function

As activation functions, we've learnt about step and sigmoid functions thus far. While the sigmoid function has been used in neural networks for a long time, the **Rectified Linear Unit (ReLU)** is now the most commonly utilized function.

If the input value is greater than 0, the ReLU function outputs the value as is. It returns 0 if the input is equal to or less than 0:

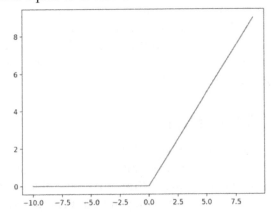

Figure 3.9: *ReLU function*

The following represents ReLU function:

$$h(x) = \begin{cases} x & (x > 0) \\ 0 & (x \le 0) \end{cases}$$

(3.7)

Equation 3.7

The ReLU function is relatively basic, as the graph and equation demonstrate. As a result, we can easily implement it, as illustrated here:

```
def relu(x):
    return np.maximum(0, x)
```

The maximum function in NumPy is utilized here. The greater of the two input values is output. While a sigmoid function will be utilized as the activation function later in this chapter, the ReLU function will be employed mostly in the second part of the book.

Multidimensional array calculation

You will be able to construct a neural network efficiently if you understand how to compute multidimensional arrays using NumPy. First, we will examine how NumPy is used for the calculation of multidimensional arrays. Then a neural network is implemented.

Multidimensional arrays

A multidimensional array is simply described as a set of integers organized in a line, in a rectangle, in three dimensions, or (more widely) in N dimensions. To construct a multidimensional table, let us utilize NumPy. First, as mentioned above, we will build a one-dimensional array:

```
>>> import numpy as np
>>> X = np.array([5, 6, 7, 8])
>>> print(X)
[5, 6, 7, 8]
>>> np.ndim(X)
1
>>> X.shape
(4,)
>>> X.shape[0]
4
```

As seen in the following example, the **np.ndim()** method may be used to get the number of array dimensions. The instance variable shape may also be used to get the array form. **X** is a one-dimensional array of four elements in the above example. The results of **X.shape** are a tuple. Please note this is because both for a single and a multidimensional array the result is returned in the same manner. For example, a tuple (4,3) for a two-dimensional array is returned and a tuple (4,3,2) for a three-dimensional array is returned. A tuple for a one-dimensional array will also be returned. Let us now build an array of two dimensions:

```
>>> Y = np.array([[5,6], [8,10], [9,7]])
```

```
>>> print(Y)
```

```
[[ 5  6]
 [ 8 10]
 [ 9  7]]
```

```
>>> np.ndim(Y)
```

```
2
```

```
>>> Y.shape
```

```
(3, 2)
```

Here is the creation of a 3x2 array, **Y**. A 3x2 array implies that the first dimension is composed of three elements and the following dimension contains two elements. Dimension 0 is the first and dimension 1 is the next (an index starts from 0 in Python). A matrix is called a double-dimensional array. As illustrated in *figure 3.10*, a row in a table is called a horizontal sequence while a column is considered a vertical sequence:

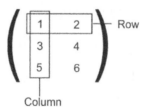

Figure 3.10: *A horizontal sequence is called a "row," and a vertical one is called a "column"*

Matrix multiplication

Consider the matrix products (two-dimensional arrays). The multiplication in the matrix is calculated for 2x2 matrices as illustrated in *figure 3.11* (specified by this technique as the calculation):

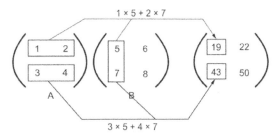

Figure 3.11: *Calculating matrix multiplication*

The multiplication of the matrix is determined by multiplying the items between the (horizontal) rows of the left matrix and the (vertical) columns of the right matrix, and adding the results. As components of a new multidimensional array, the computation result is saved. For instance, the first column of the results between **A** and **B** becomes the first column of the first row, whereas the first column between **A** and **B** becomes the first element of the second column of the first row of the first. A matrix in an equation is displayed in bold in this book. For instance, the matrix is shown as **A** to distinguish between a scalar value (such as **an** or **b**) and one element. This calculation is implemented in Python as follows:

```
>>> A = np.array([[5,6], [7,9]])
>>> A.shape
(2, 2)
>>> B = np.array([[10,12], [15,17]])
>>> B.shape
(2, 2)
>>> np.dot(A, B)
array([[140, 162],
       [205, 237]])
```

The matrices **A** and **B** are 2x2. The NumPy method **np.dot()** is used to calculate the product of matrices **A** and **B** (the **dot** here indicates a **dot** product). The **np.dot()** function calculates a internal matrix multiplication for one-dimensional array and matrix multiplication for a two-dimensional array. You need to remember that the following values are available: **np.dot(A, B)**, and **np.dot(B, A)**. Contrary to normal operations (**+**, *****, etc.), the product of matrices changes when the order of the operands (**A** and **B**) is changed.

The preceding example demonstrates the 2x2 matrix multiplication. The product of matrices with different forms can also be calculated. The product of 2x3 and 3x2 matrices, for instance, may be implemented in Python, as follows:

```
>>> A = np.array([[5, 6, 7], [10, 11, 12]])
>>> A.shape
(2, 3)
>>> B = np.array([[5, 10], [6, 12], [7, 14]])
>>> B.shape
(3, 2)
>>> np.dot(A, B)
array([[110, 220],
       [200, 400]])
```

The preceding code demonstrates how the product of the 2x3 matrix **A** and the 3x2 matrix **B** may be implemented. You have to pay attention to the form of the matrices here. In particular, the number of elements (number of columns) in dimension 1 of matrix **A** must be equal to the number of elements (number of rows) in dimension 0 of matrix **B**. Matrix **A** is 2x3 and matrix **B** is 3x2 in the previous example. In dimension 1 of matrix **A(3)**, the number of components is same to that of dimension 0 of matrix **B(3)**. If different, it is not possible to calculate the product of the matrices. If, then, the product of 2x3 matrix **A** and 2x2 matrix **C** in a Python are calculated, the following error occurs:

```
>>> C = np.array([[5, 7], [1, 9]])
>>> C.shape
(2, 2)
>>> A.shape
(2, 3)
>>> np.dot(A, C)
Traceback (most recent call last):
 File "<stdin>", line 1, in <module>
ValueError: shapes (2,3) and (2,2) not aligned: 3 (dim 1) != 2 (dim 0)
```

This mistake shows that dimensions 1 of matrix **A** and 0 of matrix **C** differ in their numbers (the index of a dimension starts from zero). In other words, the number of elements in the corresponding two matrices dimensions must be the same for the calculation of the product of a multidimensional array. Since it is an essential point, in *figure 3.12* let's check again:

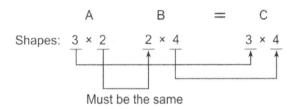

Figure 3.12: *For matrix multiplication, the*
number of elements in the appropriate dimensions must be same

The example of the 3x2 matrix **A** and 2x4 matrix **B** product, resulting in 3x4 matrix **C**, is presented in *figure 3.12*. In the respective dimensions of matrices **A** and **B**, we can see that the number of elements must be equal. The matrix **C** consists of the same number of rows as matrix **A** and the same number of columns as matrix **B**. This is essential as well.

Even if **A** is a two-dimensional matrix and **B** is a one-dimensional array, the same concept applies (that there must be equal number of items in the appropriate dimensions), as illustrated in *figure 3.13*:

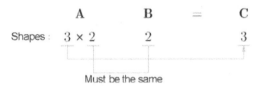

Figure 3.13: *Even if X is a two-dimensional matrix and*
Y is one-dimensional the number of elements in the respective dimensions must be the same

The sample in *figure 3.13* can be implemented in Python as follows:

```
>>> A = np.array([[5, 10], [12, 6], [7, 14]])
>>> A.shape
(3, 2)
>>> B = np.array([3, 4])
>>> B.shape
(2,)
>>> np.dot(A, B)
array([55, 60, 77])
```

Neural network matrix multiplication

Now utilize NumPy matrices as illustrated in *figure 3.14* to deploy a neural network. Bias and the function activation were excluded:

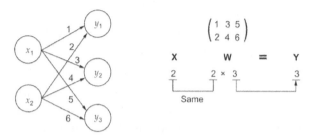

Figure 3.14: *Matrix multiplication for neural network calculation*

We need to pay attention to the shapes of **X**, **W**, and **Y** in this implementation. In the appropriate **X** and **W** dimensions, it is highly crucial that the number of elements be the same:

```
>>> X = np.array([5, 10])
>>> X.shape
(2,)
>>> W = np.array([[5, 6, 7], [10, 11, 12]])
>>> print(W)
[[ 5  6  7]
 [10 11 12]]
>>> W.shape
(2, 3)
>>> Y = np.dot(X, W)
>>> print(Y)
[125 140 155]
```

As demonstrated earlier, the value **Y** may be simultaneously calculated using the **np.dot** (**dot** product of multidimensional matrices). This implies you can compute it all at once, regardless of whether the number of elements in **Y** is 100 or 1,000. Without **np.dot** you have to remove the computational elements of **Y** (and use a statement). We may thus claim that the approach for calculating the product of multidimensional matrices by use of matrix multiplication is essential.

Implementation of a network for three layers

Now, let's set up a neural network *practical*. Here we execute the process in a neural network of three layers, as illustrated in *figure 3.15*, from its input to its output (a process in the forward direction). The NumPy multidimensional arrays will be used for implementation (as mentioned in the last section). You can create quick code in a neural network for a forward process by making effective use of NumPy arrays.

Examining the symbols

Here, we will use symbols such as $w_{12}^{(1)}$ and $a_1^{(1)}$ to explain the processes performed in the neural network. They may seem a little complicated. You can skim through this section because the symbols are only used here:

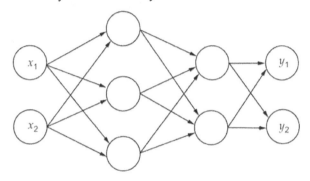

Figure 3.15: Three-layer neural network, including two neurons in input layer (layer 0), three neurons in first hidden layer (layer 1), two neurons in second hidden layer (layer 2), and two neurons in the output layer (layer 3)

In this part, it is necessary to calculate a neural network collectively as a matrix. A collective matrix multiplication may be used to calculate each layer in a neural network (this can be considered from a larger viewpoint). So, even if you forget precise regulations about these symbols, there is no trouble comprehending the further explanations.

Let's start with the symbols defined in *figure 3.16*. This graph shows how much the input layer x^2 to the neuron in the next layer weighs. As illustrated in *figure 3.16*, a neuron of the weight or buried layer (1) is put in the upper right corner. The layer 1 weight or neuron is given by (1). The weight of the neurons in the preceding and succeeding layers is two numbers on the right bottom.

For example, $w_{12}^{(1)}$ indicates that it is the weight from the second neuron (x_2) in the previous layer to the first neuron $a_1^{(1)}$ in the next layer.

In the sequence of the number for the succeeding and the preceding layers, the bottom-right weight indicator numbers have to be:

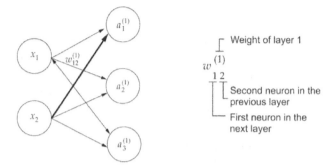

Figure 3.16: Weight symbols

Transmission of signal in each layer

Let's take a look at the transmission of signals from the input layer to the first neuron in layer 1. This is shown in *figure 3.17*:

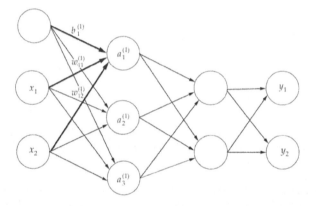

Figure 3.17: Transmitting signals from the input layer to layer 1

As shown in *figure 3.17*, ① is added as a neuron for a bias. Note that there is only one index at the lower right of the bias. This is because only one bias neuron (① neuron) exists in the previous layer. Now, let's $a_1^{(1)}$ express as an equation to review what we have learned so far. is the sum of the weighted signals and the bias and is calculated as follows:

$$a_1^{(1)} = w_{11}^{(1)} x_1 + w_{12}^{(1)} x_2 + b_1^{(1)}$$

Equation 3.8

By using matrix multiplication, you can express the weighted sum of layer 1 collectively as follows:

$$\mathbf{A}^{(1)} = \mathbf{X}\mathbf{W}^{(1)} + \mathbf{B}^{(1)}$$

Equation 3.9

Here, $\mathbf{A}^{(1)}$, $\mathbf{X}$, $\mathbf{B}^{(1)}$, and $\mathbf{W}^{(1)}$ are as follows:

Let us now use multidimensional arrays of NumPy to build a balance (*3.9*). For input signals, weights, and biases, arbitrary values are set here:

```
A = np.array([2.0, 1.0])
W1 = np.array([[0.2, 0.4, 0.6], [0.3, 0.5, 0.7]])
B1 = np.array([0.5, 1.0, 0.7])
print(W1.shape) # (2, 3)
print(X.shape)  # (2,)
print(B1.shape) # (3,)
A1 = np.dot(X, W1) + B1
```

This is the same computation as the last one. **W1** is a 2x3 array and **X** is a double-element one-dimensional array. The number of elements in the respective sizes of **W1** and **X** are also equal in this scenario. Take into account the procedures of the activation function in layer 1. The procedures are graphically shown in *figure 3.18*.

As illustrated in *figure 3.18*, weighted sums are displayed as *a's* and signals transformed with a hidden layer (total of weighted signals and biases) are displayed as *z's*. Here, **h()** is displayed as the activation function using sigmoid function:

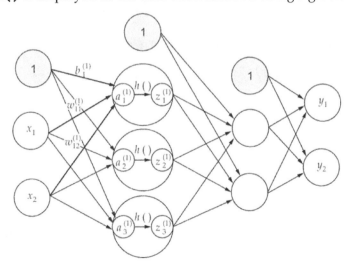

Figure 3.18: Transmitting signals from the input layer to layer 1

This process is implemented in Python as follows:

```
Z1 = sigmoid(A1)
print(A1) # [ 4.5  8.  10.7]
print(Z1) # [0.98901306 0.99966465 0.99997746]
```

This **sigmoid()** function is the function we previously defined. It accepts a NumPy array and returns the same number of elements in a NumPy array.

Please proceed to layer 1 through layer 2 implementation (*figure 3.19*):

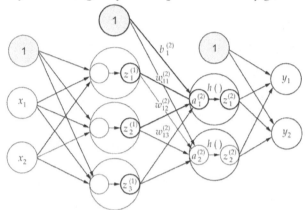

Figure 3.19: *Transmitting signals from layer 1 to layer 2*

The layer is identical to the previous layer, except that the layer 1 output (**Z1**) is the layer 2 output. As you can see, by utilizing NumPy arrays, signals can be sent simply from one layer to another:

```
W2 = np.array([[0.2, 0.7], [0.6, 0.9], [0.5, 0.7]])
B2 = np.array([0.2, 0.3])
print(Z1.shape) # (3,)
print(W2.shape) # (3, 2)
print(B2.shape) # (2,)
A2 = np.dot(Z1, W2) + B2
Z2 = sigmoid(A2)
```

Finally, allow signals from layer 2 to the output layer to be sent (*figure 3.20*). The output layer can be implemented almost the same manner as we have looked at the previous implementation. Only the last function to activate is distinct from the previously hidden layers:

```
def identity_function(a):
    return a
```

```
W3 = np.array([[0.2, 0.5], [0.7, 0.8]])

B3 = np.array([0.2, 0.3])

A3 = np.dot(Z2, W3) + B3

Y = identity_function(A3) # or Y = A3
```

In the following diagram, we construct an **identity_function()** and utilize it as an output layer activation function. The input as it is produces an identity function. Although **identity_function()** does not have to be specified in this example, this is used so that it is compatible with the preceding ones. In *figure 3.20*, the output layer's activation function appears as "()" to demonstrate that it is distinct from the hidden layers' activation, **h()** (is termed sigma):

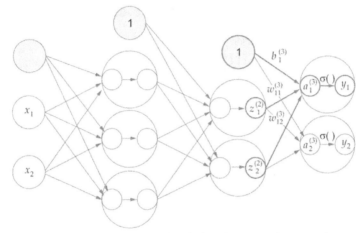

Figure 3.20: *Transmitting signals from layer 2 to the output layer*

Depending on the sort of problems you want to resolve, you may choose the activation function in the output layer. An identity function is generally utilized for a regression problem, a sigmoid function for a two-class grading problem, and a softmax feature for a multi classification problem. In the next part we will discuss in detail the activation function of an output layer.

Summary of implementation

This concludes our study of the neural network of three layers. The following sums up the implementation we have accomplished so far. In the case of neural networking, only weights are recorded in uppercase (for example, **W1**), while others are written down (for example, bias and intermediate outcome), as is customary:

```
import numpy as np


def sigmoid(x):
```

```
        return 1 / (1 + np.exp(-x))


def identity_function(a):
    return a


def init_network():
    network = {}
    network['W1'] = np.array([[0.2, 0.4, 0.6], [0.3, 0.5, 0.7]] )
    network['b1'] = np.array([0.5, 1.0, 0.7])
    network['W2'] = np.array([[0.2, 0.7], [0.6, 0.9], [0.5, 0.7]] )
    network['b2'] = np.array([0.2, 0.3])
    network['W3'] = np.array([[0.2, 0.5], [0.7, 0.8]])
    network['b3'] = np.array([0.2, 0.3])
    return network


def forward(network, x):
    W1, W2, W3 = network['W1'], network['W2'], network['W3']
    b1, b2, b3 = network['b1'], network['b2'], network['b3']
    a1 = np.dot(x, W1) + b1
    z1 = sigmoid(a1)
    a2 = np.dot(z1, W2)  +  b2
    z2 = sigmoid(a2)
    a3 = np.dot(z2,  W3)  +  b3
    y = identity_function(a3)
    return y


network = init_network()
x =  np.array([1.5, 1.0])
y = forward(network, x)
print(y) [0.99251484 1.42079246]
```

Here we have defined the methods **sigmoid()**, **identity_function()**, **init_network()**, and **forward()**. The **init_network()** initializes weight and distortion by storing it in a dictionary-type variable, which is a network that holds necessary layer, weight and bias information. Together, the **forward()** function translates an input signal into an output signal.

The term "*forward*" implies the process of transmission from the input to the output. Then, when we train a neural network, we examine this process backwards (from output to input). The implementation of a neural three-layer network in the future is completed. By using NumPy's multidimensional arrays, we were able to implement a neural network efficiently.

The output layer design

You may use a neural network both for a problem with classification and regression. However, depending on what issues for which you utilize a neural network, you will have to modify the activation function of the output layer. Usually, an identity function is used for a problem of regression and softmax is used with a problem of classification.

> **The difficulties of learning machines may often be split into issues of *classification* and *regression*. One problem of classification is identifying which class the details are; for example, classifying a person as a man or a woman in an image, whereas the problem of regression consists of the prediction of a (continuous) number of specific input data, such as predicting the weight of a person in an image.**

Softmax identity feature and function

The input produces an identity function. An identity function is the function which produces what is entered without doing anything. Therefore, an input signal is returned as it is when an identity function is utilized for the output layer. You may demonstrate the process using an identity function (as shown in *figure 3.21*) using the neural network diagram we utilized so far. The conversion process using the identity function may be represented by the same arrow as the activation function that we have seen so far:

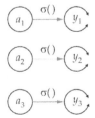

Figure 3.21: *Identity function*

The following equation is used to express the softmax function used for a classification problem:

$$y_k = \frac{\exp(a_k)}{\sum_{i=1}^{n} \exp(a_i)}$$

Equation 3.10

Here, *e* is Napier's constant, 2.7182...

The *ex(x)* is an exponential function indicating *ex(c)*. The equation yields the *k*-th output, y_k, if the total number of output layers is *n*. The softmax function numerator is the exponential function of the input signal, a_k, and the denominator is the sum of the exponential functions of all the input signals. As illustrated in equation (*3.10*).

The softmax function is graphically illustrated in *figure 3.22*. As you can see, all input signals with arrows are connected to the output of the softmax function:

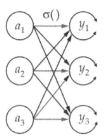

Figure 3.22: *Softmax function*

Now, let's implement the softmax function, using the Python interpreter to check the results, one-by-one:

```
>>> x = np.array([0.6, 4.9, 8.0])

>>>

>>> exp_x = np.exp(x) # Exponential function
>>> print(exp_x)
[1.82211880e+00 1.34289780e+02 2.98095799e+03]

>>>

>>> sum_exp_x = np.sum(exp_x) # Sum of exponential functions
>>> print(sum_exp_x)
3117.0698855270543

>>>

>>> y = exp_x / sum_exp_x
```

```
>>> print(y)
```

```
[5.84561421e-04 4.30820561e-02 9.56333382e-01]
```

The softmax equation function (*3.10*) with Python is presented in this implementation. No particular description is therefore necessary. We shall then define the softmax function as a Python function as follows:

```
def softmax(x):

    exp_x = np.exp(x)

    sum_exp_x = np.sum(exp_x)

    y = exp_x / sum_exp_x

    return y
```

Issues when implementing the Softmax function

The previous softmax function implementation accurately expresses an equation (*3.10*), however for computer calculations it is faulty. This error represents a problem with overflow. The softmax function requires the calculation of exponential functions and can have a very large exponential function value. For example, e^{10} is bigger than 20,000, while e^{100} is bigger than 40 digits.

> **When a computer processes a number, a data width of four or eight bytes is saved. So there are a lot of important figures. There is restricted range of numbers to be represented. Thus, the difficulty is that it is not possible to represent a really large value. This is termed as an "*overflow*". Therefore, we have to take caution while using computer calculations.**

The following equations provide an enhanced implementation of the softmax function:

$$y_k = \frac{\exp(a_k)}{\sum_{i=1}^{n} \exp(a_i)} = \frac{C \exp(a_k)}{C \sum_{i=1}^{n} \exp(a_i)}$$

$$= \frac{\exp(a_k + \log C)}{\sum_{i=1}^{n} \exp(a_i + \log C)}$$

$$= \frac{\exp(a_k + C')}{\sum_{i=1}^{n} \exp(a_i + C')}$$

Equation 3.11

First, equation (*3.11*) is changed by multiplying both the numerator and the denominator by an arbitrary constant C (the same calculations are performed because both the numerator and the denominator are multiplied by the same constant). Then, C is transferred to an exponential (**exp**) function as *log C*. Then, *log C* is finally replaced by another sign, *C'*.

The equation (*3.11*) states that when the exponential function is calculated, the addition or removal of a particular constant does not affect the outcome. Although any number like *C'* may be used here, it is common to use the highest value from the input signals to prevent an overflow. Consider the following example:

```
>>> a = np.array([9090, 3000, 110])
>>> np.exp(a) / np.sum(np.exp(a)) # Calculating the softmax function
array([nan, nan,  0.]) # Not calculated correctly
>>>
>>> c = np.max(a) # 1010
>>> a - c
array([    0, -6090, -8980])
>>>
>>> np.exp(a - c) / np.sum(np.exp(a - c))
array([1., 0., 0.])
```

You may correctly compute the function by subtracting the larger value of the input signals (**c**, here). Alternatively, nan (not a number: unstable) values are returned. Based on this description, we may implement the softmax function as follows:

```
def softmax(x):
    c = np.max(x)
    exp_x = np.exp(x - c) # Prevent an overflow
    sum_exp_x = np.sum(exp_x)
    y = exp_x / sum_exp_x
    return y
```

Softmax feature characteristics

To calculate the output of the neural network, you may use the **softmax()** function:

```
>>> a = np.array ([0.6, 4.9, 8.0])
>>> y = softmax(a)
>>> print(y)
[5.84561421e-04 4.30820561e-02 9.56333382e-01]
```

```
>>> np.sum(y)
```

```
1.0
```

The softmax function produces a real 0 to 1.0 value. The total of softmax function outputs is 1. The fact that the total number is 1 is a crucial feature of the softmax function, since this implies that we may interpreted the softmax function's output as a *"probability"*.

For example, in this case, the **y[0]** probability might be interpreted as 0.018 (1.8%), **y[1]** probability may be interpreted as 0.245 (24.5%) and **y[2]** likely as 0.737. (73.7%). From these chances, we may infer that *because the second element is most likely, the second class is the solution.* We could even say, probably, that *the answer is the second class with a 74 percent probability, the first class with a 25 percent likelihood, and the zeroth class with a 1 percent probability.* You may thus utilize the softmax function to probabilistically (statistically) manage an issue.

Note that the use of softmax does not alter the order of the elements. This is due to the monotonic growth of an exponential function, (**y = exp(x)**). In fact, the order of the elements in the previous example is the same as that of the elements in **y**. The second element is the highest value in **a**, and the second element is the highest value in **y**.

The categorization of neural network classes often only identifies the class that matches the neuron with the highest output. The location of the neuron at the greatest output does not change with the softmax function. You may therefore exclude softmax from neural network classification for the output layer. In fact, the softmax function for the output layer is often left out because it takes certain computations for the exponential function.

There are two steps in the process of addressing a problem of machine learning: training and predicting. In the training phase, you train a model and then use the learned model to predict (classify) unknown data during the inference phase. As previously mentioned, the softmax function for the output layer in the inference phase is generally ignored. We choose softmax function for the output layer when the neural network trains are important (for more details, refer to the next chapter). Number of neurons in layer of output

Depending on the problem to be resolved, you must determine the number of neurons in the output layer. The number of classes to be classified is normally utilized as the number of neurons in the output layer for classification tasks. For example, 10 neurons are inserted in the output layer, as illustrated in *figure 3.23* to predict a number from 0 to 9 of the input image (classification 10).

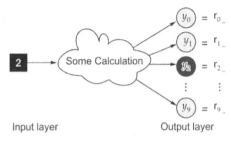

Input layer   Output layer

Figure 3.23: *The neuron in the output layer corresponds to each number*

The neurons in the output layer are 0, 1, ..., 9 from the top as seen in *figure 3.23*. Here, the different grey tones depict the values of the output layer neurons. In this case, y_2 is the darkest hue, as the y_2 neuron produces the highest value. This neural network indicates that the input belongs to the class corresponding to y_2, that is, 2.

Handwritten digit recognition

Let's explore a real situation now that we've studied the mechanics of the neural network. Some manuscript digital images will be classified. Once we have completed the training, we will use training settings to implement neural network inference. This deduction is also termed "**neural network propagation**".

> **Like the process to solve a machine learning issue (which has two stages, training and inference), we utilize training data to train weight parameters and then use learned parameters to forecast the input data. To resolve the problem using the neural network.**

MNIST dataset

We'll utilize a set of images called **MNIST** with handwritten digits. MNIST is one of the most renowned machine learning data sets that is utilized from simple tests to research in many methods. While reading image recognition or machine learning research articles, you typically realize that the MNIST dataset may be utilized as experimental information.

The MNIST data collection includes numerical images from 0 to 9 (*figure 3.24*). It comprises of 60,000 training images and a total of 10,000 test images. In the usage of the MNIST dataset, trainings are normally used to assess how the trained model categorizes the test images correctly:

Figure 3.24: Examples from the MNIST image dataset

Image data of MNIST is a 28x28 grey image (one channel) with a value of 0 to 255 for every pixel. The image data, such 7, 2, and 1, are marked for each image.

This book has a handy Python script, **mnist.py**, placed in the directory of the **dataset**. It allows the download and conversion of the MNIST dataset into NumPy arrays. The current folder should be **chapter01**, **chapter02**, **chapter03**,... or **chapter08**, in order to utilize the **mnist.py** script. You can simply load MNIST data by using the **load_mnist()** method in **mnist.py**:

```
import sys, os

sys.path.append(os.pardir) # Configure to import the files in the parent
directory

from dataset.mnist import load_mnist

# Waits for a few minutes for the first call ...

(a_train, b_train), (a_test, b_test) =
    load_mnist(flatten=True, normalize=False)

# Output the shape of each data

print(a_train.shape) # (60000, 784)

print(b_train.shape) # (60000,)

print(a_test.shape) # (10000, 784)

print(b_test.shape) # (10000,)
```

First, set up the files in the parent directory for import details. Then, from **data set/ mnist.py**, import the **load_mnist** function. Use the imported **load_mnist** function to load the MNIST dataset. When you first run **load_mnist**, you have to download the MNIST data through an internet connection. A call will be completed as soon as it only loads the files stored locally (pickle files).

In the **dataset** directory the source code in this book contains the files for loading the MNIST images. This MNIST dataset is supposed to only be used in the directories **chapter01**, **chapter02**, **chapter03**, ... or **chapter08**.

The **sys.path.append(os.pardir)** line is thus necessary to use the dataset. The reason is that the files must be imported in the parent directory (directory of the data collection).

The method **load_mnist** returns the loaded MNIST data (workout image, training label) (test image, test label). Three arguments can be used: **load_** mnist(normalize=False, flatten=Article, one hot label=Corrective). The first option, normalize, indicates if the input image may be normalized between 0.0 and 1.0. The input image pixel stays between 0 and 255 if **False** is specified. The second option, flatten, indicates if the supplied image should be flattened (convert it into a one-dimensional array).

If **False** is set, an array of three dimensions $(1 = 28 + 28)$ is saved in the input image. If the **True** is set, the array containing 784 entries is stored as one-dimensional. One hot label, the third parameter, indicates whether the label should be stored using one-hot encoding. Only 1 items for the right label is in a one-hot encoded array and 0, as in [0,0,1,0,0,0,0,0,0,0], for the remaining elements. Only the right label, such 7 or 2, is saved when one hot label is **False**. If one hot label is **True**, then the labels are saved as an encoded one-hot array.

> Python includes a comfortable feature called pickle that stores objects as files throughout execution of the application. You can recover the object that you used when running the programme instantly by loading the stored pickle file. Pickle is used for the method **load_mnist()**, which loads the MNIST dataset (for the second or subsequent loading phases). You may prepare MNIST data rapidly by using the **pickle** functionality.

Let us now display images from MNIST for data inspection. We will show the images using the **Python Image Library** (**PIL**). The first training image, as illustrated in *figure 3.25* (source code **@ chapter03/mnist show.py**), is presented when the following code is executed:

```python
import sys, os
sys.path.append(os.pardir)
import numpy as np
from dataset.mnist import load_mnist
from PIL import Image
def img_show(img):
    pil_img = Image.fromarray(np.uint8(img))
    pil_img.show()
(a_train, b_train), (a_test, b_test) = /
    load_mnist(flatten=True, normalize=False)
    img = a_train[0]
    label = b_train[0]
    print(label) # 5
```

```
    print(img.shape) # (784,)

    img = img.reshape(28, 28) # Reshape the image based on the original
size

    print(img.shape) # (28, 28)

    img_show(img)
```

This results in the following output:

Figure 3.25: *Displaying an MNIST image*

Note that the loaded image is saved as a NumPy array on one line when it is **flatten=True** (one-dimensionally). You must thus change it to an original 28x28 size in order to see the image. To redesign a NumPy array, you can use the **reshape()** procedure to set a parameter to the desired form. The image data saved in a NumPy array must also be converted into the PIL data object. This conversion may be done with **image.fromarray()**.

Inference for neural network

Let us now implement this MNIST dataset to create a neural network. The network is made up of a 784-neuron input layer and a ten-neuron input layer. The 784 for the input layer comes in the image size (28 x 28 = 784), the 10 for the output layer in 10 classes (10 classes of numbers 0 to 9). The first one has fifty neurons, whereas the second one has hundred neurons. The numbers 50 and 100 can be changed as you wish. First, let's provide the methods, **get_data()**, **init_network()**, and **prediction()**. The source code in **chapter03/ NeuralNetwork_MNIST.py** is:

```
def get_data():
    (a_train, b_train), (a_test, b_test) = /
        load_mnist(normalize=True, flatten=True, one_hot_label=False)
    return a_test, b_test
def init_network():
    with open("sample_weight.pkl", 'rb') as f:
        network = pickle.load(f)
```

```
    return network
def predict(network, x):
    W1, W2, W3 = network['W1'], network['W2'], network['W3']
    b1, b2, b3 = network['b1'], network['b2'], network['b3']
    a1 = np.dot(x, W1) + b1
    z1 = sigmoid(a1)
    a2 = np.dot(z1, W2) + b2
    z2 = sigmoid(a2)
    a3 = np.dot(z2, W3) + b3
    y = softmax(a3)
    return y
```

The **init_network()** loads the weight parameters which are contained in the **sample_weight.pkl pickle** file. This file includes weight and bias parameters as a dictionary-type variable. The following two functions are nearly the same as those given in previous implementations so they don't have to be detailed. These three functions are now to be used to predict the neural network. We want to assess the accuracy of recognition, that is, how to categorize it correctly:

```
x, t = get_data()
network = init_network()
accuracy_cnt = 0
for i in range(len(x)):
    y = predict(network, x[i])
    p = np.argmax(y) # Obtain the index of the most probable element
    if p == t[i]:
        accuracy_cnt += 1
print("Accuracy:" + str(float(accuracy_cnt) / len(x)))
```

Here we get and create a network with the MNIST dataset, then apply a command for each data of the image to be kept in **x** and use **predict()** to categorizes. The **predict()** method produces a NumPy array with each label's probability. For example, an array like [0.1, 0.3, 0.2, ..., 0.04] is returned, indicating that the likelihood of "0" is 0.1, "1" is 0.3, etc. A prediction result is the index with the greatest value in this list of probabilities and indicates the most probable element. The index of the biggest member in an array may be obtained using **nP.argmax(x)**.

It returns the **x** parameter index of the biggest item in the array. Finally, we compare the prediction replies from the neural network with the right label and present the accuracy of the predictions (accuracy).

Accuracy:0.9352 appears when the previous code is performed. This demonstrates that 93.52% of the category was right. We won't talk about the recognition accuracy now since we want to run a trained neural network, but then we will enhance the neural network structure and training process to get more accuracy. Actually, the accuracy is above 99%. The **load_mnist** function parameter, standardized, is set to **True** in this example. When **normalize** is **True**, each pixel in the image is divided by a function of 255, such that the values of a data are from 0.0 to 1.0. The conversion of data to fit in a particular range is termed as "**standardization**" and preprocessing is used to transform the data for the neural network in a given way. Here, the incoming image data was standardized as preprocessing.

> **Preprocessing is commonly utilized in practical applications in a neural network (deep learning). Experiments have demonstrated the validity of preprocessing, such as enhanced discrimination and faster learning. In this example, the value of each pixel was split by 255 by preprocessing, to make straightforward normalization. Preprocessing is typically carried out while the distribution of the entire data is being considered. The standard average deviation of the entire data is applied to normalize the entire data so as to dispense all the data around 0 or to fit in a specific range. Furthermore, all data are also whitening to ensure that they are more uniformly dispersed.**

Batch processing

This technique involves the creation of the MNIST dataset to create a neural network. Here, we review the previous method while taking the shapes of the input data and the weight factors into account.

Use the Python interpreter to produce the form of the weights for each layer of the previous neural network the shape of the weights:

```
>>> x, _ = get_data( )
>>> network = init_network( )
>>> W1, W2, W3 = network['W1'], network['W2'], network['W3']
>>>
>>> x.shape
(10000, 784)
>>> x[0].shape
(784,)
```

```
>>> W1.shape
(784, 50)
>>> W2.shape
(50, 100)
>>> W3.shape
(100, 10)
```

Let us check that in the matching multidimensional arrays, the number of elements are the same as in the previous result (biases are omitted). This is visually shown in *figure 3.26*. The number of items in the appropriate multidimensional array is the same here. Make sure that the end output is a one-dimensional array with 10 items **Y**:

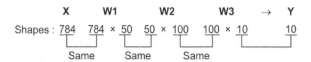

Figure 3.26: *Transition of the shapes of arrays*

The preceding figure depicts the flow in which a one-dimensional array with 784 items is supplied and a one-dimensional array with 10 elements is reinstated (originally the two-dimensional 28x28 array). This is the procedure when an image is entered.

Let us now think about the procedure when several photos are input simultaneously. Suppose, for example, that 100 image are processed in conjunction with the **predict()** method. To accomplish so, you can modify the form of **x** to 100 digits 784 to enter 100 images as input data collectively. This is graphically shown in the following figure:

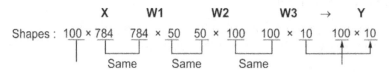

Figure 3.27: *Transition of the shapes of arrays in batch processing*

The input data is 100x784 and output data is 100x10 as shown in *figure 3.27*. This means that the results are returned in one go for the supplied data of 100 images. Examples include **x[0]** and **y[0]** store the image and forecast the results of the 0th image, **x[1]** store, and **y[1]** predict the first image result, etc.

An organized group of data is referred to as a batch, as detailed below. A batch is an image stack, like a bundle of letters.

In computer calculation, batch processing offers a great benefit. The processing time of each image may significantly be reduced as many libraries that manage numerical operations are well tuned to efficiently compute huge arrays. If data transport causes a bottleneck in the computation of the neural network, batch processing might minimize the bus load (that is, the ratio of operations to data loading can be increased).

Although a large array has to be created for batch processing, computing a large array in one go is faster than calculating tiny arrays. Now, let's utilize batch processing for our implementation. Here you can see the differences from the previous code in bold:

```
x, t = get_data( )

network = init_network( )

batch_size = 100 # Number of batches

accuracy_cnt = 0

for i in range(0, len(x), batch_size):

    a_batch = x[i:i+batch_size]

    b_batch = predict(network, a_batch)

    p = np.argmax(b_batch, axis=1)

    accuracy_cnt += np.sum(p == t[i:i+batch_size])

print("Accuracy:" + str(float(accuracy_cnt) / len(x)))
```

Now, each part will be described in bold. Let's first see the function **range()**. You may use **range()** to produce the list of integer(s) from **start** to **end-1**; for example, **range(start and end)**. Three integer numbers as provided in the **range(start, end, step)** will allow the list of integer values to be generated with the value supplied in the step, as in the following example:

```
>>> list( range(0, 10) )

[0, 1, 2, 3, 4, 5, 6, 7, 8, 9]

>>> list( range(0, 10, 3) )

[0, 3, 6, 9]
```

The **x[i:i+batch size]** object is used to extract a batch from the input data, based on the list provided by the **range()** method. The **x[i:i+batch n]** object receives in the data entry data from **i**-th to **i+batch n**-th. Hundred pieces of data, including **x[0:100]**, **x[100:200]**, and so on, are collected from the beginning.

The index of the biggest value is **argmax()**. Please note here is an argument, **axis=1**. It states that the index of the greatest value of the elements of dimension 1 may be located in the 100x10 array (the axis is roughly the same as the dimension), as demonstrated in the following:

```
>>> a = np.array([[0.2, 0.9, 0.5], [0.7, 0.5, 0.1], [0.4, 0.9, 0.1], [0.5,
0.3, 0.2]])
>>> b = np.argmax(a, axis=1)
>>> print(b)
[1 0 1 0]
```

Finally, the results of each categorization are compared to real replies for each batch. To do this, the NumPy arrays are compared through a comparison operator (==). A **True**/**False** Boolean array is returned and the number of **Trues** is computed as follows:

```
>>> a = np.array([2, 1, 0, 1])
>>> b = np.array([2, 1, 0, 1])
>>> print(a==b)
[ True  True  True  True]
>>> np.sum(a==b)
4
```

This is for batch processing implementation. Batch processing makes processing quick and efficient. In the following chapter, batches of image data are utilized to train when we learn about neural networks. We will also develop a batch processing solution like we have done in this chapter.

Conclusion

This chapter covered advanced neural network propagation. The neural network we discussed in this chapter is the same as the neural signals that were transmitted hierarchically in the previous chapter. In activation functions, however, the signal changes when transmitted to the next neurons. There is a substantial difference. A neural network employs a sigmoid function as an active function, which changes signals gradually, while a perceptron uses a step function, which significantly changes signals. In neural network training, this distinction is essential and will be discussed in the next chapter.

CHAPTER 4
Training Neural Network

This chapter covers training in neural networks. When we talk about *training*, we mean automatically acquiring optimum weight parameters from training data. We shall use a method called **gradient method** to detect the least loss function value that utilizes the gradient of a function.

Structure

- Learning from data
- Data-driven
- Training data and test data
- Loss function
- Sum of squared errors
- Cross-entropy error
- Mini-batch learning
    - Implementing cross-entropy error (using batches)
    - Why configure a loss function
- Numerical differentiation
    - Derivative

     o Examples of numerical differentiation
- Partial derivative
- Gradient
  - Gradient method
  - Gradients for a neural network
- Implementing a training algorithm
  - Presupposition
- A two-layer neural network as a class
- Implementing mini-batch training
- Using test data for evaluation

Objective

In this chapter a criterion called **loss function** is introduced; this allows a neural network to study. The aim of the training is to identify the weight parameters which lead to the lowest loss function value.

Learning from data

The key attribute of the neural network is its ability to learn from data. Data training implies that the values of the weight parameter may be calculated automatically. It's hard to work if you need to manually determine all the settings. For example, we manually computed parameter values when looking at the truth table for an example perceptron, as illustrated in *Chapter 2: Perceptron in Depth*. The number of parameters may nevertheless vary among thousands and tens of thousands in a real neural network. The number of parameters might approach hundreds of millions for deeper learning with additional layers. This chapter covers how to select data parameter values or how to use neural network training and a model that learns handwritten digits using Python's MNIST dataset.

A perceptron can automatically learn from data for a linearly separable issue. This training can solve a linearly separable issue that is known as *the convergence theory of perceptron* when finished a finite number of times. A nonlinear separation problem cannot be addressed automatically on the other hand.

Data-driven

In machine learning, data is important. Machine learning searches for a response in the data, discovers a model in the data, and presents a story on that basis. Without data, it can accomplish nothing. Hence, there are *data* at the machine learning center. We may argue that this method, based on facts, is a turning point of a *man* approach.

Usually, we must examine several factors to get a reply while resolving a problem — especially when we need to identify a pattern. "It seems that this problem has this pattern." We advance this activity by trial and error, based on our experience and intuition. Machine learning prevents as much as possible human involvement. It seeks a reply (pattern) from the data it has collected. In addition, a neural network and deep knowledge have an essential feature in common, since more than standard machine learnings may avoid human involvement.

Let's look here at a particular situation. Suppose we want a software that recognizes for instance the number 2. Suppose we develop a software to identify if hand-written pictures are "2 or not" as illustrated in *figure 4.1*. It looks quite straightforward. How can we utilize the algorithm?

Figure 4.1: *Sample handwritten digits – how "2" is written varies from person to person*

You'll find this more challenging than imagined when you try to create a software that can categorize "2" accurately. We can readily identify "2", however the criterion for identifying a picture as "2" is tough to define. How it is written changes from person to person as seen in *figure 4.1*. This tells us that it is difficult to discover the rule to recognize "2" and it might take a lot of time.

We would want to leverage data to solve the problem efficiently, rather than *developing* an algorithm recognizing "2" from scratch. One technique we may do is to extract images from their functionality and apply machine learning to understand the characteristics pattern. A feature shows a converter intended to correctly extract vital information (important data) from input data (input picture). The visual characteristic is often described as a **vector**. In the computer vision sector, SIFT, SURF, and HOG are well known characteristics. These characteristics may be used to convert picture data to vectors and to learn converted vectors from a classifier in machine learning, such as SVM or KNN.

A *machine* develops a pattern from the data acquired during this kind of learning. This is more efficient in solving a problem and reduces *human* load when compared to inventing an algorithm. However, the characteristics utilized for converting pictures into vectors are developed by a *person*. This is because good outcomes cannot be achieved without proper characteristics for the problem (or without designing the features). For example, a person must pick characteristics which differ from the ones to recognize "2" to recognize the face of a dog. After all, it may even be necessary to use features and machine learning. After all, even the approach of using features and machine learning may need suitable features to be selected by a *man*, depending on the problem.

Even a *man*, depending upon the situation, may require appropriate features to be picked for the technique of employing features and machine learning.

We have explored two difficulties with machine learning. In the high lines in *figure 4.2* these two techniques are displayed. In the lower row of *figure 4.2*, you can find the technique for employing a neural network (profound learning). It's represented as an uninterfered block.

A neural network learns *as they are*, as seen in *figure 4.2*. In the second method, the example using the features and machine training, known as human-designed features, is utilized, while a *machine* learns significant characteristics from pictures in a neural network:

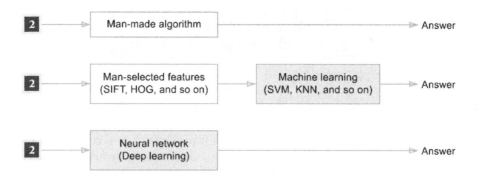

Figure 4.2: *A paradigm shift from man-made rules to a "machine" learning from data – a block without human intervention is shown in gray*

Deep learning is also referred to as end-to-end learning. End-to-end denotes the collection of the desired outcome from the raw data from one end to the other (input).

The benefit of a neural network is that it can handle all of the issues in the same flow. For instance, a neural network learns the supplied data patiently and seeks to uncover a pattern of the specific issue, whether by attempting to identify "5," a dog or a human face. An end-to-end neural network can learn data, regardless of the challenge.

Training data and test data

We will discuss neural network training in this chapter, starting with certain standard practices in data management in machine learning.

We generally utilize training data and test data to suit the purpose in machine learning difficulties. First, the only way to identify optimum settings is through training data. In order to assess the capability of the trained model, we also need test data. Why should we split information on training and testing? Because we want the model's capacity to generalize. The training data and test data should be separated since we want to properly assess this generalization.

Generalization is the capacity of unknown data (data not observed in training data), and this generalization is the ultimate aim of machine learning. In an automated system for reading postal codes on postcards, for example, handwritten digit recognition may be utilized. In such a case, *someone* characters should be distinguished by manual digit recognition. *This someone is not an individual's distinctive character, but an arbitrary character for an arbitrary person.* Even if the model can only identify your information, the data can only learn specific characteristics of the person's handwriting.

Therefore, if you just have a data set to learn and evaluate parameters, a proper assessment will not be provided. This leads to a model that can handle but cannot manage a specific data collection. Too much overfitting arises if a model is changed to just one dataset. Avoiding overfitting is a major challenge in machine learning.

Loss function

On the question, "How happy are you now?" How do you reply? We may usually answer loosely: "I'm so slightly happy" or "I'm not happy." If someone answers, "My current rate of happiness is 10.23," you may be startled, since they can assess their pleasure with only one figure. If there is such a person, he can conduct his life on the basis of his "feelings of happiness."

This 'feeling core' is an allegory that is used to represent specific topics like neural network training. The current state of the neural network training is represented by a *score*. Based on the score, weight parameters are searched ideally. In seeking ideal living based on the happiness score, this individual searches for a network of neurons as a guide for optimal set-ups. The score used in neural network training is called a **loss function**. Even if a loss function is utilized, square mistakes or cross-entropy errors are usually summed up.

An indication of a loss function is the "*poor character*" of the neural network capacity. This illustrates how inappropriate the current neural network is for the data labelled and how it is not for the data labelled. It can seem strange to have the "*poor capacity*" score, however the loss function multiplied by a negative number can be understood as 'how poor the capacity is' (that is, the score of "*how good the ability is*"). "The decrease in the capacity" is the same as "the maximization of skill goodness." Therefore the *poverty* capacity indicator is basically the same as the *goodness* capacity indicator.

Sum of squared errors

Some features are utilized as losses. Perhaps the most famous are the total squared errors. The following equation states:

$$E = \frac{1}{2} \sum_k (y_k - t_k)^2$$

Equation 4.1

In this regard, YK is the result of the neural network and **tk** is the label for the data. For example, in *Chapter 3: Neural Network*, neural networks, **yk** and **tk** are data items consisting of ten elements;

```
>>> a = [0.1, 0.05, 0.6, 0.0, 0.05, 0.1, 0.0, 0.1, 0.0, 0.0]
>>> b = [0, 0, 1, 0, 0, 0, 0, 0, 0, 0]
```

The output may be seen as the softmax function probability. **0** is **0.1**, **1** is **0.05**, **2** is **0.6**, etc., in the following example. The **0** in this instance **a** data are indicated in the meanwhile. The correct marker for the data on the label is **1** and the other labels are **0**. The label **2** is 1 that shows that the answer is **2**. The one hot display is **1** for the correct label and **0** for other labels.

The total squared errors are the total squares of differential squares between the outputs of the neural system and the relevant elements of the correct instructor data (*4.1*). Let's now utilize the total squared errors of Python:

```
def sum_squared_error(a,  b):
    return 0.5 * np.sum((a-b)**2)
```

NumPy arrays are the **a** and **b** parameters here. We're not going to discuss this here as it just implements equation (*4.1*). Now we're going to utilize this function to calculate:

```
>>> # Assume that "2" is correct
>>> a = [0, 0, 1, 0, 0, 0, 0, 0, 0, 0]
>>>
>>>  # Example 1: "2" is the most probable (0.6)
>>> b = [0.1, 0.05, 0.6, 0.0, 0.05, 0.1, 0.0, 0.1, 0.0, 0.0]
>>> sum_squared_error(np.array(a), np.array(b))
0.0975000000000000031
>>>
>>>  # Example 2: "7" is the most probable (0.6)
```

```
>>> a = [0.1, 0.05, 0.1, 0.0, 0.05, 0.1, 0.0, 0.6, 0.0, 0.0]
>>> sum_squared_error(np.array(a), np.array(b))
0.25
```

Two instances are given here. The first response is **2** and the neural network output is **2**. The second answer is **2**. In the second, the answer is **2**, but the neural network output is the greatest at **7**. The loss function of the first case is smaller, showing that the difference in the labelled data is lower. As a result of this experiment. This means that the sum of squared errors shows that, in the first case, the output matches better the labelled data.

Cross-entropy error

A cross-entropy error is commonly used as a loss function, rather than the sum of squared errors. The following equation expresses this:

$$E = -\sum_k t_k \log y_k$$

Equation 4.2

The logarithm at the bottom of e indicates here the natural logarithm (loge). The yk is the neural network output and t_k is the right label. In t_k just the right label index is 1; the remaining indices are 0. (one-hot representation). Equation (4.2) so only calculates the output logarithm that is the right label, 1.

For example, if the label index is "2" and the neural network output is 0.6, a cross-entropy error is *-log 0.6 = 0.51.*

When the "2" output is 0.1, *-log 0.1 = 2.30* is a mistake. The output result of the right label depends on a cross-entropy mistake. This natural logarithm is seen in *figure 4.3:*

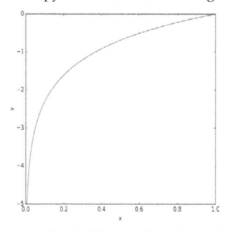

Figure 4.3: Graph of the natural logarithm y = log x

The value of y is lower as x approaches 0, as seen in *figure 4.3*, when x is 1, y. Since the result for the right label is bigger, the equation (4.2) is 0. The cross-entropy error is 0 when the output is 1 The equation value (4.2) is greater when the output of the proper label is less.

Let the cross-entropy error now be implemented:

```
def cross_entropy_error(a, b):
    s = 1e-7
    return -np.sum(b * np.log(a + s))
```

NumPy arrays are the **a** and **b** parameters here. A tiny number, **s**, is added to the calculation of **np.log**. If the calculation is made of **np.log(0)**, **-inf** is returned, indicating the minus infinity. The computation cannot be further developed at this moment. A very little value is added to avoid that, so that there is no infinite. Let's now use cross entropy **error(a, b)** to calculate easily:

```
>>> a = [0, 0, 1, 0, 0, 0, 0, 0, 0, 0]
>>> b = [0.1, 0.05, 0.6, 0.0, 0.05, 0.1, 0.0, 0.1, 0.0, 0.0]
>>> cross_entropy_error(np.array(a), np.array(b))
  6.447238200383332
>>>
>>> a = [0.1, 0.05, 0.1, 0.6, 0.05, 0.1, 0.0, 0.6, 0.0, 0.0]
>>> cross_entropy_error(np.array(a), np.array(b))
2.1927228474611695
```

In the first case, the accurate label output is **0.6** and the error of cross-entropy is **6.44**. In the following example, the right label output is as little as **0.1**, with an error of **2.1**. These findings are in line with what we spoke about up to now

Mini-batch learning

Training data are utilized for training for a machine learning issue. To be precise, it implies determining the loss function for the data and identifying the factors that reduce the value. All training data should thus be used to achieve the loss function. If 100 training data are collected, the total of their 100 loss functions as index should be utilized.

The loss function for one piece of data was used in the example of the loss function mentioned earlier. The sum of loss functions may be calculated for all training data for an error of cross-entropy (4.3):

$$E = -\frac{1}{N} \sum_{n} \sum_{k} t_{nk} \log y_{nk}$$

Equation 4.3

Suppose the data element number is N. The *tnk* is the *n-th* data *k-th* value (y_{nk} is the output of the neural network, and t_{nk} is labelled data). Although this equation appears rather difficult, it's simply a prolonged equation (4.2) that shows that one piece of data has a loss function for N items. Finally, for normalization it is divided by *N*. The *average loss function* is calculated by Division *N* by data. Regardless of the amount of training data, the average may be utilized as constant index. For example, you may calculate the average loss function per data element, even when the numbers of training data pieces are 1,000 or 10,000.

The data set of the MNIST includes 60,000 training pieces. It takes a time for all these data to calculate the amount of loss functions. Sometimes big data comprises millions or tens of millions of data items. In this instance, it is not feasible to calculate loss functions for all data. Consequently, some data are removed to estimate all the data. Furthermore, training data for each set of information, which is termed mini-batches is picked in neural network training (small collection). For instance, out of 60,000 training items utilized for training purposes, 100 pieces of data are chosen randomly. This technique of training is known as mini-batch training.

Now, let's build a method to randomly choose the given quantity of data from the training set for mini-batch training. The code to load the MNIST dataset is as follows before:

```
import sys, os
sys.path.append(os.pardir)
import numpy as np
from dataset.mnist import load_mnist
(a_train, b_train), (a_test, b_test) = /
    load_mnist(normalize=True, one_hot_label=True)
print(a_train.shape) # (60000, 784)
print(b_train.shape) # (60000, 10)
```

The **load_mnist** function loads the MNIST data collection, as explained in *Chapter 3: Neural Networks*. It may be found in the **dataset/mnist.py** file that this book contains. The training and test data are charged in this function. You can utilize one hot display with the proper label 1 and the other labels 0 by supplying the **one hot label=True** parameter.

You will see that the training data quantity is **60,000**, and the input data includes **784** rows of picture data when loading the above MNIST data (originally 28x28). Data with 10 rows are labelled data. Therefore, the forms **(60000, 784)** and **(60000, 10)** of **x_train** and **t_train** respective.

How can we now randomly extract 10 data bits from the training data? By utilizing the **np.random.choice()** method of NumPy we can write the following code:

```
train_size = a_train.shape[0]

batch_size = 10

batch_mask = np.random.choice(train_size, batch_size)

a_batch = a_train[batch_mask]

b_batch = b_train[batch_mask]
```

You may choose the required number of numerals randomly from the given numbers by using **np.random.choice()**. The **np.random.choice(60000, 10)**, for example, picks 10 numbers randomly among numerals ranging from 0 to under 60,000. The indexes for the selection of small batches may be obtained as a table in the real code as shown here:

```
>>> np.random.choice(60000, 10)

array([41393, 51485,  4356, 45474, 59514, 46761, 28387, 17344, 58536,
       15045])
```

Now, to extract micro lots, you may provide randomly picked indexes. These mini-batches will be used for the loss functions calculations.

Not all homes but chosen ones are aimed at measuring television viewing. For instance, you may approximate viewership in Tokyo by monitoring the viewing of 1,000 randomly selected households. The sighting of these 1,000 families is not precisely the same as the total sighting, but may be used as an approximation figure. The loss function of a mini-batch is assessed using spectrum data to mimic the entire data like the viewing mentioned here. In summary, the entire training data is approximated by a small number of randomly picked data (mini-batch).

Implementing cross-entropy error (using batches)

How do you incorporate cross-entropy errors with batch data such as micro batch data? We can implement it easily by improvement of the cross-entropy mistake previously, which only targets one piece of data. The input of a single data item and the input of data as batches are supported as:

```
def cross_entropy_error(a, b):

    if a.ndim == 1:
```

```
    b = b.reshape(1, b.size)

    a = a.reshape(1, a.size)

batch_size = a.shape[0]

return -np.sum(b * np.log(a + 1e-7)) / batch_size
```

The **a** is the neural network output here and t is the data labelled. The form of the data is modified if **a** is one-dimensional (that is, for one piece of data to determine the error of a cross-entropy). The standardization based on the data in a batch is the average cross-entropy error per data.

If label data are supplied as labels (not as a one-hot display, but as labels like "2" and "7," then a **cross_entropy_error** may be implemented as follows:

```
def cross_entropy_error(a, b):

    if a.ndim == 1:

        b = b.reshape(1, b.size)

        a = a.reshape(1, a.size)

    batch_size = a.shape[0]

    return -np.sum(np.log(a[np.arange(batch_size), b] + 1e-7)) / batch_
size
```

Please note that when **b** is 0 for an element in a single-hot representation, it also contains 0 for cross-entropy, and this computation can be ignored. In other words, you can compute the cross-entropy error if you can acquire the neural network output for a valid label. Therefore, **b*np.log(a)** is utilized for **b** as a one-heat representation, **b*np.log(a[np.arange(batch size), b])** is used in the same treatment as **b** for labels (here, the description of "a very small value, **1e-7**" has been omitted for visibility).

We can discuss np.log briefly for reference (**a[np.arange(batch size), b]**). The **np.arange (batch size)** produces a 0-to-batch-size-1 array. The **np.arange (batch size)** creates an array of NumPy, [0, 1, 2, 3, 4] when batch size is 5. The b includes a label that is the appropriate label for each piece (in this example, **a[np.arange(batch size), b]** creates NumPy arrays, [and[0,2], **a[1,7]**, **a[2,0]**, and **a[3,9]**, **a[4,4]]**). The **b** parameter includes the NumPy labels as in the neural network output corresponded to that of every piece of data.

Why configure a loss function?

Some individuals may ask why the loss function is introduced. For example, we want parameters to increase the detection accuracy in the case of number recognition. Is it not more labor to implement a loss function? Our aim is to obtain the maximum accuracy of recognition using a neural network. So, certainly, should we utilize the accuracy of recognition as a result?

This question may be answered by paying attention to the role of *"derivatives"* in training of the neural network. The following section will discuss this in depth. Neural network training is concerned with optimum parameters (weights and preconditions) in order to reduce the value of the loss function. The derivative (gradient) of a parameter is calculated in order to seek for the location of the lowest loss function, and the parameter value is changed gradually depending on the derivative value.

Suppose there is, for example, a virtual neural network. In the neural network, we shall be careful about one weight parameter. Here, the derivative of the weight parameter loss function illustrates how the weight parameter value varies when the weight value is slightly adjusted. If the derivative turns into a negative number, you can lower the weight function by a positive change in the weight parameter. On the other hand, you may lower the loss function by shifting the weight parameter into the negative direction when the derivative has a positive number.

We can't use accuracy as the score, as the derivative is 0 at nearly every location, which prevents updating parameters. Now, let's sum up this carefully.

We should not utilize accuracy of reconnaissance as a score while training a neural network. That is because the derivative of parameters is 0 in most areas if you use recognition accuracy as the score.

Why, therefore, does accuracy of recognition as the parameter score lead to 0 in virtually all positions? Let's use another example to demonstrate this. Tell that 32 out of 100 training items can be identified by a neural network. In other words, accuracy of recognition is 32%. If the accuracy of recognition is used, the weight parameter will be slightly changed to 32%, without causing any difference. Little parameter adjustment does not enhance accuracy of recognition. The change, however, is not continuous, like 32 0123 ...%, but rather discontinuous, like 33% and 34%, even as the identification accuracy improves. On the other hand, when the loss feature is utilized as the score, the current loss feature value, like 0.92543, must be shown as a value. The parameter value also varies somewhat, the loss function, like 0.93432, continually.

The parameter only alters the accuracy of the recognition a little-by-little adjustment, which makes any changes discontinuous. The step function of the activation function is also applicable. A neural network cannot learn correctly for the same reason if you use a step function for an activation function. The cause is that the stepping function derivatives are practically 0 (other than 0) anywhere, as seen under *figure 4.4*. When using a step function, the step function deletes a little change in the parameter, and even if you use it to make a score, the loss function value does not change.

Only at certain times a step function changes, like a *shishi odoshi* or a scarecrow. On the other hand, the output (value of the vertical axis) varies constantly for the derivative (tangent) of a sigmoid function, as illustrated in *figure 4.4*, and the curve size is likewise continuously changing. In brief, the derivative of a `sigmoid` function is 0. This is crucial for neural network *training*. Since the gradient never is 0, a neural network can properly learn:

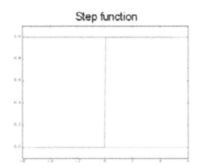
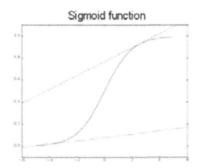

Figure 4.4: *Step function and sigmoid function – the gradient of a step function is 0 at almost all positions, while the gradient of a sigmoid function (tangent) is never 0*

Numerical differentiation

The gradient technique uses gradient information to decide the direction to be taken. This section discusses the nature and features of a gradient, starting with the descent.

Derivative

For instance, we may imagine you were in a complete marathon 2 kilometers in ten minutes from the beginning. The speed of 2/10 =.2 may be calculated [km/minute]. At 0.2 kilometers per minute, you were running.

In this example, the change in "running distance" over "time" was computed. Strictly speaking, this figure shows the "average pace," because in 10 minutes you walked 2 kilometers. A derivative indicates at "a specific instant" the amount of change.

Thus, you may achieve the amount of change at a specific point when minimizing the duration of 10 minutes (the last 1 minute, the distance for the last 1 second, the distance for the last 0.1 seconds etc.). (Instantaneous speed).

A derivative therefore reveals at a particular instant the amount of change. The following equation defines this:

$$\frac{df(x)}{dx} = \lim_{h \to 0} \frac{f(x+h) - f(x)}{h}$$

Equation 4.4

The derivative of a function is indicated in equation (4.4). The left side displays the *f(x)* derivative for *x* – the *f(x)* change level in relation to *x*. The equation derivative (4.4) shows how the function value *f(x)* varies due to a *minor change* lim Here, the slight change, *h*, is brought close to 0 infinitely, which is indicated as $h \to 0$.

Write a software to obtain an equation-based function derivative (4.4). You can provide a modest value to h for calculation reasons to execute equation (4.4) directly:

```python
# Bad implementation sample
def numerical_diff(f,  x):
    h = 10e-50
    return (f(x+h) - f(x)) / h
```

After a number differentiation, the function is called numerical *diff(f,x)*. Two parameters are used: function, *f*, arguments, *x*, functions, *f*. This method appears to be correct, however there can be two enhancements.

The previous approach utilizes a tiny value of *10e-50* ("0,00…1") as h since we want to use as little value as h as feasible (we want to bring h infinitely close to 0 if possible). However, here is the problem of a rounding mistake.

In the final computation result, an error arises by omitting a numerical value inside a tiny decimal range (for example, by omitting eight or more places of decimals). A rounding mistake is shown in Python in this example:

>>> np.float32(1e-50)

0.0

If the float32 value (a 32-bit floating point number) is *1e-50*, this value is 0.0. You can't put it right. A computer computation issue results from the usage of too tiny a number. The first improvement has now been made. As a modest number, you can use 10–4, *h*. A number of around 10–4 is known to provide satisfactory outcomes.

The second improvement relates to the function difference, *f*. The previous implementation calculates the difference between *x + h* and *x* in function *f*. You should note that in the first instance this computation creates an error. As illustrated in *figure 4.5*, the *true derivative* is the gradient for the location of the function at *x* (called a tangent) and is the gradient between (*x + h*) and *x* for that implementation. The actual derivative (true tangent) hence does not precisely match its value. This change is because you can't indefinitely bring *h* close to 0:

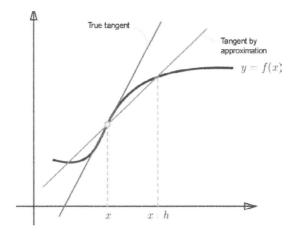

Figure 4.5: *True derivative (true tangent) and numerical differentiation (tangent by approximation) are different in value*

A numerical differential has an inaccuracy as seen in *Figure 4.5*. You can use the difference between (f), $(x+h)$ or $(x+h)$ to compute this mistake $(x - h)$. This difference is called a central difference since it is calculated around x (on the other hand, a forward difference is referred to as a difference between $(x + h)$ and x). Let us now build a numerical (numerical) differentiation based on both of these improvements:

```
def numerical_diff(f,  x):

    h = 1e-4 # 0.0001

    return (f(x+h) - f(x-h)) / (2*h)
```

As the previous code demonstrates, numerical differentiation is called by computing a derivative using a very small value difference. By contrast, a derivative is derived utilizing the expansion, for example by using the phrase "analytic," as "analytical solution" or "analytical derivative getting" You can obtain the derivative of y = x2 analytically as $\left.\frac{dy}{dx} = 2x\right|$. Therefore, you can calculate the derivative of y as x = 2, and this is 4. An analytic derivative is the "true derivative" without errors.

Examples of numerical differentiation

By utilizing numerical differentiation let us differentiate a simple function. The first example is the quadratic function represented in:

$$y = 0.01x^2 + 0.1x$$

Equation 4.5

Implement equation (*4.5*) in Python as follows:

```
def function_1(a):

    return 0.01*a**2 + 0.1*a
```

Draw this feature's graph. The code to draw a chart and the resulting chart (*figure 4.6*) are shown in the following:

```
import numpy as np

import matplotlib.pylab as plt

a = np.arange(0.0, 20.0, 0.1) # The array x containing 0 to 20 in increments of 0.1

b = function_1(a)

plt.xlabel("a")

plt.ylabel("f(a)")

plt.plot(a, b)

plt.show()
```

Now calculate the differentials of the function when **a=5** and **a=10**:

```
>>> numerical_diff(function_1, 5)
```

```
0.1999999999990898
```

```
>>> numerical_diff(function_1, 10)
```

```
0.2999999999986347
```

The differential calculated here is the amount of change of *f(x)* for *x*, which corresponds to the gradient of the function. By the way, the analytical solution of *f* $(x) = 0.01x2 + 0.1x$ is $= 0.02x + 0.1$. The true derivative when $x=5$ and 10 are 0.2 and 0.3, respectively. They are not exactly the same as numerical differentiation findings, although the mistake is extremely minor. In fact, the mistake is so tiny that it is virtually the same values:

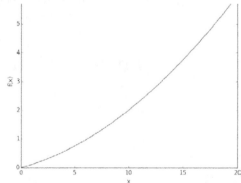

Figure 4.6: *Graph of f (x) = 0.01x2 + 0.1x*

In plotting the graphs of the lines with gradients which are useful for numerical differentiation, we will utilize our results before. The *figure 4.7* shows the results. The derivatives **match** function tangents (source code **@chapter04/Gradient_1D. py**) here. Here you may see:

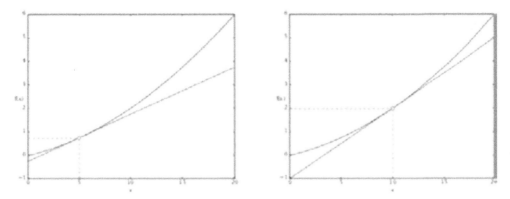

Figure 4.7: *Tangents when x = 5 and x = 10 – using
the values from numerical differentiation as the gradients of lines*

Partial derivative

Then let's look at the equation function (4.6). This simple equation calculates the quadratic sum. Note that, unlike the previous example, it has two variables:

$$f(x_0, x_1) = x_0^2 + x_1^2$$

Equation 4.6

You can implement it in Python as follows:

```
def function_2(x):
    return x[0]**2 + x[1]**2
    # or return np.sum(x**2)
```

Here, NumPy arrays are supposed to be given through as arguments. This feature just squares each member of the arrays and adds it up (the same operation can be done using **np.sum(x**2))**. Now, let's draw this feature's graph. The following is a 3-dimensional diagram:

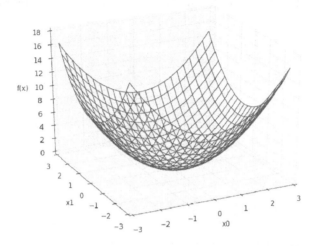

***Figure 4.8**: Graph of f(x₀, x₁)= x_0^2+x_1^2*

Now, the derivative of the equation is calculated (4.6). Please notice that there are two variables in equation (4.6). You must thus provide the differentials generated for the two variables *x0* and *x1*. The derivative of a multi-variant function is termed a **partial derivative**. They are expressed as $\dfrac{\partial f}{\partial x_0}$, $\dfrac{\partial f}{\partial x_1}$.

Consider the two partial derivatives problems and their answers in order to show this:

Question 1: Calculate the partial derivative, $\dfrac{\partial f}{\partial x_0}$, for *x0* when *x0 = 3* and *x1 = 4*:

```
>>> def function_tmp1(x0):
....     return x0*x0 + 4.0**2.0
...
>>> numerical_diff(function_tmp1, 3.0)
6.00000000000378
```

Question 2: Calculate the partial derivative, $\dfrac{\partial f}{\partial x_1}$, for *x1* when *x0 = 3* and *x1 = 4*:

```
>>> def function_tmp2(x1):
....     return 3.0**2.0 + x1*x1
...
>>> numerical_diff(function_tmp2, 4.0)
7.999999999999119
```

A function with one variable is determined and the function derivatives are generated to answer these difficulties. For instance, a new function for **x1=4** is constructed in *Question 1*, and for the purpose of calculating a numerical differentiation a function which contains one single variable, **x0** is transferred. Based on the findings *Question 1* has been answered by **6.000000000378**, while *Question 2* has received **7.999999999999119**. Most of them are the same as the analytical differentiation solutions.

However, one of the variables is targeted for the partial derivative and a particular value is set for the remaining variables. A new function was built to hold the other variables at a specified value in the previous implementation. To calculate the partial derivative, the newly constructed function has been given to the prior numerical difference.

Gradient

In the example above, the **x0** and **x1** halves of each variable were computed. We now wish to jointly calculate **x0** and **x1** partial derivatives. For example, let's calculate the partial derivatives of (**x0, x1**) when **x0 = 3** and **x1 = 4** as ($\frac{\partial f}{\partial x_0}$, $\frac{\partial f}{\partial x_1}$)The vector that collectively indicates the partial differentials of all the variables, such as () is called a **gradient**. You can implement a gradient as follows:

```
def numerical_gradient(f,    x):
    h = 1e-4 # 0.0001
    grad = np.zeros_like(x) # Generate an array with the same shape as x
    for idx in range(x.size):
        tmp_val = x[idx]
        # Calculate f(x+h)
        x[idx] = tmp_val + h
        fxh1 = f(x)
        # Calculate f(x-h)
        x[idx] = tmp_val - h
        fxh2 = f(x)
        grad[idx] = (fxh1 - fxh2) / (2*h)
        x[idx] = tmp_val # Restore the original value
    return grad
```

It looks a little hard to implement the number **gradient(f,   x)** function but procedures for one variable are nearly identical to those in numerical difference.

Note that **np.zeros** like (**x**) produces an array with the same structure as **x**, all of which have zero entries.

The **numerical_gradient(f,x)** function accepts the inputs **f** (function) and **x** (NumPy array) and gets numerical differentiations for every NumPy member, **x**. Now let us compute a gradient by using this function. Here, at locations (**3, 4**), (**0, 2**), and (**3, 0**) we shall receive the gradients:

```
>>> numerical_gradient(function_2, np.array([3.0, 4.0]))
array([ 6., 8.])
>>> numerical_gradient(function_2, np.array([0.0, 2.0]))
array([ 0., 4.])
>>> numerical_gradient(function_2, np.array([3.0, 0.0]))
array([ 6.,    0.])
```

> The present results are [7.9.999999999991188]   [6.000000000000037801, but [6., 8.] returned. The reason for this is that a returned NumPy array is structured to improve value visibility.

So, at any location of the gradient we may compute (**x0, x1**). The preceding example demonstrates that the point gradient (**3, 4**) is (**6, 8**) that is (**0, 4**) and (**3, 0**) that is (**0, 2**). (**6, 0**). What do these gradients mean? To understand this, let's look at the gradients of .

$f(x_0,x_1) = x_0^2 + x_1^2$. Here, the gradients are turned down and the vectors are drawn (source code is in **chapter04/Gradient_2D.py**).

The gradients of $f(x_0,x_1) = x_0^2 + x_1^2$ are shown as the vectors (arrows) that have the direction toward the lowest point, as shown in *figure 4. 9*. In *figure 4.9, the lowest location (smallest value)* appears in the gradients, **f (x0, x1)**. The arrows points to one spot, much like a compass. The farther they are from the *lowest position*, the greater the arrow size:

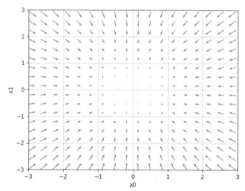

Figure 4.9: Gradients of $f(x_0, x_1) = x_0^2 + x_1^2$

The gradients point to the lowest location in the example shown in *figure 4.9*, but this is not always the case. In reality, at each place, the gradient points downwards. More accurately, the direction of a pitch is one which at each location most decreases the value of the function.

Gradient method

Many machine learning issues include looking for appropriate training settings. An ideal parameters (weights and biases) should also be found during training in a neural network. The parameter value is the optimum parameter if the loss function gets the least value. A loss function can, however, be difficult. The space of the parameter is huge and we can't imagine where the minimal value is taken. A gradient technique uses gradients to locate the function's lowest (or minimum) value.

A gradient displays the direction which at each location most decreases the function value. Thus, it cannot be guaranteed if the position of a gradient is indeed the least value of the function, that is to say whether the direction really is the one to choose. In fact, the direction that a gradient indicates is not of most cases the least value in a complex function.

> **The gradient is 0 at a minimum local, minimum and the saddle point of a function at a location. A local minimum is the lowest value locally, which in a narrow range is the lowest value. A saddle point is the local maximum position in one direction and the local minimum position in another. A gradient technique searches for where a gradient is 0, but where the position is not necessarily the least global position (it can be the local minimum or a saddle point). When a function has a complex and deformed form, learning reaches a nearly flat terrain and a motionless time, dubbed a "plateau."**

Even though the direction of a gradient is not necessarily the global lowest value, it might lower the value of the function the most by travelling in that direction. Therefore, you should identify the direction of movement based on information about gradients in order to find the point of the minimal value or find the place where the function possesses the lowest possible value.

Let's now examine the method of gradient. You travel a fixed distance from the present position in the direction of the gradient with the gradient technique. This gives you a pitch at the new place and moves back in the direction of the gradient. So you travel in the direction of the gradient over and again. The method of gradient is known as the reduction of the value of a function gradually by travelling in the gradient direction. This approach is often used in machine learning optimization problems. It is usually used in neural networks training.

> If it seeks for the minimum or maximum value, a gradient method is called by a different name. To put it accurately, the minimal value technique is known as the gradient descent method, and the highest value method is known as the gradient ascending method. If the sign of a loss function is reversed it might convert it from a minimum value problem into a maximum value problem.

Thus, it does not matter particularly if *descent* or *ascent* differ. A *gradient descent* approach is usually employed in neural networks (deep learning).

Now, let's express a gradient method with an equation. The equation (4.7) shows a gradient method:

$$x_0 = x_0 - \eta \frac{\partial f}{\partial x_0}$$

$$x_1 = x_1 - \eta \frac{\partial f}{\partial x_1}$$

Equation 4.7

Adjust the quantity to be updated in equation (4.7). This is known as a neural network learning rate. An apprenticeship rate defines how much the parameters must be updated and how much.

The equation (4.7) for one training instance displays an update equation, and this procedure is repeated. As illustrated at equation (4.7), each step updates the variable values and repeats the step multiple times to progressively lower the function's value. This example is a case of two variables, but a similar equation—a partial difference for every variable—is utilized to upgrade even when the number of variables is doubled.

The value of the learning rate must be indicated in advance, for example **0.01** and **0.001**. In general, you can't achieve the *good spot* if that value is too high or too little. We generally examine if training is effective by changes of the learning rate in neural network training.

Now, let's apply a Python technique of gradient descent. The following can be done:

```
def gradient_descent(f, init_x, lr=0.01, step_num=100):
    x = init_x
    for i in range(step_num):
        grad = numerical_gradient(f, x)
        x -= lr * grad
    return x
```

The parameter **f** is a feature to optimize, the argument **init_x** is an initial value, the argument **lr** is a study rate, and the argument **step_num** is the number of repetitions in a gradient method. The function gradient is obtained by the **numerical_gradient(f, x)** and is updated by the gradient, multiplied by the rate of learning repeated by the **step_num** number.

You may use this to get the minimal local feature and even the lowest value, if you are fortunate. Let's try to solve an issue

Question: Obtain the minimum value of $f(x_0,x_1) = x_0^2 + x_1^2$ with a gradient method:

```
>>> def function_2(x):
...     return x[0]**2 + x[1]**2

...

>>> init_x = np.array([-3.0, 4.0])
>>> gradient_descent(function_2, init_x=init_x, lr=0.1, step_num=100)
array([ -6.11110793e-10, 8.14814391e-10])
```

In this context, enter **(-3.0, 4.0)** as the beginning value and use a gradient technique to start looking for the least value. The ultimate outcome is almost close **(-6.1e-10, 8.1e-10) (0, 0)**. The real minimum value is actually **(0, 0)**. Using a gradient technique, you achieved nearly perfect results. The updating process using a gradient technique may be shown in *figure 4.10*. The bottom position is the origin, and you can see that it steadily approaches. The **chapter04/Gradient.py** has the source code to generate this graph (**chapter04/Gradient.py** does not provide snapped lines showing the contour lines in the picture):

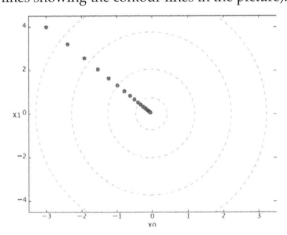

Figure 4.10: *Updating $f(x_0, x_1) = x_0^2 + x_1^2$ with a gradient method – the dashed lines show the contour lines of the function*

As noted previously, there are no positive results in an extremely big or small learning rate. Let's make some experiments in these two cases:

```
# When the learning rate is too large: lr=10.0
```

```
>>> init_x = np.array([-3.0, 4.0])
>>> gradient_descent(function_2, init_x=init_x, lr=10.0, step_num=100)
array([ -2.58983747e+13, -1.29524862e+12])
# When the learning rate is too small: lr=1e-10
>>> init_x = np.array([-3.0, 4.0])
>>> gradient_descent(function_2, init_x=init_x, lr=1e-10, step_num=100)
array([-2.99999994, 3.99999992])
```

As this experiment illustrates, if the learning rate is too high, the result will differ. On the other side, there are hardly any updates if the rate of education is too low. Setting a suitable learning rate is needed.

The hyperparameter is a parameter like a learning rate. The features of the neural network differ from parameters (weights and biases). With trainings and a training method, weight parameters in a neural network may be automatically generated while explicitly specifying a hyperparameter. In general, the hyperparameter must be changed to several values in order to obtain a value which allows excellent training. In neural network training, you also need to compute gradients. The gradients are those of a weight loss function.

Gradients for a neural network

You must also calculate gradients in neural network training. The gradients here are those of a loss function for weight parameters. For example, let's assume that a neural network has the weight W (2:$\frac{\partial L}{\partial W}$array) only, and the loss function is L. In this case, we can express the gradient as $\frac{\partial L}{\partial W}$. The following equation shows this:

$$\mathbf{W} = \begin{pmatrix} w_{11} & w_{12} & w_{13} \\ w_{21} & w_{22} & w_{23} \end{pmatrix}$$

$$\frac{\partial L}{\partial \mathbf{W}} = \begin{pmatrix} \frac{\partial L}{\partial w_{11}} & \frac{\partial L}{\partial w_{12}} & \frac{\partial L}{\partial w_{13}} \\ \frac{\partial L}{\partial w_{21}} & \frac{\partial L}{\partial w_{22}} & \frac{\partial L}{\partial w_{23}} \end{pmatrix}$$

Equation 4.8

Each element of $\frac{\partial L}{\partial W}$ is the part$\frac{\partial L}{\partial W}$ erivative for each element. For example, the element at the first row and column, $\frac{\partial L}{\partial W_{11}}$, indicates how a slight ch$\frac{\partial L}{\partial W}$ge in $w11$ changes the loss function, L. What is important here is $\frac{\partial L}{\partial W}$t the shape of $\frac{\partial L}{\partial W}$ is the same as that of W. Actually, in equation (4.8), both W and $\frac{\partial L}{\partial W}$ are the same (2x3) in shape.

Now let's use the easy neural networks to develop a software that calculates a gradient. To achieve this, we are implementing a class called **SimpleNet** (in the **chapter04/SimpleNet.py** the source code is:

```
import sys, os
```

```
sys.path.append(os.pardir)

import numpy as np

from common.functions import softmax, cross_entropy_error

from common.gradient import numerical_gradient

class SimpleNet:

    def __ init __ (self):

            self.W = np.random.randn(2,3) # Initialize with a Gaussian
distribution

    def predict(self, x):

        return np.dot(x, self.W)

    def loss(self, x, t):

        z = self.predict(x)

        y = softmax(z)

        loss = cross_entropy_error(y, t)

        return   loss
```

In **common/functions.py**, **softmax** and **cross_entropy_error** are utilized here. The **common/gradient.py** numerical gradient technique is also used. The **simpleNet** class contains just one instance variable, which is 2x3 shaped weight parameters. It has two methods: one is a **prediction(x)** and the other is a **loss(x,t)** for the loss function. Here, the **x** argument is the input data and the **t** argument is a correct label. Now, let's try using **simpleNet**:

```
>>> net = simpleNet()

>>> print(net.W) # Weight parameters

[[ 0.47355232 0.9977393 0.84668094]

[ 0.85557411 0.03563661 0.69422093]]

>>>

>>> x = np.array([0.6, 0.9])

>>> p = net.predict(x)

>>> print(p)

[ 1.05414809 0.63071653 1.1328074]

>>> np.argmax(p) # Index for the maximum value

2

>>>
```

```
>>> t = np.array([0, 0, 1]) # Correct label
```

```
>>> net.loss(x, t)
```

```
0.92806853663411326
```

Then let's get the **numerical_gradient (f,x)**. A dummy parameter is used for the here specified **f(W)**, **W**. Since **f(x)** is performed within **numerical_gradient(f,x)**, for consistency **f(W)** is defined: **f(x)**

```
>>> def f(W):
```

```
...     return net.loss(x, t)
```

```
...
```

```
>>> dW = numerical_gradient(f, net.W)
```

```
>>> print(dW)
```

```
[[ 0.21924763 0.14356247 -0.36281009]
 [ 0.32887144 0.2153437 -0.54421514]]
```

The number **gradient(f,x)** argument **f** is a function, and the **x** is the function parameter **f**. A new function, **f**, is therefore here defined. The argument of **net.W** is taken and the loss function is calculated. The new function is transferred to **numerical_gradient (f,x)**.

numerical_gradi $\frac{\partial L}{\partial W}$ **(f,n** $\frac{\partial L}{\partial W}$**.W)** returns **dW**, which is a two-dimensional 2x3 array. The **dW** shows that $\frac{\partial L}{\partial W_{11}}$ for ∂W is around **0.2**, for example. This indicat $\frac{\partial L}{\partial W}$ at when *w11* is increased by **h**, the value of the loss function increases by **0.2h**. $\frac{\partial L}{\partial W_{23}}$ is about **-0.5**, which indicates that when *w23* is increased by **h**, the value of the loss function decreases by **0.5h**. Therefore you should update *w23* in a positive direction and *w11* in a negative direction in order to minimize the loss function. The update *w23* also reduces the rate of updating *w11* more than it does.

The new function is written as **def(x)** in the previous implementation. You may define and implement a basic function with a lambda notation in Python, like follows:

```
>>> f = lambda w: net.loss(x, t)
```

```
>>> dW = numerical_gradient(f, net.W)
```

Using a gradient technique to upgrade the weight parameters once you have obtained the gradients for a neural network. All these training procedures are implemented for a two-layer neural network in the next section.

We utilized a **numerical_gradient()** function to handle multiple-dimensional arrays like weight parameters, **W** somewhat different from prior approach. These modifications are nevertheless basic and are for multidimensional arrays alone. See the source code (**common/gradient.py**) for additional details.

Implementing a training algorithm

We have learnt the basics of training in neural networks so far. Important terms have been published in sequence, such as *loss function, mini-batch, gradient,* and *gradient descent technique.* Here we shall examine the method for review purposes for neural network training. Let's go through the training method for the neural network.

Presupposition

The weight and bias of a neural network are adjustable. It is termed *training* to change them to suit the training data. Four steps are included in the neural network training:

Step 1 (Mini-batch)

Choose some data from the training data randomly. A mini-batch is the selected data. The aim is to minimize the value of the mini-batch loss function.

Step 2 (Calculating gradients)

Calculate the gradient for each weight parameter to decrease the loss function for the mini-batch. The gradient displays the direction which most lowers the loss value.

Step 3 (Updating parameters)

Update the gradient direction of weight parameters slightly.

Step 4 (Repeating)

Repeat steps 1, 2, and 3.

For neural network training, the previous four stages are employed. This technique is used to update parameters with a gradient descent approach. As the data utilized here are randomly picked as a mini-batch, it is called stochastic descent. *Stochastic* refers to *stochastically choosing data at random.* Therefore, *the method of gradient descent for randomly picked data* indicates stochastic descent. Stochastic descent is normally implemented in many deep learning systems as the SGD function, named after its initials.

Let's now implement the neural network that learns handwritten numbers the MNIST training dataset is used here by a two-layer neural network (with one cache layer).

A two-layer neural network as a class

Let's first create a class neural double layer network. The **TwoLayerNet** class is implemented as follows (**TwoLayerNet** implementation is based on Python source code supplied by Stanford University's Convolutionary Neural Networks (CS231n). The **chapter04/TwoLayerNet.py** has a source code:

```python
import sys, os
sys.path.append(os.pardir)
from common.functions import *
from common.gradient import numerical_gradient
class TwoLayerNet:
    def __ init __ (self, input_size, hidden_size, output_size,
                        weight_init_std=0.01):
        # Initialize weights
        self.params = {}
        self.params['W1'] = weight_init_std * /
                        np.random.randn(input_size, hidden_size)
        self.params['b1'] = np.zeros(hidden_size)
        self.params['W2'] = weight_init_std * /
                        np.random.randn(hidden_size, output_size)
        self.params['b2'] = np.zeros(output_size)
    def predict(self, x):
        W1, W2 = self.params['W1'], self.params['W2']
        b1, b2 = self.params['b1'], self.params['b2']
        a1 = np.dot(x, W1) + b1
        z1 = sigmoid(a1)
        a2 =  np.dot(z1, W2) + b2
        y = softmax(a2)
        return y
    # x: input data, t: label data
    def loss(self, x, t):
        y = self.predict(x)
        return cross_entropy_error(y, t)
    def accuracy(self, x, t):
        y = self.predict(x)
```

```
        y = np.argmax(y, axis=1)
        t = np.argmax(t, axis=1)
        accuracy = np.sum(y == t) / float(x.shape[0])
        return accuracy
    # x: input data, t: teacher data
    def numerical_gradient(self, x, t):
        loss_W = lambda  W:  self.loss(x,  t)
        grads = {}
        grads['W1'] = numerical_gradient(loss_W, self.params['W1'])
        grads['b1'] = numerical_gradient(loss_W, self.params['b1'])
        grads['W2'] = numerical_gradient(loss_W, self.params['W2'])
        grads['b2'] = numerical_gradient(loss_W, self.params['b2'])
        return grads
```

This class is a little lengthy in its implementation, but nothing new appears. The implementation of a new neural network discussed in the previous chapter has several aspects in common. Let's first examine the variables and methods utilized in this class. The main variables are given in *table 4.1*, while all techniques are shown in *table 4.2*:

Variable	Description
params	Dictionary variable (instance variable) that contains the parameters of the neural network.
	params['W1'] is the weights for layer 1, while params['b1'] is the biases for layer 1.
	params['W2'] is the weights for layer 2, while params['b2'] is the biases for layer 2.
grads	Dictionary variable that contains gradients (return value of the numerical_gradient() method).
	grads['W1'] is the gradients of the weights for layer 1, while grads['b1'] is the gradients of the biases for layer 1.
	grads['W2'] is the gradients of the weights for layer 2, while grads['b2'] is the gradients of the biases for layer 2.

Table 4. 1: Variables used in the TwoLayerNet class

Method	Description
`__init__(self, input_ size, hidden_size, output_size)`	Initialize. The arguments are the numbers of neurons in the input layer, in the hidden layer, and the output layer in order from left to right.
`predict(self, x)`	Conduct recognition (making predictions). The **x** argument is image data.
`loss(self, x, t)`	Obtain the value of the loss function. The **x** argument is image data, and the **t** argument is the correct label (the same is true for the arguments of the following three methods).
`accuracy(self, x, t)`	Obtain recognition accuracy.
`numerical_gradient(self, x, t)`	Obtain the gradient for the weight parameter.
`gradient(self, x, t)`	Obtain the gradient for the weight parameter. The fast version of the `numerical_gradient()` method. This will be implemented in the next chapter.

Table 4.2: Methods used in the TwoLayerNet class

The **TwoLayerNet** class has as instance variables two dictionary variables, **parameters** and **grades**. The weight parameters of the **parameter** variable are present. For example, the layer 1 weight parameters are kept as a NumPy array in **params['W1']**. You may use **parameters['b1']** to access layer 1. An example is provided here:

```
net = TwoLayerNet(input_size=784, hidden_size=100, output_size=10)

net.params['W1'].shape # (784, 100)

net.params['b1'].shape # (100,)

net.params['W2'].shape # (100, 10)

net.params['b2'].shape # (10,)
```

The variable parameters contain all necessary parameters for this network. As seen above. For forecasting the weight parameters of the variable parameters are used (forward processing). A forecast can be made as follows:

```
x = np.random.rand(100, 784) # Dummy input data (for 100 images)

y = net.predict(x)
```

The **gradient** variable for each parameter is contained such that it meets the **parameter** variable. By utilizing the digital **gradient()** technique, gradient information is saved in the gradients variable as follows when calculating gradients:

```
x = p.random.rand(100, 784) # Dummy input data (for 100 images)

t = np.random.rand(100, 10) # Dummy correct label (for 100 images)

grads = net.numerical_gradient(x, t) # Calculate gradients
```

```
grads['W1'].shape # (784, 100)

grads['b1'].shape # (100,)

grads['W2'].shape # (100, 10)

grads['b2'].shape # (10,)
```

Now, let's consider implementing the **TwoLayerNet** methods. The method for starting the class is **init (self, input_size, hidden_size, output_size)**. The parameters are the number of neurons in the input layer, in the hidden layer and the output layer. A total of 784 input pictures with 28x28 sizes and 10 classes are supplied for manual digit recognition. Therefore, the **input_size=784** and **output_size=10** parameters are specified and the hidden size value is set as the number of layers hidden.

This function also initializes the parameters of weight. For successful neural network training it is necessary to determine what values to put as the initial weight parameters. We shall cover **weight** parameter setup later in detail. Here, with the random numbers based on Gaussian distribution, weights are initialized and biases initialized by 0. The **Predict(self, x)**, and **accuracy(self, x, t.)** are nearly identical to those we looked at in the previous chapter while implementing a prediction in respect to the neural network. Please go to the previous chapter if you have any questions.

The remaining digital **gradient (self, x, t)** generates each parameter's gradient. The calculation of the gradient for the loss of each parameter employs numerical differentiation. In the following chapter the method of **gradient(self, x, t)** is implemented.

> The numerical_gradient(self, x, t) **calculates the parameter gradients by use of numerical differentiation. In the following chapter, we will look at how gradients may be swiftly calculated using backpropagation. The outcome is essentially identical to numerical difference, but with quicker processing.**

In the following chapter, the way to get a gradient through back propagation is used as a **gradient(e, x, t)**. You may use **gradient (self, x, t)** instead of number **gradient (self, x, t)** if you wish to save time, because training for neural networks takes time.

Implementing mini-batch training

Here, we employ miniatures for neural training in the network. We take some data from the training data (called a **mini-batch**) by random during mini-batch training and utilize it to update parameters using a gradient approach. Let's conduct training for the **TwoLayerNet** class by using the **MNIST** dataset (the source code is located at **chapter04/NeuralNet_Training.py**):

```python
import numpy as np
from dataset.mnist import load_mnist
from two_layer_net import TwoLayerNet
(x_train, t_train), (x_test, t_test) = \
    load_mnist(normalize=True, one_hot_label=True)
train_loss_list = []
# Hyper-parameters
iters_num = 10000
train_size = x_train.shape[0]
batch_size = 100
learning_rate = 0.1
network = TwoLayerNet(input_size=784, hidden_size=50, output_size=10)
for € in range(iters_num):
    # Obtain a mini-batch
    batch_mask = np.random.choice(train_size, batch_size)
    x_batch = x_train[batch_mask]
    t_batch = t_train[batch_mask]
    # Calculate a gradient
    grad = network.numerical_gradient(x_batch, t_batch)
    # grad = network.gradient(x_batch, t_batch) # fast version!
    # Update the parameters
    for key in ('W1', 'b1', 'W2', 'b2'):
        network.params[key] -= learning_rate * grad[key]
    # Record learning progress
    loss = network.loss(x_batch, t_batch)
    train_loss_list.append(loss)
```

The mini-batch size here is 100. 100 pieces of data are recovered by random extraction from 60,000 pieces of training data, each time (images and accurate label information). Then the steps are acquired for mini-batch, and stochastic gradient descent updates the parameters (SGD). In this context, the number of updates using a gradient technique is 10,000. Each update calculates the loss function for the training data and adds the result to the array. The diagram illustrates how this loss function changes value in *figure 4.11*.

The value of the loss function diminishes as the amount of training rises. It shows that training is good. The neural network's weight parameters are gradually adapted to the data. In fact, the neural network teaches. When repeatedly exposed to data, the optimum weight parameters are approached:

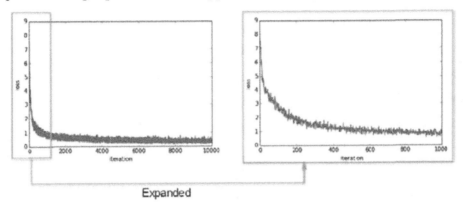

Figure 4.11: *Transition of the loss function – the image on the left shows the transition up to 10,000 iterations, while the image on the right shows the transition up to 1,000 iterations*

Using test data for evaluation

The outcome of *figure 4.11* demonstrates that the data are steadily reduced by the repeated training. The value of the loss function, however, is *the loss function of the training data mini-batch*. The decrease in the loss function value of the training data shows that the neural network is learning successfully. However, this outcome does not demonstrate that it can manage and manage a distinct data collection.

We must verify that input other than training can be identified appropriately in neural network training. We must verify that there is no *overfitting*. Surface-service indicates that it is only possible to accurately recognize the number of pictures in the training data and that they are not recognizable, for example.

The aim of training the neural network is to achieve widespread capacity. To this end, data not included in the training information must be used to evaluate the neural network generalization capabilities. In the next implementation, during training, we regularly record the accuracy of recognition for the test data and training data. For each stage, we will record the accuracy of recognition for the test data and training data.

An era is an enclosure. One time shows how many iterations were utilized when all data for training were used. Suppose, for example, that there are 10,000 pieces of training data with 100 mini-batches. Following the repeated 100 times of a stochastic gradient decay procedure, all data were viewed from the training. 100 iterations Equals 1 epoch, in this example.

Now we will slightly alter the prior execution to get a proper assessment. Here we may highlight boldly the changes from the prior execution:

```python
import numpy as np
from dataset.mnist import load_mnist
from two_layer_net import TwoLayerNet
(x_train, t_train), (x_test, t_test) = \
    load_mnist(normalize=True, one_hot_label=True)
train_loss_list = []
train_acc_list = []
test_acc_list = []
# Number of iterations per epoch
iter_per_epoch = max(train_size / batch_size, 1)
# Hyper-parameters
iters_num = 10000
batch_size = 100
learning_rate = 0.1
network = TwoLayerNet(input_size=784, hidden_size=50,
output_size=10)
for € in range(iters_num):
    # Obtain a mini-batch
    batch_mask = np.random.choice(train_size, batch_size)
    x_batch = x_train[batch_mask]
    t_batch = t_train[batch_mask]
    # Calculate a gradient
    grad = network.numerical_gradient(x_batch, t_batch)
    # grad = network.gradient(x_batch, t_batch) # Quick version!
    # Update the parameters
    for key in ('W1', 'b1', 'W2', 'b2'):
        network.params[key] -= learning_rate * grad[key]
    loss = network.loss(x_batch, t_batch)
    train_loss_list.append(loss)
```

```
# Calculate recognition accuracy for each epoch
if € % iter_per_epoch == 0:
    train_acc = network.accuracy(x_train, t_train)
    test_acc = network.accuracy(x_test, t_test)
    train_acc_list.append(train_acc)
    test_acc_list.append(test_acc)
    print("train acc, test acc | " + str(train_acc) + " , " + str(test_
acc))
```

For all the training and test data, the accuracy of the recognition is measured in the above example and for each period of time the results are recorded. The accuracy of recognition is computed for each epoch as it takes time for a statement to calculate it repeatedly.

We also don't usually need to record correctness (all we need is the approximate transition of recognition accuracy). Consequently, during each stage of the training, the accuracy transition is recorded.

Let us now display in a diagram the outcomes of the previous code:

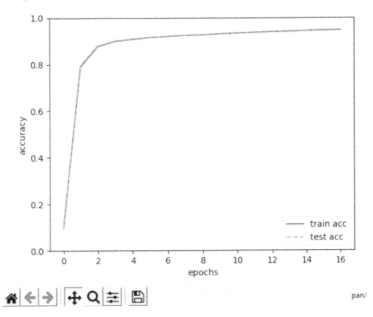

Figure 4.12: *Transition of recognition accuracy for training data and test data. The horizontal axis shows the epochs*

The *figure 4.12* illustrates the accuracy of the identification of the training data, while the struck line represents the accuracy of the test data. As you can see, the recognition accuracy for both training data and test data is improving as the number of periods grows (training progress). Here, we can see the two accuracies of recognition about equal to the overlapping of the two lines. This shows that there was no overfitting here.

Conclusion

This section covered training in the neural network. First, we put a score known as a loss function so a neural network might learn. The objective of neural network training is to find the weight parameters that cause the loss function to be of lowest value. We next learnt how to get the least loss function value with a gradient of a function named the gradient technique. The following points are discussed in this chapter:

We utilize training data and test data for machine learning. Training data are utilized for training, whereas test data are used to evaluate the capacity of the learned model for generalization. In neural network training, a loss function is employed as a scoring. Weight parameters are changed in order to reduce the value of the loss function.

The weight parameters are updated by their gradients to update their values periodically in the gradient direction. A derivative calculation is referred to as numerical differentiation based on the difference when extremely tiny numbers are supplied. To obtain the weight parameters gradients, you may use numerical differentiation. It takes time to compute numerical differentiations, but its realization is straightforward. On the other hand, it is slightly complex to reverse propagate, which is discussed in the next chapter, but can compute gradients.

CHAPTER 5
Backpropagation

The previous chapter outlined the training of neural networks. The gradient of a weight parameter in a neural network was determined by using numerical differentiation (that is, the loss function gradient for a weight parameter). Numerical differentiation is straightforward and easy to carry out, but it takes time to calculate. Backpropagation, explained in this chapter, is a more effective technique to determine the weight parameter gradients.

There are two approaches to accurately comprehend backpropagation. One employs equations, whereas the other uses computational graphs. The former is a shared way, and many machine learning books focus on formulae for this approach. This is excellent since it is rigorous and concise, but it might obscure crucial information or end up as a list of useless equations. Writing code will further improve your comprehension and persuade you. Andrej Karpathy's blog, *Hacker's Guide to Neural Networks* **(http://karpathy**.github.io /neuralnet/), and the course, CS231n: Convolutional Neural Networks for Visual Recognition (**http://cs231n.github.io/**), provided by *Karpathy* and Professor *Fei-Fei* Li at Stanford University provides guidance on the use of computational graphs to explain backpropagations and deep learning.

Structure

- Computational graphs
    - Using computational graphs to solve problems

- Local calculation
  - Why do we use computational graphs?
- Chain rule
- Backward propagation in a computational graph
  - What is chain rule?
- Chain rule and computational graphs
- Backward propagation
  - Backward propagation in an addition node
  - Backward propagation in a multiplication node
- Implementing a simple layer
- Implementing a multiplication layer
  - Implementing an addition layer
- Implementing the activation function layer
- ReLU layer
- Sigmoid layer
- Implementing the affine and softmax layers
  - Affine layer
- Batch-based affine layer
- Softmax loss layer
- Implementing backpropagation
  - Overview of neural network training
  - Presupposition
  - Implementing a neural network that supports backpropagation
- Gradient check
- Training using backpropagation

Objective

This chapter will thus employ computational graphs in order to visually comprehend backpropagation.

Computational graphs

The process of calculation is expressed on a computational graph. This graph is used as a data structure network that represents several nodes and edges (that is, straight lines that connect nodes). In this section, we solve basic problems in order to understand computational graphs before progressing step-by-step into more complicated backpropagation.

Using computational graphs to solve problems

The problems in this section are easy enough to answer with mental arithmetic, but it is here that computational graphs are understood. Learning computational graphs is crucial for the complex computations we discuss later on; so first mastering how to utilize them here is vital.

Question 1: Taro purchased two oranges of 1000 yen each. If a 10 per cent consumption tax is levied, calculate the amount of money he pays.

The calculating procedure with nodes and arrows is shown in the computational graph. A node, shown as a circle, describes an operation. The intermediate result above the arrow shows the outcome of every node flowing from left to right. The following diagram illustrates the computational graph that solves Question 1:

Figure 5.1: Answer to Question 1 using a computational graph

As shown in the preceding graph, 100 yen for an oranges flows into node x2 and becomes 200 yen, which is then passed to the next node. The 200 yen then flows into node x1.1 and becomes 220 yen. This computational graph indicates that the answer is 220 yen.

Each circle in the previous figure contains x2 or x1.1 as one operation. In the operation, you may also position only x in a circle. In such a scenario, you may set 2 and 1.1 as the *"number of oranges"* and *"consumption tax"* variables outside of circles as illustrated in the following diagram:

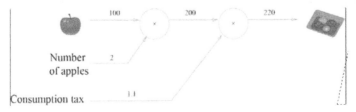

Figure 5.2: Answer to Question 1 using a computational graph: the "Number of mangoes" and "Consumption tax" variables are placed outside circles

Question 2: Taro purchased two oranges and three mangoes. The cost of one orange was 100 yen and of one mango was 150 yen. A tax of 10% was levied on consumption. The amount of money that he paid may be calculated.

We will utilize a computational graph in order to solve Question 2 like in Question

1. The following figure displays the computational graph:

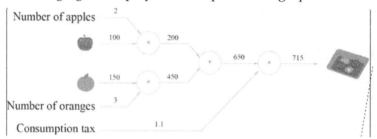

Figure 5.3: *Answer to Question 2 using a computational graph*

In this question, an addition node, "+", was added to sum the amounts of oranges and mangoes. After creating a computational graph, we make the calculation from left to right. Like an electric current that runs in a circuit, the calculation result goes from left to right, and computation terminates once the result reaches the right. The graph above illustrates that 715 yen is the answer.

In order to solve an issue by utilizing a computational graph, the following must be done:

1. Build a computational graph.

2. Promote calculation on the computational graph from left to right.

Step 2 is called forward propagation. The calculation spreads from the beginning to the end of a computational graph during forward propagation. If there is a forward propagation, propagation from right to left can also be taken into consideration. This is termed backward propagation and is referred to as backpropagation (or backprop). When we compute derivatives later, it will play an essential role.

Local calculation

The essential feature of a computational graph is that a "local calculation" propagates the ultimate conclusion. The word "local" refers to the node's "limited range". The local calculation returns the subsequent result of node information, regardless of what happens.

A concrete example allows us to split down local calculations. Let us imagine that we bought two oranges and several other items at a store. You may construct a computational graph like the following:

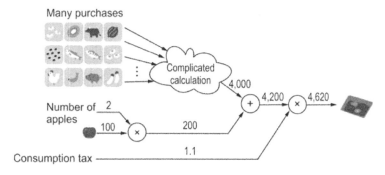

Figure 5.4: *Example of buying two oranges and many other things*

Let's say that we bought a lot and that, as indicated in *figure 5.4*, the total amount was 4,000 yen (after a complicated calculation). Here, it is necessary to calculate the local calculation in each node. You may add up the purchase of the oranges and other things without contemplating how 4,000 was obtained (4000 + 200 = 4200). In other words, just the computation linked to the node is necessary in each node; in this example, the addition of the two numbers provided. We do not have to worry about the full graph.

In a computational graph you may therefore concentrate on local calculations. However difficult the entire computational graph is, local calculation for the target node can be done at each node. You may get the result of complicated calculates that make up the complete graph by passing the results of simple local calculations.

> For example, assembling a vehicle is difficult, yet it is generally carried out on an assembly line, based on the division of labor. Every employee (or machine) does simple tasks. The result of one process will go to the next worker and, finally, a car will be created. In the same way that an automotive is sent to an assembly line, a computational graph splits difficult computations into simple and local calculations to send the result into the next node. Thus like the installation of an automobile, complicated calculations may be reduced into simple calculations.

Why do we use computational graphs?

By means of computational graphs we have solved two problems and can now take account of the advantages. One of them, as stated previously, is local calculation. While the entire computation is complex, local calculations highlights the emphasis to simplify the problem in its entirety on basic calculations in each node.

Another advantage is that all intermediate calculation results may be kept in a computational graph (for example, in *figure 5.3*, 200 yen after 2 oranges is calculated, and 650 yen before consumption tax is added). The main reason you use computational graphs is, however, because you can efficiently calculate derivatives by propagating it backwards.

Consider Question 1 again so that we may define backpropagation in a computational graph. In this example, we calculated the total price for two oranges and the consumption tax. Now assume that you need to know how the total amount paid would be influenced when the price of the orange increases. This corresponds to obtaining the derivative of the amount paid with respect to the price of an orange. It corresponds to obtaining $\frac{\partial L}{\partial x}$ when the price of an orange is x and the amount paid is L. The amount paid for this derivative shows by how much the price of an orange lightly rises.

As previously indicated, you might utilize backpropagation in a computational graph to acquire a value, such as the derivative of the amount spent in relation to an orange's price. We're just going to see the result first. The following diagram demonstrates how you may acquire derivatives via backpropagation in a computational graph:

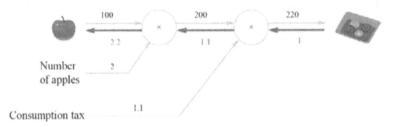

Figure 5.5: Propagating differential values using backward propagation

As illustrated in \, backpropagation is visually depicted with arrows (thick lines) in the reverse direction. The backpropagation goes through local differentials, and values are shown underneath the arrows. The derivative values are transferred from right to left, that is, 1 1.1 2.2. The result shows that the value derived from the amount spent with regards to the price of a orange is 2.2.

This shows that if the orange's price rises by 1 yen, the final amount paid will increase by 2.2 yen. Similarly, you can also obtain, using identical procedures, the derivative of the amount paid for the consumption tax and the derivative of the amount paid for the number of oranges.

In those steps, the intermediate results of the derivatives (derivatives passed half-way) may be shared so that many derivatives can be effectively calculated. The benefit of a computational graph is therefore that forward and backward propagation allows you to easily retrieve every variable's derivative value.

Chain rule

Forward propagation in a computational graph propagates the calculation results in the forward direction, that is, from left to right. These are natural computations since they are generally performed. In backpropagation, on the other hand, a local derivative is transmitted from right to left, that is, in the reverse direction. The idea of the local derivative is based on the chain rule. Let us examine the chain rule and clarify how it corresponds to backpropagation in a computational graph.

Backward propagation in a computational graph

We will now look at a backpropagation example utilizing a computational graph. Suppose the calculation y = f(x) exists.

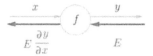

Figure 5.6: *Backward propagation in a computational graph – the local derivative is multiplied in the backward direction*

As shown in the *Figure 5.6.* backpropagation multiplies the signal E by the local derivative of the node, $\left(\frac{\partial y}{\partial x}\right)$, and propagates it to the next node. The local derivative here means obtaining the derivative of the calculation, $y = f(x)$, in forward propagation, and indicates obtaining the derivative, y, with respect to x $\left(\frac{\partial y}{\partial x}\right)$; for example, $y = f(x) = x2$, $\left(\frac{\partial y}{\partial x}\right) = 2x$. The local derivative is multiplied by the value propagated from the upper stream € and passed to the previous node.

This is the backpropagation method. The derivative values can be obtained efficiently. The reason why this is feasible is described in the next section by the notion of the chain rule.

What is chain rule?

We have to discuss about composite functions before introducing the chain rule. A composite function is a function with multiple functions. For example, as seen in equation *(5.1)*, the equation $z = (x+y)^2$ has two equations:

$$z = t^2$$

$$t = x + y$$

Equation 5.1

The chain rule is the feature of the derivative of a composite function and is defined as follows.

When a function is expressed by a composite function, the derivative of the composite function can be expressed by a product of the derivative of each function that comprises the composite function.

This is the principle of the chain $\left(\frac{\partial z}{\partial x}\right)$ Although it may seem difficult, it is actually quite simp $\left(\frac{\partial z}{\partial t}\right)$ equation (5.1), $\left(\frac{\partial z}{\partial x}\right)$ (a derivative of $\left(\frac{\partial t}{\partial x}\right)$ th respect to x) is the product of $\left(\frac{\partial z}{\partial t}\right)$ (a derivative of z with respect to t) and $\left(\frac{\partial t}{\partial x}\right)$ (a derivative of t with respect to x).

$$\frac{\partial z}{\partial x} = \frac{\partial z}{\partial t}\frac{\partial t}{\partial x}$$

Equation 5.2

You can remember equation (5.2) easily because ∂t's cancel each other out, as shown here:

$$\frac{\partial z}{\partial x} = \frac{\partial z}{\partial t}\frac{\partial t}{\partial x}$$

Now, let's use the chain rule to obtain the derivative of equation (5.2), $\left(\frac{\partial z}{\partial x}\right)$. First, obtain the local differential (partial differential) of equation (5.2):

$$\frac{\partial z}{\partial t} = 2t$$

$$\frac{\partial t}{\partial x} = 1$$

Equation 5.3

As shown in equation (5.3), $\frac{\partial z}{\partial t}$ is $2t$ and $\frac{\partial t}{\partial x}$ is 1. $\frac{\partial z}{\partial x}$ This result is analytically obtained from the differentiation formula. The final result, $\frac{\partial z}{\partial x}$, can be calculated by the product of the derivatives obtained in equation (5.4):

$$\frac{\partial z}{\partial x} = \frac{\partial z}{\partial t}\frac{\partial t}{\partial x} = 2t \cdot 1 = 2(x+y)$$

Equation 5.4

Chain rule and computational graphs

Now let's use a computational graph to describe the chain rule calculation made in equation (5.4). We may create a diagram for the square with the **2 node as follows:

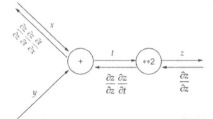

Figure 5.7: *Computational graph of equation*
(5.4) – local derivatives are multiplied and passed in the backward direction

The backpropagation in a graph propagates a signal from right to left, as illustrated in *Figure 5.7*. Returning the signal of the local derivative (partial derivative) of the node to a node multiplies and transmits it to the next node. For example, the $\frac{\partial z}{\partial z}$ input to node **2 in backpropagation is $\frac{\partial z}{\partial z}$.. It is multiplied by the local derivative, $\frac{\partial z}{\partial t}$ (in forward propagation, the input is t and the output is z, so the local derivative at this node is $\frac{\partial z}{\partial t}$) and then multiplied and passed to the next node. In the preceding diagram, the first signal in backward propagation, $\frac{\partial z}{\partial z}$, did not appear in the previous equation. It was omitted there because $\frac{\partial z}{\partial z} = 1$.

What we should note from the preceding diagram is the result of backpropagation at the leftmost position. It corresponds to the derivative of z with respect to x because

$\frac{\partial z}{\partial z}\frac{\partial z}{\partial t}\frac{\partial t}{\partial x} = \frac{\partial z}{\partial t}\frac{\partial t}{\partial x} = \frac{\partial z}{\partial x}$ due to the chain rule. What backpropagation performs is based on the principle of the chain rule.

When you assign the result of equation (5.3), as shown in the preceding diagram, the result is as follows. Thus, $\frac{\partial z}{\partial x}$ is 2(x + y):

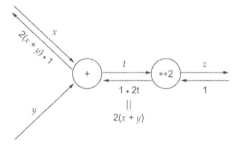

Figure 5.8: *Based on the result of backward propagation in the computational graph, is 2(x + y)*

Backward propagation

The previous section showed how backpropagation in a computational graph is based on the chain rule. We will now examine how backpropagation works using examples of operations like "+" and "x".

Backward propagation in an addition node

First, let's examine an addition node with backward propagation. Here, we shall look at the backpropagation for the equation z = x + y. The derivatives of z = x + y can be analytically achieved as follows:

$$\frac{\partial z}{\partial x} = 1$$

$$\frac{\partial z}{\partial y} = 1$$

Equation 5.5

As shown by equation (5.5), both $\frac{\partial z}{\partial x}$ and $\frac{\partial z}{\partial y}$ are 1. Therefore, we can represent them in a computational graph, as shown in the following diagram. In backpropagation, the derivative from the upper stream—in this example, $\frac{\partial L}{\partial z}$—is multiplied by 1 and passed to the lower stream. In short, backpropagation in an addition node multiplies 1, so it only passes the input value to the next node.

In this example, the differential value from the upper stream is expressed as $\frac{\partial L}{\partial z}$. This is because we assume a large computational graph that finally outputs L, as shown in *Figure 5.10*. The calculation, $z = x + y$, exists somewhere in the large computation graph, and the value of $\frac{\partial L}{\partial z}$ is passed from the upper stream. The values of $\frac{\partial L}{\partial x}$ and $\frac{\partial L}{\partial y}$ are propagated downstream:

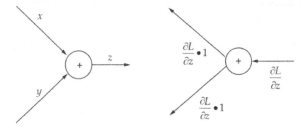

Figure 5.9: *Backward propagation in an addition node*
– forward propagation on the left and backward propagation on the right.

As illustrated on the right, backpropagation in an addition node travels from the upper to the lower stream without altering it:

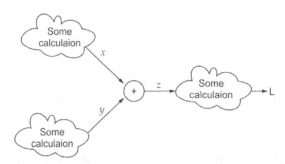

Figure 5.10: *This addition node exists somewhere in the final output calculation.*

In backpropagation, local derivatives are transmitted from node to node in the reverse direction from the rightmost output.

Let us now look at a backpropagation example. For example, the calculation $10 + 5 = 15$ exists and a value of 1.3 flows backward from the upper stream. This is illustrated in the following computational graph:

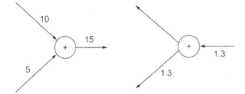

Figure 5.11: *Example of backward propagation in an addition node*

As backpropagation only sends the input signal to the next node in an addition node, 1.3 is sent to the next node.

Backward propagation in a multiplication node

Let's look at a backpropagation in a multiplication node by using an example equation, z = xy. The difference between this equation and equation (5.6) is as follows:

$$\frac{\partial z}{\partial x} = y$$

$$\frac{\partial z}{\partial y} = x$$

Equation 5.6

You may create a computational graph (*Figure 5.12*) based on the above equation (5.6).

For backpropagation in multiplication node, the value of the upper stream multiplied by the reversed value of the input signal for forward propagation will be transmitted downstream. A reversed value implies that if the signal is x is in forward propagation, then the value to multiply is y at backpropagation, and that if the signal is y at forward, the value to multiply in backpropagation is x, as seen in the following graph.

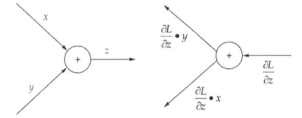

Figure 5.12: *Backward propagation in a multiplication node – forward propagation on the left and backward propagation on the right*

Let us look at an example. Assume that a 10 x 5 = 50 computation exists, and the result of 1.3 is reversed from the top stream. This is shown by a computational graph in *Figure 5.13*.

The inverted input signals are multiplied in the backpropagation of multiplication so as to get 1.3 x 5 = 6.5 and 1.3 x 10 = 13. The upstream value was only transferred downstream in the backpropagation of addition. The input signal value is therefore not necessary for forward propagation. In contrast, the input signal value in forward propagation is necessary for the backpropagation of multiplication. The input signal of forward propagation is therefore preserved to implement a multiplication node:

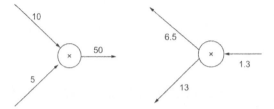

Figure 5.13: Example of backward propagation in a multiplication node

Orange example

Let us think about the example at the start of this chapter, that is, the purchase two oranges and the consumption tax levied on it. We need to determine how the final amount paid is influenced by each of the three variables (prices of a mango, quantity of mangoes, and consumption tax).

That means we need to find the derivative of the amount paid for the mango's prices, the derivative of the amount payable with respect to the number of mangoes, and the derivative of the amount paid as far as consumption tax is concerned. This may be solved by employing backpropagation in a computational graph, as seen in the accompanying diagram:

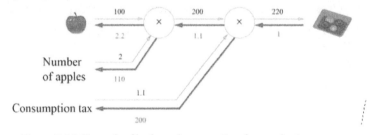

Figure 5.14: Example of backward propagation for purchasing oranges

As already established, the input signals in the backpropagation of a multiplication node are inverted and transmitted downstream. The price disparity of oranges is 2.2 according to the results given in the preceding graph; 110 oranges are available and the consumption tax is 200.

It states that when the consumption tax and price of the orange increases by the same amount, the consumption tax influences the final amount paid in the amount of 200 and that the price of an orange has an impact on it in the size of 2.2.

But this outcome is due to the difference in units between the consumption tax and the orange (1 for the consumption tax is 100 percent, while 1 for the price of an orange is 1 yen).

Finally, let's solve the backpropagation of purchasing oranges as a practice. Request the derivatives of the various variables and enter the numbers in the squares of the following diagram (you may get the answer in the next section):

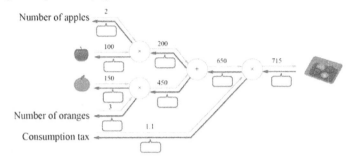

Figure 5.15: *Example of backward propagation for purchasing oranges and mangoes – complete this calculation by putting figures in the squares*

Implementing a simple layer

In this section, we'll use the multiplication node as the multiplication layer (**MulLayer**) and the addition node as the addition layer (**AddLayer**) to implement the orange example we mentioned in Python.

> We shall implement in the next part the layers in one class which form a neural network. The layer here is a functional unit within a neural network – the silver layer for a sigmoid function and the affine layer for matrix multiplication. We will thus implement multiplication and addition nodes as layers.

Implementing a multiplication layer

We construct a layer to have two common methods: **forward()** and **backward()**, which correspond to forward propagation and backward propagation. Now, as a class called **MulLayer** you may construct a multiplication layer as follows (source code is in **chapter05/MulLayer.py**):

```
class MulLayer:
    def __init__ (self):
        self.x = None
        self.y = None
    def forward(self, x, y):
```

```
        self.x = x
        self.y =y
        out = x * y
        return out
    def backward(self, dout):
        dx = dout * self.y # Reverse x and y
        dy = dout * self.x
        return dx, dy
```

Example variables, **x** and **y**, are initialized by **__init__** () for retaining input data in forward propagation. The **forward()** function accepts two variables, **x** and **y**, and their products are multiplied and shown as outputs. On the other hand, the **backward ()** is multiplied by the reverse value of forward propagation and transmits the result from upstream (**dout**) to downstream.

Now use **MulLayer** to implement the purchase of the oranges, that is, two oranges and a consumption tax. For this calculation, as illustrated in the accompanying graph, we employed the forward and backward propagation in the preceding section:

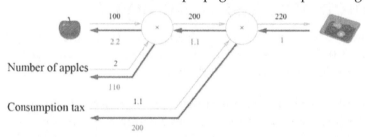

Figure 5.16: *Purchasing two oranges*

We may do forward multiplication by utilizing the multiplication layer (the source code lies at **chapter05/BuyOrange.py**) as follows:

```
orange = 1000
orange_num = 3
tax = 1.5

mul_orange_layer = MulLayer()
mul_tax_layer = MulLayer()

# forward
```

```
orange_price = mul_orange_layer.forward(orange, orange_num)

price = mul_tax_layer.forward(orange_price, tax)

print(price) # 220
```

You can use **backward()** to obtain the differential of each variable.

```
# backward

dprice = 1

dorange_price, dtax = mul_tax_layer.backward(dprice)

dorange, dorange_num = mul_orange_layer.backward(dorange_price)

print(dorange, dorange_num, dtax) # 2.2 110 200
```

Here, the order of calling **backward()** is the reverse of calling **forward ()**. Note that **backward()** is the derivative in forward propagation with respect to the output variable. For example, **mul_orange** layer returns **dorange_price** in forward propagation while taking the derivative value of **dorange_price** as a backward propagating input. The result of the execution corresponds to the results given in *figure 5.16*.

Implementing an addition layer

Now, we will implement an addition layer, which is an addition node, as follows:

```
class AddLayer:
    def __init__ (self):
        pass
    def forward(self, x, y):
        out = x + y
        return out
    def backward(self, dout):
        dx = dout * 1
        dy = dout * 1
        return dx, dy
```

No initialization is necessary for an addition layer; thus **__init__ ()** does nothing (the passing statement is *"does nothing"*). The **forward()** accepts two arguments for the addition layer, **x** and **y**, and adds them for output. The **backward()** translates the upper stream to the lower stream differential (**dout**).

Let us now utilize the addition and multiplication layers to purchase two oranges and three oranges as indicated in the following graph:

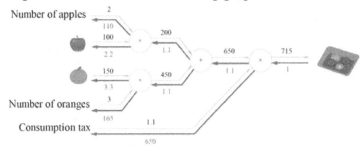

Figure 5.17: Purchasing two oranges and three oranges

This computational graph may be implemented in Python in the following manner (the source code is in **chapter05/BuyOrangeMango.py**):

```
orange = 1000

orange_num = 3

mango = 1500

mango_num = 4

tax = 1.5


# layer

mul_orange_layer = MulLayer()

mul_mango_layer = MulLayer()

add_orange_mango_layer = AddLayer()

mul_tax_layer = MulLayer()


# forward

orange_price = mul_orange_layer.forward(orange, orange_num)

mango_price = mul_mango_layer.forward(mango, mango_num)

all_price = add_orange_mango_layer.forward(orange_price, mango_price)

price = mul_tax_layer.forward(all_price, tax)


# backward

dprice = 1

dall_price, dtax = mul_tax_layer.backward(dprice)
```

```
dorange_price, dmango_price = add_orange_mango_layer.backward(dall_price)

dmango, dmango_num = mul_mango_layer.backward(dmango_price)

dorange, dorange_num = mul_orange_layer.backward(dorange_price)


print("price:", int(price)) #13500

print("dOrange:", dorange) #4.5

print("dOrange_num:", int(dorange_num)) #1500

print("dMango:", dmango) #6.0

print("dMango_num:", int(dmango_num)) #2250

print("dTax:", dtax) #9000
```

This is a bit lengthy, but every statement is straightforward. You build the needed layers and the forward propagation method, **forward()**, is invoked in a suitable order. The backward propagation method, **backward()** is then called to propagate to acquire the required derivatives.

This makes it straightforward to implement layers (addition and multiplication layers in this implementation) in a computational graph and to generate complex derivatives. Next, the layers utilized in a neural network will be implemented.

Implementing the activation function layer

The notion of a computational graph will now be applied to a neural network. Here, the layers which form a neural network are used for activation functions in one class utilizing the ReLU and sigmoid layers.

ReLU layer

An activation function of a rectified linear unit (ReLU) is expressed in the following equation (5.7):

$$y = \begin{cases} x & (x > 0) \\ 0 & (x \le 0) \end{cases}$$

Equation 5.7

The derivative of y with respect to x using equation (5.8) may be obtained from the previous equation (5.7):

$$\frac{\partial y}{\partial x} = \begin{cases} 1 & (x > 0) \\ 0 & (x \le 0) \end{cases}$$

Equation 5.8

As shown in equation (5.8), if x is greater than 0 in forward propagation, the backpropagation passes upstream value downstream without any alterations. However, if x is equal to or less than 0, the signal ceases in backwards propagation. You may represent this in a computational graph as follows:

Figure 5.18: Computational graph of the ReLU layer

Next, let's use the ReLU layer. We presume that the **forward()** and **backward()** arrays are used for the implementation of a layer in a neural network. The ReLU layer is implemented on **common.layers.py**:

```
class Relu:
    def __init__ (self):
        self.mask = None
    def forward(self, x):
        self.mask = (x <= 0)
        out = x.copy()
        out[self.mask] = 0
        return out
    def backward(self, dout):
        dout[self.mask] = 0
        dx = dout
        return dx
```

An instance variable, mask, is available for the **Relu** class. The mask variable is a NumPy array of **True/False** value. If the input element, **x**, is equal to or less than 0 in forward propagation, the matching element of the mask variable is **True**. The element is **False** otherwise (if **x** is greater than 0). For example, the **mask** variable includes a NumPy array of **True** and **False**, as seen in the following code:

```
>>> x = np.array( [[1.0, -0.5], [-2.0, 3.0]] )
>>> print(x)
[[ 1.   -0.5]
 [-2.    3. ]]
>>> mask = (x <= 0)
>>> print(mask)
```

```
[[False True]
[ True False]]
```

As illustrated above, the value of backpropagation is 0 if the input value is 0 or less. The mask variable maintained for the forward propagation is therefore utilized to establish **dout** from the upper stream in backpropagation. The matching element in question is set to 0 if an element of the mask is **True**.

> A "switch" in one circuit is the ReLU layer. If the electrical current goes through it and the switch does not flow through it in forward propagation, it turns on the switch. In backpropagation, if the switch is ON and no longer flows when the switch is OFF, the electrical current continues to flow.

Sigmoid layer

Next, let's implement a **sigmoid** function. This is expressed by equation (5.9):

$$y = \frac{1}{1 + \exp(-x)}$$

Equation 5.9

The following diagram shows the computational graph that represents equation (5.9):

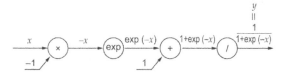

Figure 5.19: Computational graph of the Sigmoid layer (forward propagation only)

Here, the *exp* and / nodes appear in addition to the *x* and + nodes. The *exp* node calculates $y = exp(x)$, while the / node calculates $y = \frac{1}{x}$.

Equation (5.9) involves local calculations being propagated. Next, analyze the backpropagation displayed in the *figure 5.19* and consider the flow of backpropagation step-by-step to summarize everything we have explained so far.

Step 1

The / node represents $y = \frac{1}{x}$. Its derivative is analytically expressed by the following equation:

$$\frac{\partial y}{\partial x} = -\frac{1}{x^2}$$

$$= -y^2$$

Equation 5.10

The node multiplies the upstream value by $-y^2$, based on equation (5.10) and transfers the value to the lower stream, in backpropagation. This is demonstrated in the following diagram:

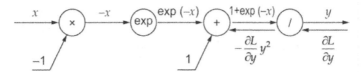

Figure 5.20: *Computational graph of the Sigmoid layer (with the additive inverse of the square)*

Step 2

The + node transfers the value from upstream to the lower stream only. This is demonstrated in the following diagram:

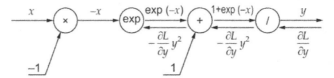

Figure 5.21: *Computational graph of the Sigmoid layer (with passing upstream value)*

Step 3

The *exp* node represents $y = exp(x)$ and the following equation expresses its derivatives:

$$\frac{\partial y}{\partial x} = \exp(x)$$

Equation 5.11

The node multiplies the upstream value by the output in the forward spread (*exp(-x)*, in this case) and passes the value to the lower stream, as shown in the following computational graph:

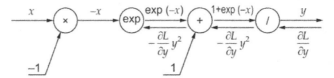

Figure 5.22: *Computational graph of the Sigmoid layer*

Step 4

In forward propagation, the x node reverses the values for multiplication. Consequently, −1 is multiplied here:

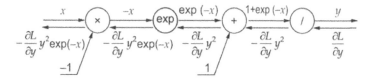

Figure 5.23: Computational graph of the sigmoid layer (reversed values)

So, in the computational network depicted in *figure 5.23*, we can demonstrate backpropagation of $\frac{\partial L}{\partial y} y^2 exp(-x)$ layer. According to the result, the output of backpropagation $\frac{\partial L}{\partial y} y^2 exp(-x)$ and it is propagated to the downstream nodes. Note here that $\frac{\partial L}{\partial y} y^2 exp(-x)$ can be calculated from the input, x, and output, y, of forward propagation. Therefore, we can draw the computational graph shown in the preceding diagram as a grouped sigmoid node (*figure 5.24*):

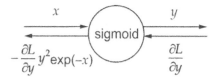

Figure 5.24: Computational graph of the sigmoid layer (simple version)

The computational graph in *figure 5.23* and the simplified computational graph in *figure 5.24* provide the same calculation result. The simple version is more efficient because it can omit the intermediate calculation in backpropagation. It is also important to note that you can only concentrate on the input and output, without caring about the details of the sigmoid layer, by grouping the nodes.

You can also organize $\frac{\partial L}{\partial y} y^2 exp(-x)$ as follows:

$$\frac{\partial L}{\partial y} y^2 exp(-x) = \frac{\partial L}{\partial y} \frac{1}{(1 + exp(-x))^2} exp(-x)$$

$$= \frac{\partial L}{\partial y} \frac{1}{1 + exp(-x)} \frac{exp(-x)}{1 + exp(-x)}$$

$$= \frac{\partial L}{\partial y} y(1 - y)$$

Equation 5.12

Therefore, you can only compute the backpropagation in the sigmoid layer (illustrated in the previous diagram) from the output of forward propagation:

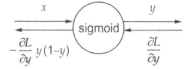

Figure 5.25: Computational graph of the Sigmoid layer –
you can use the output, y, of forward propagation to calculate the backward propagation

Let us now implement the sigmoid layer in Python. The following may be implemented according to the preceding diagram (this implementation is in **common/layers.py**):

```python
class Sigmoid:
    def __init__ (self):
        self.out = None
    def forward(self, x):
        out = 1 / (1 + np.exp(-x))
        self.out = out
    return out
def backward(self, dout):
    dx = dout * (1.0 - self.out) * self.out
    return dx
```

The implementation maintains the output of forward propagation in the output variable and subsequently uses the output variable in backpropagation for calculation purposes.

Implementing the affine and softmax layers

Affine layer

In forward propagation in a neural network, the weighted signals were added via the product of matrices (**np.dot()** in NumPy). For details, refer to the section, *Multidimensional array calculation* in *Chapter 3: Neural Network*. Do you recall, for example, the following Python implementation?

```python
>>> X = np.random.rand(2) # Input values
>>> W = np.random.rand(2,3) # Weights
>>> B = np.random.rand(3) # Biases
>>>
>>> X.shape # (2,)
>>> W.shape # (2, 3)
>>> B.shape # (3,)
>>>
```

```
>>> Y = np.dot(X, W) + B
```

Assume here that X, W and B are multidimensional arrays of the form (2,), (2, 3), and (3,). In this, the weighted sum of neurons may be calculated as **Y = np.dot(X, W) + B**. Y is propagated to the next layer via the activation function which is the flow of forward propagation in a neural network. Note that for multiplication of matrices, the number of elements in the respective dimensions must be the same. This indicates that the number of components in the product of X and W must be the same in the respective dimensions, as seen in the following figure. The form of the matrix is shown in parentheses as (2, 3) (that is, for consistency with the output of the NumPy's form):

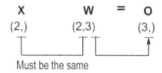

Figure 5.26: *The number of elements in corresponding dimensions must be the same for matrix multiplication*

The product of matrices propagated (forward) in the neural network is known in the field of geometry as affine transformation. We shall thus implement the method of affine transformation (affine layer).

Let us look at the calculation in a computational graph—the product of matrices and the sum of biases. The following computational graph shows the calculation **np.dot (X, W) + B**, while representing the node that calculates the product of matrices as dot. The variable's form is shown above each variable (for example X's shape is (2,) and Y's shape is (3,)):

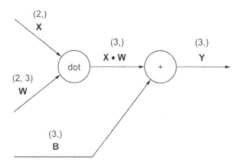

Figure 5.27: *Computational graph of the affine layer. Note that the variables are matrices. Above each variable, the shape of the variable is shown*

The above is a reasonably easy computational graph. Note, however, the multidimensional arrays **X**, **W**, and **B**. In the previous examples of computational graphs, the scalar values flow between nodes, whereas in this example, multidimensional arrays propagate across nodes.

Let us consider the backpropagation in the previous computational graph. In order to achieve backpropagation for multidimensional arrays, you may write each element from the multidimensional arrays using the same method as that used in earlier computational graphs for scalar values. This allows us to achieve the following (how we acquire equation (5.13) is omitted here):

$$\frac{\partial L}{\partial X} = \frac{\partial L}{\partial Y} \cdot W^T$$

$$\frac{\partial L}{\partial W} = X^T \cdot \frac{\partial L}{\partial Y}$$

Equation 5.13

In equation (5.13), T in WT indicates transpose. Transpose switches the (I, j) elements of W to the (j, i) elements, shown in the following equation:

$$W = \begin{pmatrix} w_{11} & w_{12} & w_{13} \\ w_{21} & w_{22} & w_{23} \end{pmatrix}$$

$$W^T = \begin{pmatrix} w_{11} & w_{21} \\ w_{12} & w_{22} \\ w_{13} & w_{23} \end{pmatrix}$$

Equation 5.14

As shown in equation (5.14), when the form of W is (2, 3), the form of a W^T becomes (3, 2).

Let's write backpropagation in the computation graph based on equation (5.13). The results are shown in the following diagram:

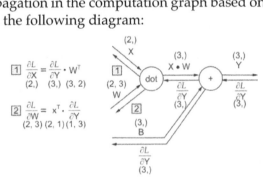

Figure 5.28: *Backward propagation of the Affine layer.*
Note that the variables are matrices. Below each variable, the shape of the variable is shown

Let's consider the shape of each $\frac{\partial L}{\partial X}$ variable carefully. Please note that X and $\frac{\partial L}{\partial X}$ are the same shape, and that W and $\frac{\partial L}{\partial W}$ are the same in terms of shape because of the following equation:

$$X = (x_0, x_1, \cdots, x_n)$$

$$\frac{\partial L}{\partial X} = \left(\frac{\partial L}{\partial x_0}, \frac{\partial L}{\partial x_1}, \cdots, \frac{\partial L}{\partial x_n} \right)$$

Equation 5.15

The shapes of matrices are important since the number of elements in the respective dimensions must be the same for multiplication of the matrices. For example, consider ∂Le product of $\frac{\partial L}{\partial Y}$ and W so that the shape of $\frac{\partial L}{\partial X}$ becomes $(2,)$ when the shape of ∂Y is $(3,)$ and that of W is $(3,2)$. Then, equation (5.13) follows. This can be seen in the following diagram:

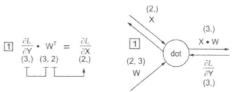

Figure 5.29: *Product of matrices (you can create backward propagation of the "dot" node by configuring a product so that the number of elements in the corresponding dimensions is the same in the matrices)*

Batch-based affine layer

A piece of data, X, is used as input for the affine layer. This section takes a batch-based affine layer into account, which jointly spreads N data parts (a group of data is called a batch). Let us start with a computational graph of a batch-based affine layer (*figure 5.30*).

The only change is that the form of the input, X, is currently $(N, 2)$. We only need to calculate the matrices in the computational graph as we had done earlier. For backward propagation, we m∂Lst be ∂L reful regarding the shapes of the matrices. Only after that can we obtain ∂X and ∂W in the same way.

When introducing bias, you need to be careful. Bias is added for each piece of data $X \cdot W$ in forward propagation. For example, if $N = 2$ (two pieces of data), biases are applied to each of the two pieces of data (to each calculation result). The following graph illustrates such an example:

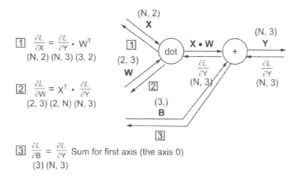

Figure 5.30: *Computational graph of the batch-based Affine layer*

```
>>> X_dot_W = np.array([[0, 0, 0], [20, 20, 20]])
>>> B = np.array([1, 2, 3])
```

```
>>>
>>> X_dot_W
array([[  0,   0,   0],
       [ 20,  20,  20]])
>>> X_dot_W + B
array([[ 3,   4,   6],
       [23,  24,  26]])
```

The biases are applied to each piece of data for forward propagation (the first, the second, and so on). Therefore, the values of each piece of data in backpropagation must be included in the elements of biases when backpropagation takes place. This is indicated by the following code:

```
>>> dY = np.array([[5, 6, 7,], [4, 5, 6]])
>>> dY
array([[5, 6, 7],
       [4, 5, 6]])
>>> dB = np.sum(dY, axis=0)
>>> dB
array([ 9, 11, 13])
```

In this example, we assume there are two data items ($N = 2$). For each piece of data, the derivatives with respect to the two data items are totaled in backpropagation of the biases. To achieve this the items of axis 0 are summed in **np.sum()**.

The affine layer is therefore implemented as follows. (The implementation of affine in **common/layers.py** differs somewhat from the version given here because it takes into account when the input information is a tensor):

```
class Affine:
    def __init__ (self, W, b):
        self.W = W
        self.b = b
        self.x = None
        self.dW = None
        self.db = None
    def forward(self, x):
        self.x = x
```

```
    out = np.dot(x, self.W) + self.b

    return out

def backward(self, dout):

    dx = np.dot(dout, self.W.T)

    self.dW = np.dot(self.x.T, dout)

    self.db = np.sum(dout, axis=0)

    return dx
```

Softmax loss layer

Finally, a softmax function, which is the output layer, must be considered. The softmax function normalizes and returns the entered values (as described earlier). The *figure 5.31*, for example, shows the output for the handwritten digit recognition of the softmax layer.

The softmax layer normalizes and outputs the entered values (that is, the total output values are 1). There are 10 inputs in the softmax layer because handwritten digital recognition dials data into 10 classes.

Two steps are involved in neural network processing: inference and training. The softmax layer usually does not employ inference in a neural network. For example, the output of the last affine layer is utilized to determine the network inference depicted in the accompanying figure.

The unnormalized output of the neural network (as seen in the Affine layer output before the softmax layer in the accompanying diagram,) is frequently known as a "*score*". You just need to calculate the maximum score to get just one response in neural network inference; therefore you do not require a softmax layer.

In neural network training, however, you require a softmax layer.

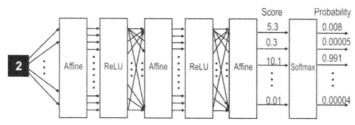

Figure 5.31: *The images are converted by the Affine and ReLU layers and 10 input values are normalized by the softmax layer*

In this example, the "0" score is 5.3 and is translated into a softmax layer of 0.008 (0.8 percent). The value for score "2" is 10.1, which is 0.991 (99.1 percent).

Now we shall implement the softmax loss layer, which also incorporates a loss function cross-entropy error. The following computational graph depicts the softmax loss layer (softmax and cross-entropy error):

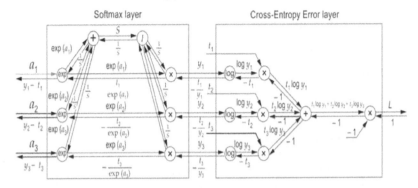

Figure 5.32: Computational graph of the softmax loss layer

As you can see, the softmax loss layer is slightly complicated. Only the result is shown here. If you are interested in how the softmax loss layer is created, refer to the computational graph of the softmax loss Layer section in the Appendix.

Here is a simplified outcome of the complex softmax loss layer:

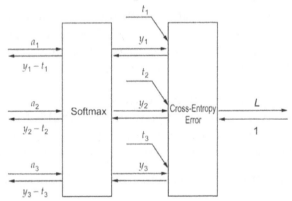

Figure 5.33: "Simplified" computational graph of the softmax-with-Loss layer

In *figure 5.33*, the softmax layer represents the softmax function whereas the layer of cross-entropy error indicates a cross-entropy error. We assume here that the data from the previous layer is received, which is categorized into three classes and three inputs (scores). As you can see, the inputs (a_1, a_2, a_3) and outputs of softmax ($y1$, $y2$, and $y3$) are normalized. The output of softmax (y_1, y_2, y_3) and the label (t_1, t_2, t_3) and loss L on the basis of this data is obtained by the cross-entropy error layer.

The softmax layer returns backpropagation (y_1 t_1, y_2 t_2, and t_3) to that is called a clean output. Since the output of the softmax layer (y_1, y_2, y_3) and and (t_1, t_2, t_3) the label, ($y_1 - t_1$, $y_2 - t_2$, $y_3 - t_3$) is the difference between the label and softmax layer. When a neural network propagates backwards, an error is given to the preceding layer which is the difference. This is crucial when a neural network is formed.

Please note that neural network training is intended to modify weight parameters to bring the output of a neural network (softmax output) close to the label. To achieve this, we have to efficiently pass the error between the output of the neural network and the label to the preceding layer. The preceding result (y1 − t1, y2 − t2, y3 − t3) is the precise difference between the label and the softmax layer output; the present failure between the neural network output and the label is clearly indicated.

If the loss function of the softmax function is a cross-entropy error, the backpropagation produces a beautiful result, (y1−t1, y2−t2,y3−t3). The result is not an accident. This is accomplished via a function that calls for a cross-entropy error. An identity function is applied to the output layer in a regression problem and for the same reason, the sum of squared errors is employed for the loss function (see the section, *The output layer design*, in *Chapter 3: Neural Network*). If we utilize the sum of squared errors as the loss function of an identity fun ction, backpropagation gives a beautiful result, (y1 − t1, y2 − t2, y3 − t3).

Let us consider another example: Say that, for one piece of data, the label is (0, 1, 0) and softmax layer output is (0.3, 0.2, 0.5). The neural network at this point does not identify it correctly as the probability of it being the right label is 0.2 (20 percent). Here a major error (0.3, −0.8, 0.5) is propagated from the softmax layer. Because that major error propagates through the preceding layers, a great deal may be learned from the major error in layers before the softmax layer.

As another example, for one piece of data, the label shall be (0, 1, 0), and the softmax layer's output shall be (0.01, 0.99, 0) (this neural network recognizes quite accurately). A tiny inaccuracy (0.01, −0.01, 0) is propagated backwards from the layer softmax in this example. This little error spreads to the previous levels. Only limited information is available in the layers preceding the softmax layer, as it is tiny.

Now, the softmax loss layer must be implemented. The softmax loss layer can be implemented as follows:

```python
class SoftmaxWithLoss:
    def __init__ (self):
        self.loss = None # Loss
        self.y = None       # Output of softmax
        self.t = None       # Label data (one-hot vector)
    def forward(self, x, t):
        self.t = t
        self.y = softmax(x)
```

```
        self.loss = cross_entropy_error(self.y, self.t)
        return self.loss
    def backward(self, dout=1):
        batch_size = self.t.shape[0]
        dx = (self.y - self.t) / batch_size
        return dx
```

The **softmax()** and cross entropy **error()** methods are used in that implementation. They have been implemented in the sub-section, *Issues when implementing softmax function* of *Chapter 3: Neural Network*, and *Implementing cross-entropy error (using batches)* of *Chapter 4: Training Neural Network*. The execution is thus extremely straightforward here. Note that the error per data propagates backwards to the earlier layers, because the propagation value is split by batches (**batch_size**).

Implementing backpropagation

You can build a neural network by combining the layers implemented in the previous sections as if you were assembling Lego blocks. Here, we will build a neural network by combining the layers we've implemented so far.

Overview of neural network training

Because the description was a little long, let us check the overall view of neural network training again before proceeding with its implementation. Now we will take a look at the procedure for neural network training.

Presupposition

A neural network has adaptable weights and biases. Adjusting them so that they fit the training data is called training. Neural network training consists of the following four steps:

Step 1 (mini-batch)

Select some data at random from the training data.

Step 2 (calculating the gradients)

Obtain the gradient of the loss function for each weight parameter.

Step 3 (updating the parameters)

Update the parameters slightly in the gradient's direction.

Step 4 (repeating)

Repeat steps 1, 2, and 3.

Backpropagation occurs in step 2. In the previous chapter, we used numerical differentiation to obtain a gradient. Numerical differentiation is easy to implement, but calculation takes a lot of time. If we use backpropagation, we can obtain a gradient much more quickly and efficiently.

Implementing a neural network that supports backpropagation

A two-layer neural network named **TwoLayerNet** is implemented in this part. First, in *tables 5.1* and *table 5.2*, we shall examine the variables and methods of this class.

The implementation of this class is a little long, but contains many portions that are common with the implementation, such as in the *Implementation of a training algorithm* section of *Chapter 4: Training Neural Network*. A major difference compared to the previous chapter is the introduction of layers. When using layers, you may get recognition results (**predict()**) and **gradient()** by propagating between layers: **Gradient()**

Instance variable	Description
params	A dictionary variable that contains the parameters of the neural network.
	params['W1'] is the weights for layer 1, while params['b1'] is the biases for layer 1.
	params['W2'] is the weights for layer 2, while params['b2'] is the biases for layer 2.
layers	An **ordered dictionary** variable that contains the parameters of the neural network layers. An **ordered dictionary** such as layers['Affine1'], layers['Relu1'], and layers['Affine2'] retains each layer.
lastLayer	The last layer of the neural network.
	In this example, it is the SoftmaxWithLoss layer.

Table 5.1: Instance variables in the TwoLayerNet class

Method	Description
__init__(self, input_size, hidden_size, output_size, weight_init_std)	Initializes the arguments.
	The arguments are the numbers of neurons in the input layer, in the hidden layer, and the output layer, and the scale of the Gaussian distribution at weight initialization, in order from left to right.
predict(self, x)	Conducts recognition (makes a prediction).
	Argument **x** is the image data.
loss(self, x, t)	Obtains the value of the loss function.
	Argument **x** is the image data, while argument **t** is the label.
accuracy(self, x, t)	Obtains the recognition accuracy.
numerical_gradient(self, x, t)	Uses numerical differentiation to obtain the gradient for the weight parameters (the same as in the previous chapter).
gradient(self, x, t)	Uses backpropagation to obtain the gradient for the weight parameters.

Table 5.2: Methods in the TwoLayerNet class

Now, let's implement **TwoLayerNet**:

```python
import sys, os
sys.path.append(os.pardir)
import numpy as np
from common.layers import *
from common.gradient import numerical_gradient
from collections import OrderedDict
class TwoLayerNet:
    def __init__ (self, input_size, hidden_size, output_size,
            weight_init_std=0.01):
    # Initialize weights
    self.params = {}
    self.params['W1'] = weight_init_std * \
                    np.random.randn(input_size, hidden_size)
    self.params['b1'] = np.zeros(hidden_size)
    self.params['W2'] = weight_init_std * \
                    np.random.randn(hidden_size, output_size)
    self.params['b2'] = p.zeros(output_size)
    # Create layers
    self.layers = OrderedDict( )
    self.layers['Affine1'] = \
        Affine(self.params['W1'], self.params['b1'])
    self.layers['Relu1'] = Relu( )
    self.layers['Affine2'] = \
    Affine(self.params['W2'], self.params['b2'])
    self.lastLayer = SoftmaxWithLoss( )
    def predict(self, x):
        for layer in self.layers.values( ):
            x = layer.forward(x)
        return x
    # x: input data, t: label data
    def loss(self, x, t):
        y = self.predict(x)
        return self.lastLayer.forward(y, t)
```

```python
def accuracy (self, x, t):
    y = self.predict(x)
    y = np.argmax(y, axis=1)
    if t.ndim != 1 : t = np.argmax(t, axis=1)
    accuracy = np.sum(y == t) / float(x.shape[0])
    return accuracy
# x: input data, t: teacher data
def numerical_gradient(self, x, t):
    loss_W = lambda W: self.loss(x, t)
    grads = {}
    grads['W1'] = numerical_gradient(loss_W, self.params['W1'])
    grads['b1'] = numerical_gradient(loss_W, self.params['b1'])
    grads['W2'] = numerical_gradient(loss_W, self.params['W2'])
    grads['b2'] = numerical_gradient(loss_W, self.params['b2'])
    return grads
def gradient(self, x, t):
    # forward
    self.loss(x, t)
    # backward
    dout = 1
    dout = self.lastLayer.backward(dout)
    layers = list(self.layers.values( ))
    layers.reverse( )
    for layer in layers:
        dout = layer.backward(dout)
    # Settings
    grads = {}
    grads['W1'] = self.layers['Affine1'].dW
    grads['b1'] = self.layers['Affine1'].db
    grads['W2'] = self.layers['Affine2'].dW
    grads['b2'] = self.layers['Affine2'].db
    return grads
```

Please note the code here in bold. It is particularly crucial to retain a neural network layer as **OrderedDict** (that is, a commanded dictionary) as this implies that the dictionary can remember the order of the items it adds. Therefore during forward propagation, you may finish the processing by invoking the **forward()** layer function in the addition order in the neural network. You only have to invert the layers in reverse order during backpropagation. Internally, affine and ReLU layers appropriately process propagation and backpropagation. You therefore just need to mix the layers in the right sequence and name them in order (or in reverse order).

Thus, the components of a neural network may be readily built by using them as layers. The modular implementation with layers has a tremendous benefit. If you wish to construct a huge five-, ten-, or twenty-layer network, you may add the needed layers (as if you were assembling Lego blocks). Through a forward propagation and backpropagation in each layer, the gradients necessary to be recognized and learn are therefore correctly achieved.

Gradient check

Till now, we have seen two methods of calculation for a gradient: One utilizes numerical differentiation, while the other analytically resolves the equation. With backpropagation, the latter approach allows efficient calculation even when there are many parameters. We will thus use backpropagation to construct a gradient from now on instead of sluggish numerical differentiation.

It takes time to calculate numerical differentiation. If backpropagation is correct, numerical differentiation does not need to be carried out. So, what is beneficial for numerical differentiation? In reality, numerical differentiation is necessary to determine if backpropagation is correct.

The advantage of numerical differentiation is that it is straightforward to execute, with errors being uncommon compared to the much more complex backpropagation. Thus, numerical differentiation results are typically compared with backpropagation to evaluate whether the backpropagation process is valid.

The verification procedure is known as **gradient inspection**. The following code is used to do a gradient inspection (source code is in **chapter05/GradientCheck.py**):

```
import sys, os

sys.path.append(os.pardir)

import numpy as np

from dataset.mnist import load_mnist

from TwoLayerNet import TwoLayerNet
```

```
(a_train, b_train), (a_test, b_test) = load_mnist(normalize=True, one_
hot_label=True)


network = TwoLayerNet(input_size=784, hidden_size=50, output_size=10)


a_batch = a_train[:4]
b_batch = b_train[:4]


grad_numerical = network.numerical_gradient(a_batch, b_batch)
grad_backprop = network.gradient(a_batch, b_batch)


for key in grad_numerical.keys():
    diff = np.average( np.abs(grad_backprop[key] - grad_numerical[key]) )
    print(key + ":" + str(diff))
```

The MNIST dataset is loaded here as always. Next, a portion of the training data is utilized to verify the error between the gradient by numerical differentiation and by backpropagation. As an error, the absolute values of the differences of element are averaged in each weight parameter. The following result is obtained when the preceding code is executed:

W1:3.1284357024517484e-10

X1:1.885251360678555e-09

W2:3.609090529978871e-09

X2:1.2018078520831256e-07

The result reveals that there are very modest variations between the gradients obtained by numerical differentiation and backpropagation. In case of the error, layer 1 biases are **9.7e-13 (0.00000000000097)**. This shows that the gradient is also correct via backpropagation and enhances its accuracy.

The error between the results of a numerical differentiation t and backpropagation is seldom 0. This is because the precision of the calculations is limited (for example, 32-bit floating-point numbers are used). Since numerical accuracy is restricted, generally the error is not 0. But the error should be a tiny value approaching 0, if the implementation is right. The backpropagation execution is wrong when the value is large.

Training using backpropagation

Finally, we'll show how we can use backpropagation to accomplish neural network training. The only difference is that gradients are measured by backpropagation. We just see the code and miss out on the explanation (source code is in **chapter05/ NeuralNet_Training.py**):

```python
import sys, os
sys.path.append(os.pardir)
import numpy as np
from dataset.mnist import load_mnist
from two_layer_net import TwoLayerNet
# Load data
(x_train, t_train), (x_test, t_test) = \
    load_mnist(normalize=True, one_hot_label=True)
network = TwoLayerNet(input_size=784, hidden_size=50, output_size=10)
iters_num = 10000
train_size = x_train.shape[0]
batch_size = 100
learning_rate = 0.1
train_loss_list = [ ]
train_acc_list = [ ]
test_acc_list = [ ]
iter_per_epoch = max(train_size / batch_size, 1)
for i in range(iters_num):
    batch_mask = np.random.choice(train_size, batch_size)
    x_batch = x_train[batch_mask]
    t_batch = t_train[batch_mask]
    # Use backpropagation to obtain a gradient
    grad = network.gradient(x_batch, t_batch)
    # Update
    for key in ('W1', 'b1', 'W2', 'b2'):
        network.params[key] -= learning_rate * grad[key]
```

```
    loss = network.loss(x_batch, t_batch)

    train_loss_list.append(loss)

if i % iter_per_epoch == 0:

    train_acc = network.accuracy(x_train, t_train)

    test_acc = network.accuracy(x_test, t_test)

    train_acc_list.append(train_acc)

    test_acc_list.append(test_acc)

    print(train_acc, test_acc)
```

Conclusion

In this chapter, we learnt about computational graphs that visually illustrate calculations. We examined a computational graph that defined backpropagation in a neural network, comprising a ReLU layer, softmax loss layer, an affine layer, and softmax layer, in a neural network. These layers have forward and backward method, and can efficiently compute the weight parameters by propagating data forward as well as reverse. You may mix these layers freely into a neural network by utilizing them as modules so that the network you want can simply form. This chapter addressed the following points:

- We can graphically display calculation processes using computational graphs.

- Local calculations are a node in a computational graph. The whole calculation is made up of local calculations.

- Forward propagation in a computational graph results in a regular calculation. Meanwhile, the differential of each node may be determined in a computational graph via backpropagation.

- You can compute gradients efficiently by implementing components in a neural network as layers (backpropagation).

- You may confirm that backpropagation findings are valid by comparing results from numerical differentiation and backpropagation (gradient check).

CHAPTER 6

Neural Network Training Techniques

This chapter discusses key principles in neural network training, including the optimization strategies used for searching for the best weight parameters, the initial weight parameter values, and the hyperparameter setup procedure—all of these are major themes in neural network training. In order to prevent excessive fitness, we will look at regularization strategies such as decay and drop. Finally, we are going to examine batch normalization, which has been employed in many recent years in research.

Structure

- Updating parameters
  - Story of an adventurer
- Stochastic Gradient Descent (SGD)
  - Disadvantage of SGD
- Momentum
- AdaGrad
- Adam
- Which update technique should we use?
  - Using the MNIST dataset to compare the update techniques

- o Initial weight values
- o Distribution of hidden layers of activation
- Initial weight values for ReLU
  - o Using the MNIST dataset to compare the weight initializers
- Batch normalization
  - o Batch normalization algorithm
- Evaluating batch normalization
- Regularization
- Overfitting
- Weight decay
- Dropout
- Validating hyperparameters
  - o Validation data
  - o Optimizing hyperparameters
  - o Implementing hyperparameter optimization

Objective:

With the methods presented in this chapter, you will be able to efficiently encourage neural network training to enhance recognition accuracy.

Updating parameters

The objective of neural network training is to search for parameters that minimize the value of loss function. The challenge is to identify the optimum parameters (an optimization procedure). Sadly, optimization is hard since the set of parameters is highly complex and it is tough to identify the best solution. You cannot accomplish it by fixing an equation instantly to achieve the minimal value. Due to the large number of parameters in the deep network, it is more challenging.

So far, we have determined the optimal parameters through the gradients (derivatives) of the parameters. We gradually approach the optimal parameters by utilizing the gradients of the parameters to update their parameters in the gradient direction. This is a simple approach called **stochastic descent gradient (SGD)** but it is a smarter one than a random search of the space of the parameter. SGD is nonetheless a simple approach and there are some alternate methods that perform better (for specific situations). Let's first look at the downside of SGD and offer additional methods for optimization.

Story of an adventurer

We may look at an allegory to illustrate the circumstance we are in in relation to optimization before moving on to the main subject.

> There's an odd explorer. He travels across an extensive arid terrain every day to find a deep valley floor. His objective is to reach the deeper floor of the valley which he calls the "*deep spot*". That is why he is travelling. Furthermore, he placed two stringent restrictions on himself: One is not to use a map, the other to hide his eyes. Therefore, he knows not where in a wide area there is the deepest valley floor, and he can see nothing. How can this explorer seek for the deep spot under these severe conditions? How can he be effective in finding a deep place?

The position we are in is a realm of darkness exactly like that of this adventurer, when looking for the perfect conditions. We need to search for the deep spot in a large and intricate terrain without a map.

The inclination of the ground is crucial in this tough scenario. The explorer cannot see, but he knows where the inclination of the ground is (his feet can feel it). Thus, the strategy of SGD is to move towards the direction of steepest inclination. "I may be able to reach the 'deep spot' eventually by saying that," thought the courageous traveler.

Stochastic Gradient Descent (SGD)

Now that we have understood the challenge of optimization, let us begin with the SGD review. SGD is described in equation (*6.1*) as following:

$$\mathbf{W} \leftarrow \mathbf{W} - \eta \frac{\partial L}{\partial \mathbf{W}}$$

Equation 6.1

Here, the weight parameters to update are W and the gradients of the loss function for W is . η is the learning rate. We must set it as a value, like 0.01 or 0.001. indicates that the value on the right side of the equation is utilized to update the value on the left side. As equation (6.1) demonstrates, SGD is a simple technique which moves some distance in the direction of the gradient. In Python, we implementing SGD as a class:

```python
class SGD:
    def __init__ (self, lr=0.01):
        self.lr = lr
    def update(self, params, grads):
        for key in params.keys():
            params[key] -= self.lr * grads[key]
```

The argument in this case, **lr**, is the rate of learning. The rate of learning is kept as an instance variable. The update method, which is repeatedly called by **SGD**, will also be defined. The argument, parameter, and grade are dictionary variables (as in the implementation of neural networks so far). Each element holds a weight parameter or gradient, just such as **parameters['W1']** and **grades['W1']**. By utilizing the SGD class, you may upgrade the parameters of the neural network in the following way:

```
network = TwoLayerNet(...)

optimizer = SGD()

for i in range(10000):

    ...

    x_batch, t_batch = get_mini_batch(...)  # Mini-batch

    grads = network.gradient(x_batch, t_batch)

    params = network.params

    optimizer.update(params, grads)

    ...
```

The variable name that occurs here, **optimizer**, implies an optimizing individual. This is the job of the SGD here. The parameters are updated by the **optimizer** variable. All we have to do here is to give the information on parameters and gradient to the **optimizer**.

Thus, it is possible to modularize functionalities individually by implementing the optimized class. In the near future we are, for example, implementing another optimization approach, called **Momentum (params, grads)**. Then, we can change the **optimizer = SGD()** line to **optimizer = momentum** (by switching **SGD()** to Momentum).

Different optimization strategies are implemented and a simple mechanism is given for switching between them in many deep learning systems. For example, optimization approaches are implemented as functions in the updates.py file in a deep learning framework called Lasagne (http://github.com/Lasagne/Lasagne/blob/master/lasagne/updates.py). From these, the user may choose the approach of optimization.

Disadvantage of SGD

SGD is simple and straightforward to implement; however, for some situations, it may be inefficient. Let us consider a problem in order to illustrate the disadvantage of SGD by calculating the minimum value of the following function:

$$f(x,y) = \frac{1}{20}x^2 + y^2$$

Equation 6.2

The shape of the function in equation (6.2) appears in the following plots, as a bowl spread in the direction of the X-axis. The equation (6.2) contour lines really seem to expand ellipses in the direction of the X-axis.

Let us now look at the function gradients, which are given by equation (6.2). The gradients are displayed in *Figure 6.2*. These are wide in the direction of the Y-axis and tiny in the direction of the X-axis. That means the tilt towards the Y-axis is severe while it is progressive towards the X-axis. It should be noted that the minimum value position in equation (6.2) is $(x, y) = (0, 0)$ but that in Figure 6.2, the gradients do not show the $(0, 0)$ direction in many places.

Let us apply SGD to the function given in the following graphs. Searches are started at $(x, y) = (-7.0, 2.0)$ (initial values). The outcome is shown in *figure 6.3*:

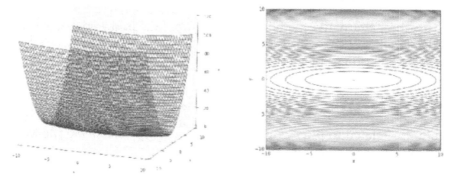

Figure 6.1: Graph of (left) and its contour lines (right)

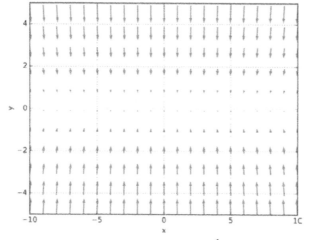

Figure 6.2: Gradients of $f(x,y) = \frac{1}{20} x^2 + y^2$

As illustrated in the accompanying graphic, SGD travels in a zigzag direction. The drawback of SDG is that if the shape of a function is not isotropic (that is, extended), its search route becomes inefficient. We thus need a technique that is more intelligent than SGD and moves only in the gradient direction. The fundamental cause of SGD's inefficient search route is that the gradients do not point to the correct minimum values:

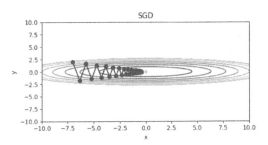

Figure 6.3: *Update path of optimization by SGD –*
inefficient because it moves in a zigzag to the minimum value (0, 0)

We will use three alternative methods: Momentum, AdaGrad, and Adam to overcome SGD's disadvantage. We will briefly explain each of these and demonstrate their Python equations and implementations.

Momentum

Momentum is related to physics; it means the *"quantity of motion"*. The Momentum technique is represented by the following equations:

$$\mathbf{v} \leftarrow \alpha\mathbf{v} - \eta\frac{\partial L}{\partial \mathbf{W}}$$

Equation 6.3

$$\mathbf{W} \leftarrow \mathbf{W} + \mathbf{v}$$

Equation 6.4

Just like SGD, W is the weight parameter to update, is the gradients of the loss function for W, and η is the learning rate. A new variable that appears here, v, is the velocity in physics. Equation (6.3) represents a physical law stating that an object receives a force in the gradient direction and is accelerated by this force. In Momentum, update functions are used as if a ball had been rolled on the ground, as shown in the following diagram:

Figure 6.4: *Image of Momentum – a ball rolls on the slope of the ground*

The term αv in equation (6.3) slows the object down gradually when it receives no force (a value such as 0.9 is set for α). This is the friction created by the ground or the air resistance. The following code shows the implementation of **Momentum** (the source code is located at **common/optimizer.py**):

```
class Momentum:
    def __ init __ (self, lr=0.01, momentum=0.9):
        self.lr = lr
        self.momentum = momentum
        self.v = None
    def update(self, params, grads):
        if self.v is None:
            self.v = {}
            for key, val in params.items():
                self.v[key] = np.zeros_like(val)
        for key in params.keys():
            self.v[key] = self.momentum*self.v[key] - self.lr*grads[key]
            params[key] += self.v[key]
```

The instance variable, **v**, retains the velocity of the object. At initialization, **v** retains nothing. When **update()** is called, it retains the data of the same structure as a **dictionary** variable. The remaining implementation is simple: it just implements equations (6.3) and (6.4).

Now, let's use **Momentum** to solve the optimization problem of equation (6.2). The following image shows the result.

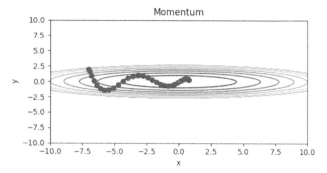

Figure 6.5: *Update path for optimization by Momentum*

As shown in the plot, the update path goes like a ball rolling around in a bowl. It can be seen that the extent of zigzag is lower than that of SGD. There is extremely minimal force in the X-axis direction but the item always receives force in the same direction and is propelled in the same direction. On the other hand, force is large in the direction of the Y-axis, yet the item receives force both positively and negatively in an alternating manner. The speed in the Y-axis is unsteady. They cancel each other out. This can speed up motion in the direction of the X-axis and minimize motion in comparison with the SGD.

AdaGrad

The value of the learning rate— in the equation— is crucial in neural network training. Training takes too long if learning rate η is too small. If it is too large, divergence develops, and proper training cannot be performed.

There is an efficient learning rate approach called "**learning rate decay**". As training progresses, it employs a decreasing learning rate. This is commonly used in the training of neural networks. A neural network initially learns much and then gradually learns less. The progressive reduction in the learning rate is identical to the reduction in learning rate values for all parameters.

AdaGrad adjusts the learning rate for each element of the parameter adaptively for training (the "Ada" in AdaGrad comes from "*adaptive*"). Now, we will show AdaGrad's update method with equations:

$$\mathbf{h} \leftarrow \mathbf{h} + \frac{\partial L}{\partial \mathbf{W}} \odot \frac{\partial L}{\partial \mathbf{W}}$$

Equation 6.5

$$\mathbf{W} \leftarrow \mathbf{W} - \eta \frac{1}{\sqrt{\mathbf{h}}} \frac{\partial L}{\partial \mathbf{W}}$$

Equation 6.6

Just like SGD, W is the weight parameters to update, is the gradients of the loss function for W, and η is the learning rate. Here, a new variable, h, appears. The h variable stores the sum of the squared gradient values thus far, as shown in equation (6.5). This equation indicates multiplication between array elements). When updating parameters, **AdaGrad** adjusts the rate of learning by multiplying . The learning rate is reduced for the parameter element that is considerably shifted (that is, has been significantly modified). You can therefore diminish the learning rate of each parameter element by gradually lowering the learning rate of the substantially shifted parameter.

Now, let's get **AdaGrad** implemented. You may use **AdaGrad** (source code is available at **common/optimizer.py**):

```
class AdaGrad:
```

```
    def __init__ (self, lr=0.01):
        self.lr = lr
        self.h = None
    def update(self, params, grads):
        if self.h is None:
        self.h = {}
        for key, val in params.items():
            self.h[key] = np.zeros_like(val)
for key in params.keys():
    self.h[key] += grads[key] * grads[key]
    params[key] -= self.lr * grads[key] / (np.sqrt(self.h[key]) + 1e-7)
```

Note that the last line has added a small value of 1*e*-7. This avoids divisions by 0 if self.h[key] has 0. This tiny amount may be set up as a parameter in many deep learning systems but a fixed value, 1*e*-7, is utilized here.

Let us now utilize AdaGrad to solve the optimization problem in equation (6.2). The outcome is seen in this screenshot:

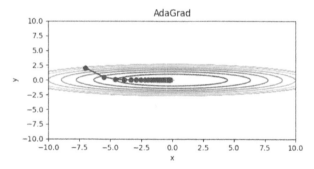

Figure 6.6: Update path for optimization by AdaGrad

In the preceding figure, the results demonstrate that parameters go to the minimal value effectively. Initially, the parameters move a lot since the gradient in the Y-axis is high. Adjustment is made in proportion to the significant motion to make the update step smaller. Thus, the degree of update in the Y-axis is reduced and the zigzag movements are reduced.

Adam

In **Momentum**, parameters move depending on the physical law, such as a ball rolling around in a bowl. **AdaGrad** modifies the update process suitably for every parameter element. How can we combine **Momentum** and **AdaGrad**, the two methods? This is the basic idea of **Adam** (the account by Adam is intuitive and does not contain any technical specifications.

Adam is a new technique that was presented in 2015. This is a really complicated hypothesis. It is like an obvious mix of **Momentum** and **AdaGrad**. The space parameter may be found effectively by combining the advantages of these two techniques. Adam also includes a specific hyperparameter called bias correction. The **Adam** class in **common/optimizer.py** is implemented in Python.

Let us now utilize Adam to tackle the problem of optimization in equation (6.2). The outcome is shown in the following screenshot:

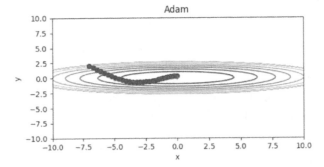

Figure 6.7: Update path for optimization by Adam

As seen in *figure 6.7*, Adam's update path travels like a ball rolling in a bowl. The action in Momentum is similar, but the left and right ball movements are less. The adaptive modification of the learning rate results in this benefit.

> Three parameters have been added to Adam. The first is the learning rate (which appears in the text as α). The others are the primary coefficient, $\beta 1$, and $\beta 2$ the secondary coefficient. It is stated in the text that the usual $\beta 1$ and $\beta 2$ values are in many situations 0.9 and 0.999.

Which update technique should we use?

We have investigated updating methods with four parameters up to now. Here we will compare the results (source code in **chapter06/Naive_OptimizerComparison. py**).

The various approaches used in the various pathways for updating parameters are depicted in *figure 6.8*. This picture seems to indicate **AdaGrad** to be the best; however, remember that the results vary according to the difficulties.

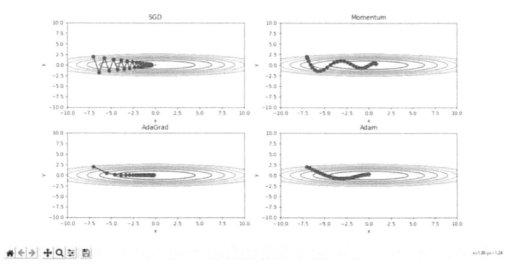

Figure 6.8: *Comparison of optimization techniques – SGD, Momentum, AdaGrad, and Adam*

Up to now, four approaches have been looked at: **SGD**, **Momentum**, **AdaGrad**, and **Adam**. But what are we supposed to use? Sadly, no approach that is good for fixing every problem is currently known. Each one has its own particular features and benefits, making it better suited than others to certain challenges. Therefore, in some cases it is vital to know which approach works best.

In much research, SGD remains in use. Momentum and AdaGrad also deserve to be tried. Recently, Adam seems to have been preferred by many researchers and developers. SGD and Adam are prominently employed in this book. The other approaches you want to attempt can be done.

Using the MNIST dataset to compare the update techniques

We will compare the four approaches we discussed so far for handwritten digit recognition: SGD, Momentum, AdaGrad, and Adam. Let's study how every approach works in advanced training. The *figure 6.9* displays the results (**chapter06/MNIST_ OptimizerComparison.py** contains the source code):

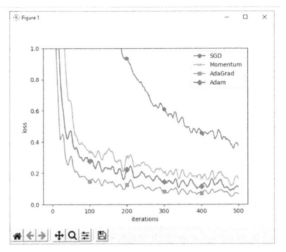

Figure 6.9: Using the MNIST dataset to compare the four update techniques – the horizontal axis indicates the iterations of learning, while the vertical axis indicates the values of the loss function

This experiment utilized a neural network of five layers with hundred neurons each layer. The activation function was utilized with ReLU.

The *figure 6.9* demonstrates that alternative approaches have learnt more quickly than the SGD. The other three approaches appear to be similarly quick in learning. Looking closer, AdaGrad appears to have learnt a bit quicker. In this experiment, the outcomes rely on the learning rate hyperparameter and the topology (the number of layers) of the neural network. However, the other three approaches are typically faster learned than SGD, and sometimes better acknowledged.

Initial weight values

For neural network training, the initial weight values are particularly essential. Initial weight settings frequently affect whether the neural network training is successful. In this part, we recommend the initial weight values, and then conduct an experiment to ensure that neural network training accelerates.

How to set the initial weight values to zero?

We will later look at a technique called weight decay that decreases overfitting and enhances the generalization performance. Briefly, weight decay is a method to lower weight parameter values to avoid overfitting.

If we wish to have smaller weights, it will probably be a smart idea to start with the smallest initial values. An initial weight value of **0.01*np.random.randn(10, 100)** is employed here. This tiny number is the Gaussian Distribution value multiplied by 0.01—a Gaussian Distribution with a standard deviation of 0.01.

How can we put the starting weight values at 0 if we want the weight values to be small? This is a misconception since it stops us from training properly.

Why should we not have 0 for the initial weight? Or, why should the weights not be consistent? Well, all weight levels have been updated in backpropagation uniformly (similarly). Thus, in a two-layer neural network, the layers 1 and 2 have 0 as their weights. Then the same value is spread to all neurons in layer 2 when the input layer is propagated forward because the weight is 0. All the weights of layer 2 are updated equally in backpropagation if the same values are entered for all neurons in layer 2. (Please see the section *Backward propagation in a multiplication node* in *Chapter 5: Backpropagation*). The weights are therefore adjusted to the same value and become symmetrical (duplicate values). Because of this, it makes no sense to have numerous weights. Random initial values are necessary to prevent weights from being uniform or breaking their symmetrical structure.

Distribution of hidden layers of activation

There is a lot of information to see the distribution of the activation data (this refers to the output data in the hidden layers following the activation function, while other literature calls the data which runs between layers as "*activation*"). This is a basic experiment to look at how the initial weight values affect hidden layers of activation. In a five-layer neural network, we enter some randomly generated data (using a **sigmoid** function as an activation function) and present the data distribution of the activation of each layer in a histogram. This experiment is based on the Stanford University courses in Visual Recognition CS231n [*Convolutional Neural Networks* (`http://cs231n.github.io/`)].

The source code for the experiment is located at **chapter06/ActivationHistogram. py**. The following is part of this code:

```
import numpy as np

import matplotlib.pyplot as plt


def sigmoid(x):
    return 1 / (1 + np.exp(-x))


input_data = np.random.randn(1000, 100)
node_num = 100
hidden_layer_size = 5
```

```
activations = {}


x = input_data


for i in range(hidden_layer_size):
    if i != 0:
        x = activations[i-1]


    # Weight value setting ============================================
========
    w = np.random.randn(node_num, node_num) * 1
    # ================================================================
========


    a = np.dot(x, w)


    # Activation function setting =====================================
========
    z = sigmoid(a)
    # ================================================================
========


    activations[i] = z
```

There are five layers here with a hundred neurons in each layer. As input data, 1,000 pieces of data are randomly generated and sent to the neural network of five layers. Sigmoid functions are employed as activation function, and activation results are recorded in the `activations` variable for each layer. The weight scale should be noted. Here, a Gaussian distributor of standard deviation 1 is employed. The aim of this experiment is to examine how activation distribution varies by altering this scale (standard deviation). Now let us display the data from each layer saved in a histogram during activation:

```
# Draw histograms

for i, a in activations.items():
    plt.subplot(1, len(activations), i+1)
```

```
    plt.title(str(i+1) + "-layer")
    if i != 0:
        plt.yticks([], [])
    plt.hist(a.flatten(), 30, range=(0,1))
plt.show()
```

The histograms presented in the accompanying image are created with this code.

This image demonstrates that each layer is predominantly activated at 0 and 1. An S-curve function is the **sigmoid** function used here. The value of the difference is 0, since the output of the **sigmoid** function approaches 0 (or 1). If the data are mostly 0s and 1s, the gradient values of the backpropagation will thus be reduced until they disappear. It's a problem called vanishing gradients. When several layers exist in deep learning, it might lead to a more significant problem of vanishing gradient.

Let us now carry out the same experiment, but with the standard deviation of the weights as 0.01. You must change the preceding code to establish the initial weight values as follows:

```
# w = np.random.randn(node_num, node_num) * 1
w = np.random.randn(node_num, node_num) * 0.01
```

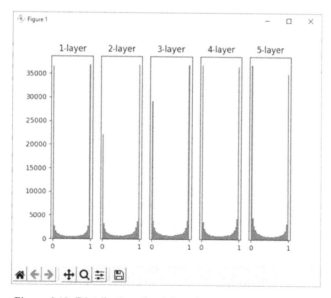

Figure 6.10: Distribution of each layer's activations where the
starting weight values are utilized by a Gaussian distribution with a standard deviation of 1

Observe the findings. The *figure 6.11* illustrates each layer's activation distribution when a Gaussian distribution with a standard deviation of 0.01 is employed:

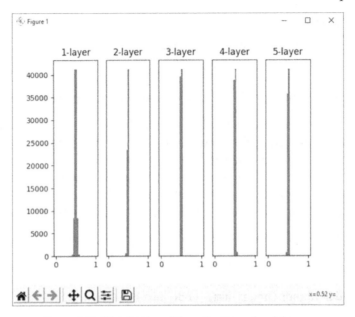

Figure 6.11: *Distribution of the activations of each layer*
if the usual 0.01 Gaussian distribution for the starting weight values is applied

The activations now focus on 0.5. Unlike the prior example, they are not skewed towards 0 and 1. There are no vanishing gradients. However, when activations are biased, their representation presents a major difficulty. There is little significance in the existence of numerous neurons if several neurons yield virtually the same results. For instance, if a hundred neurons are almost identical, one neuron may be nearly the same thing. The biased activations therefore pose a difficulty, as the representation is restricted. There needs to be an appropriate distribution of activations in each layer. This is because a neural network learns quickly when relatively different data flows in each layer.

On the other hand, the training may not go well when biased data flows because of the vanishing gradient and limited representation.

Next, in a study by *Xavier Glorot* et. al.(*Understanding the difficulty of training deep feedforward neural networks* 2010), we will utilize initial weight values. This is called "Xavier Initialization". Currently, Xavier Initialization is commonly utilized in deep learning frameworks. For example, the Xavier argument for the initial weight setting may be used with the Xavier initializer in the Caffe framework.

Xavier acquired the right weight range such that the activation of each layer was correspondingly extended. It determined that when the number of nodes in the previous layer is n, distributions with the standard deviation should be employed

(Xavier's paper proposed setting values that take into account both the number of input nodes in the previous layer and the number of output nodes in the next layer. However, just the input nodes in the preceding layer for simplicity in the framework implementations, such as Caffe, are calculated as specified here.) The following graphic shows this:

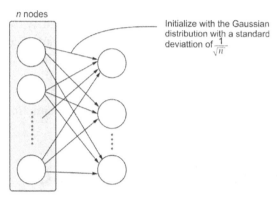

Figure 6.12: *Xavier initializer – when n nodes in the previous layer are connected, a distribution with the standard deviation of is used for initial values*

The weight scope of the original values for the target nodes is lower when the Xavier initializer is employed since the number of nodes in the preceding layer is higher. Let us now conduct some experiments using the Xavier Initializer. The original weight value simply has to be modified as follows (implementation is simplified because in all layers the number of nodes equals 100):

```
node_num = 100 # Number of nodes in the previous layer

w = np.random.randn(node_num, node_num) / np.sqrt(node_num)
```

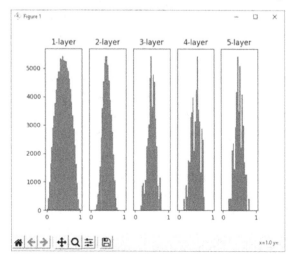

Figure 6.13: *Distribution of each layer activation when the original weight value Xavier is utilized.*

Figure 6.13 illustrates the outcomes when the Xavier Initializer is employed. It indicates distributions are more widely distributed, while a higher layer has a more deformed shape. We may anticipate to do the training well since the data flowing in every layer are correctly dispersed and the representation of the sigmoid function is not restricted.

> In addition, the distribution of the upper layers are slightly twisted in their form. When a `tanh` (hyperbolic) function is employed instead of a `sigmoid` function, the distorted form is improved. Actually, the distributions will have a bell shape when the tanh function is applied. The tanh function, like a sigmoid function, is an S-curve. Tanh is symmetrical for origin (0, 0) but the sigmoid is symmetrical for (x, y) = (0, 0.5). It is preferable to utilize the tanh function to symmetrically activate the origin.

Initial weight values for ReLU

The Xavier Initializer is predicated on the assumption that an activation function is linear. The Xavier Initializer is suitable since the function of sigmoid and tanh is symmetrical and linear in its centers. In the meanwhile, it is advised to use the original value for ReLU. This was advocated by *Kaiming He et. al*. This was known as the He initializer.

The Initializer employs a Gaussian distribution with a standard deviation when the nodes of the preceding layer are *n*. If we consider that the Xavier Initializer is, we may suppose (intuitively) that the coefficient must be doubled in order to spread further, because for ReLU a negative range is 0.

Let's see how the activation is distributed when ReLU is utilized for activation function. After three trials using a 0.01 (that is, `std=0.01`) Gaussian distribution, the Xavier Initializer and the He Initializer, which is used for **ReLU**, we will analyze the outcomes of three experiments (*figure 6.14*).

Every layer has a very small activation (average of the distribution values: **layer 1:0.0396, layer 2:0.00290, layer 3:0.000197, layer 4: 1.32e-5; layer 5: 9.46e-7**) for **std=0.01**. When little data flows through a neural network, the weight gradients of a backpropagation are small. This is a significant concern as training will not progress.

Let us next look at the Xavier Initializer findings. This demonstrates that the bias is gradually growing as the layers become deeper — like the activations. Gradient disappearance in training will be an issue. In contrast, the distribution of Gaussian in each layer is identical for the He Initializer. Even at deeper layers, the distribution of the data is comparable. Thus, we may assume that suitable values also flow backwards.

In brief, the He Initializer will be used when you are using ReLU, and the Xavier Initializer will be used for S-curve functions, such as sigmoid and tanh. This is the best practice at the time of writing this book.

Using the MNIST dataset to compare the weight initializers

Let us utilize real data to explore how different weight initializers impact neural network training. In our tests we will choose **std=0.01** (the source code is accessible at **chapter06/WeightInitComparison.py**). Initializer is also the He Initializer. The result is shown in the following screenshot:

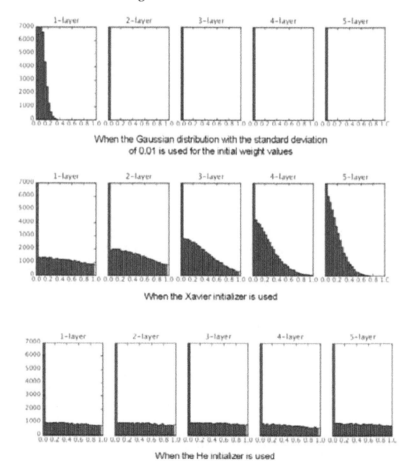

Figure 6.14: *Weight initializer change of activation distribution when the ReLU is employed to activate*

The experiment employs the activation function of a five-layer neural network (100 neurons in each layer). The findings in the next picture demonstrate that no learning occurs for **std=0.01**. This is because small values (data about 0) are being transmitted in the future as previously seen when activation was distributed. Therefore, the progression to be obtained is also limited in backpropagation, leading to a few weight updates. Training for the **Xavier** and **He** initializers is, on the other hand, smooth. The following screenshot illustrates also that training for the initializer proceeds quickly:

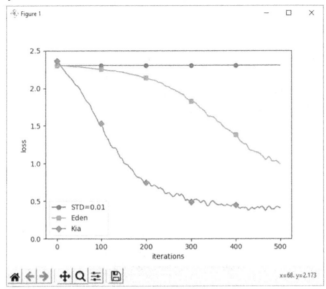

Figure 6.15: *The horizontal axis represents the iterations of the workout using the MNIST data set for compared the weight inducer, while the vertical axis shows the loss function values*

As we have seen, the initial weight values are very important in neural network training. Often they decide whether or not they succeed. While the usefulness of the initial weight values is frequently underestimated, it is vital for everybody to have the initial value.

Batch normalization

The distribution of activations on each layer was shown in the preceding section. The correct initial weight values have been learnt to ensure that the activities on each layer are distributed properly so as to allow smooth training. So how about forcefully changing the activation distribution to ensure that each layer has a correct dispersion?

This technique is based on the idea of batch normalization.

Batch normalization algorithm

In 2015, the initial proposal for batch normalization (a.k.a. batch norm) was made. While the batch norm is a novel approach, several academics and engineers have utilized it frequently. Indeed, batch norm typically produce good results in competitions around machine learning.

Batch normalization has the following advantages:

- It can speed up training (it can increase the learning rate).
- The weight of the original is not as dependent (you do not need to be cautious about the initial values).
- It lowers overfitting (it reduces the necessity of dropout).

The first benefit is very tempting as it takes a great deal of time to learn. With the batch norm the initial weight values need not be concerned, and as it reduces overfitting, this cause of worry is removed from deep learning.

As mentioned above, the objective of batch norm is to modify the distribution of activations in each layer to ensure a suitable distribution. In this way, as a batch normalization layer (also known as the batch norm layer) the layer that normalizes the distribution of data is put into a neural network as illustrated in the following diagram:

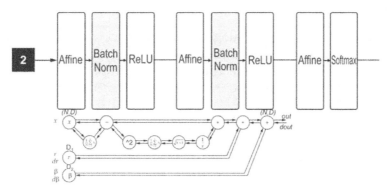

Figure 6.16: *Example of the neural network with batch normalization (the batch norm layers are shown in gray)*

The input data is normalized so that the average of the data is 0 and their variation is 1. μ is a tiny number in equation (6.7). (such as 10e-7). Division by 0 is prevented.

$$\mu_B \leftarrow \frac{1}{m}\sum_{i=1}^{m} x_i$$

$$\sigma_B^2 \leftarrow \frac{1}{m}\sum_{i=1}^{m}(x_i - \mu_B)^2$$

$$\hat{x}_i \leftarrow \frac{x_i - \mu_B}{\sqrt{\sigma_B^2 + \varepsilon}}$$

Equation 6.7

Here, a set of m input data $p = \{x_1, x_2, \dots, x_m\}$, is treated as a mini-batch and its average, μ_b, and variance, σ_b^2,, are calculated. The input data is normalized so that its average is 0 and its variance is 1 for the appropriate distribution. In equation (6.7), ε is a small value (such as 10e-7). This prevents division by 0.

The equation (6.7) simply converts the input data for a mini-batch, $\{x_1, x_2 \ldots, x_m\}$, into data with an average of 0 and a variance of 1, $\{\hat{x}_1, \hat{x}_2, \ldots, \hat{x}_{1m}\}$. By including this process before (or after) the activation function [see arXiv:1502.23167[cs] (February 2015) and the distribution bias of the data can be reduced.

The batch norm layer further converts the normalized data to a certain scale and shift. This conversion is shown as follows:

$$y_i \leftarrow \gamma \hat{x}_i + \beta$$

Equation 6.8

The parameters and β are here. It begins with = 1 and β = 0 and is modified during training to the proper values. This is the batch norm algorithm. The forward propagation in a neural network is provided by this algorithm. With the use of a computational graph, as stated in *Chapter 5: Backpropogation*, we may express the batch norm.

We will not go into depth regarding how to get backward propagation in batch standard since this is a little difficult. You may very simply calculate a backpropagation of the batch norm if you utilize a computational graph, as demonstrated in the accompanying figure. *Frederik Kratzert's* blog post, *"Understanding the Backward Pass through the Batch Normalization Layer"*.

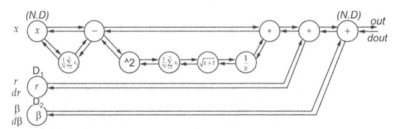

Figure 6.17: *Computational graph of batch normalization*

Evaluating batch normalization

Now let us conduct some experiments using the batch norm layer. The first step is to utilize the **MNIST** dataset to examine how the learning progress varies with and without the batch norm layer (source code at **chapter06/TestBatchNorm.py**). The outcome is displayed in *figure 6.18*.

The *figure 6.18* shows that batch norm accelerates learning. Let us examine how training progress varies when different scales are being utilized for the initial data.

The *figure 6.19* includes graphs showing how the standard deviations of initial weight values have evolved during training.

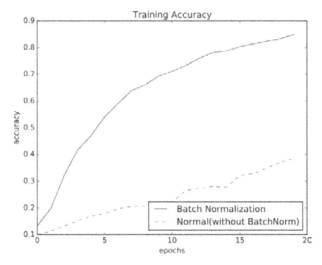

Figure 6.18: *Effect of batch norm – batch norm accelerates learning*

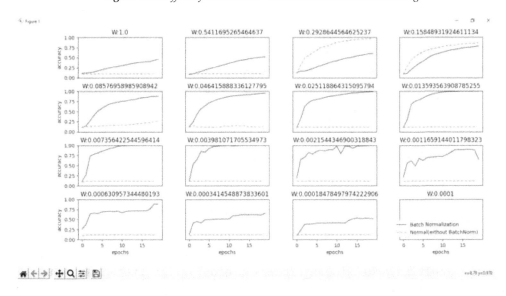

Figure 6.19: *The firm lines represent the results of the use of batch standard, while the points show the results without them - each chart title shows the standard weight deviation*

This shows that in nearly all situations, batch norm accelerates training. In reality, training cannot progress without a good range of initial values when batch norms are not utilized.

As we have shown, batch norm can speed up training and ensure the initial weight values are resistant ("initial weight values are resistant" means having a little dependence on them). Batch norm will play an active role in many instances since it has such great features.

Regularization

Overfitting frequently presents problems with machine learning. In overfitting, the model fits the training data too well and is unable to handle other variables not included in the training data adequately. Machine learning is aimed towards generalization performance. It is desirable that unknown data not present in training data be appropriately recognized by the model. While this allows you to construct a sophisticated and representative model, it is crucial to reduce overfitting.

Overfitting

The two primary reasons for overfitting are:

- The model is representative and contains numerous parameters.
- The data on training is not enough.

Here, by supplying these two reasons we produce overfitting. The **MNIST** dataset provides just 300 of over 600,000 pieces of training data, and uses a seven-layer network to enhance the complexity of the network. In every layer there are 100 neurons. ReLU is used as the activation feature.

The following is part of the source file (at **chapter06/OverfitWeightDecay.py**). First, the code loads the information:

```
(a_train, b_train), (a_test, b_test) = load_mnist(normalize=True)

# Reduce learning data to reproduce overfitting

a_train = a_train[:300]

b_train = b_train[:300]
```

Training takes place in the following code. Here recognition accuracy for both training data and all test data is calculated for each stage:

```
network = MultiLayerNet(input_size=784, hidden_size_list=[100, 100, 100,
100, 100, 100], output_size=10)

                    weight_decay_lambda=weight_decay_lambda)
optimizer = SGD(lr=0.01)


max_epochs = 31
train_size = a_train.shape[0]
batch_size = 100
```

```
train_loss_list = []
train_acc_list = []
test_acc_list = []

iter_per_epoch = max(train_size / batch_size, 1)
epoch_cnt = 0

for i in range(1000000000):
    batch_mask = np.random.choice(train_size, batch_size)
    a_batch = a_train[batch_mask]
    b_batch = b_train[batch_mask]

    grads = network.gradient(a_batch, b_batch)
    optimizer.update(network.params, grads)

    if i % iter_per_epoch == 0:
        train_acc = network.accuracy(a_train, b_train)
        test_acc = network.accuracy(a_test, b_test)
        train_acc_list.append(train_acc)
        test_acc_list.append(test_acc)

        print("Epoch:" + str(epoch_cnt) + ", Train acc:" + str(train_acc)
+ ", Test acc:" + str(test_acc))

        epoch_cnt += 1
        if epoch_cnt >= max_epochs:
            break
```

The **train_acc_list** and **test_acc_list** records the recognition accuracies for every **epoch**. An epoch shows that all training data were used. Let us draw graphs from the list of graphs (**train_acc_list**, **test_acc_list**). The outcome is shown in the following plot.

The recognition accuracies assessed using training data after 100 epochs was approximately 100%, however the recognition accuracies in the test data was considerably less than 100%. The overfitting of training data is responsible for these significant discrepancies. This graph indicates that generic data (test data), which was not used appropriately in training, cannot be handled by the model:

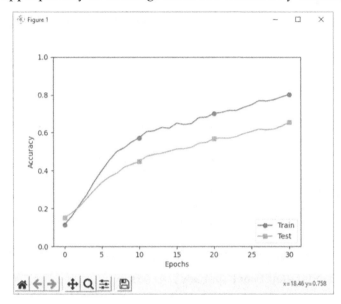

Figure 6.20: *Transition of training information (train) and test data recognition accuracies (test)*

Weight decay

The approach of weight decay was commonly employed to reduce overfitting. It prevents overfitting by putting a penalty on large weights during training. Overfitting happens commonly when a weight parameter is of a large value.

The goal of neural network training is to lower the value of the loss function, as explained before. You can, for instance, add the squared norm (*L2* norm) of the wright to the loss function. Then, you could prevent the weight $\frac{1}{2}\lambda W^2$ from being large. When the weights are *W*, the *L2* norm of the weight decay is $\frac{1}{2}\lambda W^2$. This $\frac{1}{2}\lambda W^2$ is added to the loss function. Here, λ is the hyperparameter that controls the strength of regularization. If you set a larger value to λ, you can impose a stronger penalty on a large weight. $\frac{1}{2}\lambda W^2$ the beginning of $\frac{1}{2}\lambda W^2$ is a constant for adjustment so that the differential of $\frac{1}{2}\lambda W^2$ is λW.

Weight decay adds $\frac{1}{2}\lambda W^2$ to the loss function for all weights. Consequently, while computing the weight gradient, the regularization term differential, *W*, is added to the output of backpropagation.

The *L2* norm is the sum of every element's squares. Besides the *L2* norm, there are also the *L1* and *L* norms. The *L1* norm is the total value, $|w1| + |w2| + ... + |wn|$. The total value, that is, the *L* norm is sometimes referred to as the max norm. It's the most important of all the elements' absolute values. You can use any of these norms as a time-limit. Each one has its properties, but here, we are just going to apply the *L2* norm as it is utilized most often.

Let us now conduct an experiment. To the previous experiment we will use the weight decay of ▣= *0.1*. The findings of this table are below (weight decay supportive network is at **common/multi_layer_net.py** and experiment code is at **chapter06/ OverfitWeightDecay.py**):

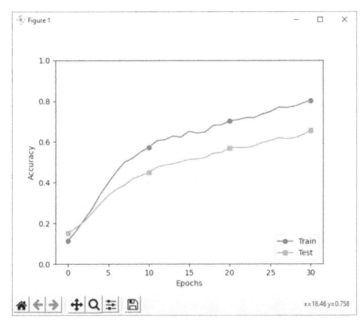

Figure 6.21: *Transition of accuracy in training data accuracy (train) and weight decline testing (test)*

The figure above indicates that the recognition accuracy of training data and test data is different but the difference is lower than in the one in *Figure 6.20* where there was no weight decay. This shows that overfitting has been minimized. Please note that the recognition accuracy of training data is not 100% (1.0).

Dropout

The weight decay approach was discussed in the preceding section. It adds to the loss function the *L2* norm of weights to reduce overfitting. Weight decay is straightforward to implement and can to some extent decrease overfitting. However, weight decay becomes insufficient as a neural network model gets more complex. This is when the dropout technique is often used.)

Dropout randomly removes neurons during training. During training, neurons in a hidden layer are randomly selected and erased. The deleted neurons do not send signals, as illustrated in the accompanying image. Each time data flows are picked at random during training, the neurons are deleted.

The signals of all neurons are spread during the training process. Each neuron's output is multiplied by the rate during exercise:

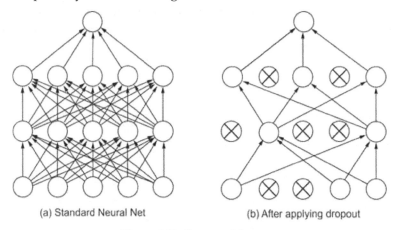

(a) Standard Neural Net　　　　　　　(b) After applying dropout

Figure 6.22: *Concept of dropout*

The *figure 6.22* is cited from the aforementioned reference.

The image on the left displays a standard neural network whereas the network on the right applies a dropout. Dropout chooses random neurons and deletes them in order to halt the continuing signal transmission.

Let us now put the concept into practice. In the implementation here, simplicity is underlined. If suitable calculations are made throughout training, forward propagation of data must be carried out (without multiplying the rate of the erased neurons). This is carried out through deep learning frameworks. For example, the dropout in the chainer framework might be beneficial for efficient implementation:

```
class Dropout:
    def __init__ (self, dropout_ratio=0.5):
        self.dropout_ratio = dropout_ratio
        self.mask = None
    def forward(self, x, train_flg=True):
        if  train_flg:
            self.mask = np.random.rand(*x.shape) > self.dropout_ratio
            return x * self.mask
        else:
```

```
                return x * (1.0 - self.dropout_ratio)

    def backward(self, dout):

        return dout * self.mask
```

Please note that, during each forward propagation, the neurons to be deleted are recorded as **False** in **self.mask**. **self.mask** produces an array of the same shape as **x** at random and sets the entries **True** if their values exceed dropout ratio. In reverse propagation, the behavior is the same as in ReLU. If a neuron transmits a signal in front of the received signal, it transmits it without affecting its backpropagation. When a neuron does not spread a signal in forward propagation, it inhibits the signal being received in backpropagation.

To check the effect of dropout, we will utilize the **MNIST** dataset. You can find the source code in **chapter06/OverfitDropout.py**. They make the implementation easier with the **Trainer** class.

In a **common/trainer.py** the **Trainer** class is implemented. It carries out network training till this chapter. See **common/trainer.py** and **chapter06/OverfitDropout. py** for further information.

We will utilize a seven-layer network to experiment with dropout (where there are 100 neurons in the layer and ReLU is the activation function), like we did in the previous experiment. One experiment will employ dropout while the other will not. The outcome is presented in the following image:

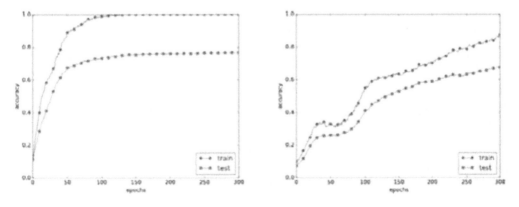

Figure 6.23: *The left picture displays the experiment without dropout and the right picture shows the dropout experiment (dropout rate=0.15)*

We can observe that with dropout, the disparity between the recognition accuracies of training data and test data is reduced. It also shows that the recognition accuracy of training data is not 100%. As a result, even in a representative network you may utilize dropout to prevent overfitting:

Ensemble learning is commonly employed in the machine learning. In this many models train separately and the average output is predicted. For example, we create five networks with the same (or similar) structure when using this system in a neural network and train them separately. Then, during testing, we average five results to achieve the outcome. Experiments have demonstrated that ensemble learning improves recognition accuracy of a neural network by several percent.

Ensemble learning is similar to dropout. Deleting random neurons can be regarded as a distinct model to learn data each time during training. The neuron output is multiplied by the erasure rate (0.5, for instance) by the mean of models when forecasting. We may argue, then, that dropout replicates ensemble learning in one network.

Validating hyperparameters

There are numerous hyperparameters in a neural network, as well as parameters such as weights and biases. Hyperparameter here includes the amount of neurons in each layer, batch size, learning rate for updating parameters and weight decay. The incorrect setting of hyperparameters impairs the model's performance. The value of these hyperparameters is highly essential, but it often needs a lot of test and error to determine them. This section shows you how to look as efficiently as possible for hyperparameter values. The data we have utilized to date is separate from the training data and test data.

Validation data

The training data and test data are distinct in the dataset we have been using up to now. The training data is utilized to train a network and the test data are used to assess generalization performance. This way, you can decide if the network matches just too well to the training data (that is, overfitting) and how large the generalization performance is.

For validation, we will employ many hyperparameter settings. Please note that the performance of hyperparameters should not be evaluated using test data. This is highly important but is frequently ignored.

Why can we not utilize test data to assess hyperparameter performance? The hyperparameter values override the test data when we utilize test data to alter hyperparameters. In other words, the hyperparameter values are "*good*" with test information, such that the hyperparameter values are solely set to the test data. In this case, the model might offer low generalization performance and cannot fit other data.

Therefore, verification data (called validation data) must be used to modify them. These data are utilized for the assessment of the quality of our hyperparameters.

Training data are utilized for parameters of learning (**weights** and **biases**). For evaluating the performance of the hyperparameters, validation data are employed. At the end of the training, test data are utilized (preferably once) to check generalization performance.

Some datasets include training data, validation data and testing data separately. Some just give training data and test data, whereas others only provide one sort of information. In this scenario, you have to manually separate the data. The simplest approach for the **MNIST** dataset to get validation data is to isolate 20% and utilize this as validation data in advance. This is shown by the following code:

```
(a_train, b_train), (a_test, b_test) = load_mnist()

# Shuffle training data

a_train, b_train = shuffle_dataset(a_train,  b_train)

# Separate validation data

validation_rate = 0.20

validation_num = int(a_train.shape[0] * validation_rate)

a_val = a_train[:validation_num]

b_val = b_train[:validation_num]

a_train = a_train[validation_num:]

b_train = b_train[validation_num:]
```

Here, before separating the training data, the input data and labeled data are mixed. This is because some datasets have biased data (for example, numbers 0 to 10 are arranged in this order). The shuffle dataset function utilizes **np.random.shuffle** in **common/util.py**.

Next, let us utilize validation data to examine the approach employed for optimizing hyperparameters.

Optimizing hyperparameters

In optimizing hyperparameters, what is crucial is that the range of excellent hyperparameter values be shrinking progressively. We will initially establish a wide range, choose random hyperparameters from the sampled range and use the sampled values to measure recognition accuracy. Then we repeat these procedures numerous times and observe the results of the recognition accuracy. Based on the outcome, the excellent hyperparameter value will be restricted. Thus, we may phase out the range of suitable hyperparameters by repeating this approach.

Random sampling before a search has been claimed to produce better results than a systemic search for hyperparameters, such as the grid search. This is because, under various hyperparameters, the extent to which the final recognition accuracy is influenced is varied.

It is advantageous to specify a wide range of hyperparameters. The range of "10-power," such as 0.001 (10–3) to 1000 (103) are specified (this is also called *specifying on a log scale*).

Please be aware that deep learning takes a lot of time to optimize hyperparameters (even a few days or weeks). Any hyperparameters that appear inadequate must thus be abandoned while looking for them. If hyperparameters are optimized, the epoch of training may be reduced to lessen the time it takes. We covered optimization of hyperparameters before. This topic is summed up as follows:

1. Input the hyperparameter range.

2. Sample a random range of hyperparameters.

3. Utilize hyperparameter values in step 1 for formation and use the validation data to measure recognition accuracy (set small epochs).

4. Repeat steps 1 and 2 a number of times (for example 100 times) and narrow down the hyperparameter range on the basis of recognition accuracy. Select a value from the hyperparameter if the range is reduced to some extent. This is a realistic technique for hyperparameters optimization.

> However, you may believe that this method is not science but the "wisdom" of engineers. You can use Bayesian optimization if you require a sophisticated approach for optimizing hyperparameters. The Bayes theorem is used to give tighter and efficient optimization using mathematical theories.

Implementing hyperparameter optimization

Now let us optimize a few hyperparameters with the **MNIST** dataset. Two hyperparameters will be looked for: the learning rate and weight decay. The weight decay rate controls the strength of weight decay. As previously mentioned, hyperparameters are validated in the log scale by random sampling from 0.001 (10–3) to 1000 (103). This can be written in Python as **10** `** np.random.uniform(-3, 3)`. This experiment will start at the weight decay rate of 10–8 to 10–4 and at the learning rate of 10–6 to 10–2. In this situation, the hyperparameters can be sampled randomly as follows:

```
weight_decay = 10 ** np.random.uniform(-8, -4)

lr = 10 ** np.random.uniform(-6, -2)
```

Here, the hyperparameters have been randomly sampled and the sampled values have been utilized for training. Then training is performed multiple times with the application of different hyperparameter values to discover the relevant hyperparameters. The implementation specifics were removed here, and only the outcome was shown. The **chapter06/HyperparameterOptimization.py** is the source code for optimizing hyperparameters.

We get the following findings when we have a 10–8 to 10-4 range for the weight decay rate and a 10–6 to 10–2 range for the learning rate. Here, we can identify transitions in learning the the validation data in descending order of high recognition accuracy:

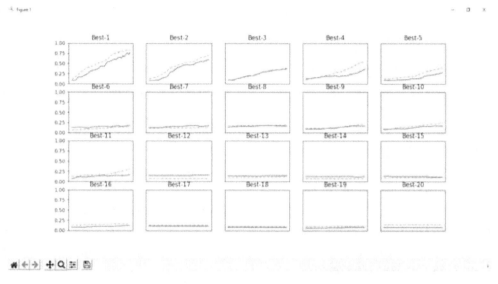

Figure 6.24: *The solid lines reflect the accuracy of the validation data recognition, whilst the points indicate the accuracy of the training data recognition*

This shows that the training progressed from Best-1 to Best-20 smoothly. Let us verify the hyperparameter values of Best-1 to Best-20 (that is the rate of learning and weight decay). These are the findings:

```
Best-1(Val      acc:0.77)      |      lr:0.007927957757502558,      Weight
Decay:1.1538127187392815e-05

Best-2(Val      acc:0.59)      |      lr:0.003910771196572644,      Weight
Decay:2.078366334975177e-08

Best-3(Val      acc:0.37)      |      lr:0.0013538283718871377,      Weight
Decay:1.0910259361067629e-07

Best-4(Val      acc:0.37)      |      lr:0.0022350576044958964,      Weight
Decay:8.385743813313609e-05

Best-5(Val      acc:0.28)      |      lr:0.0011498458989700406,      Weight
Decay:9.137303110924061e-07

Best-6(Val      acc:0.17)      |      lr:0.00036954798126304187,      Weight
Decay:4.388693192372083e-06
```

Best-7(Val   acc:0.17) | lr:0.00030437569188413826,   Weight
Decay:1.2606340765048516e-08

Best-8(Val   acc:0.17) | lr:0.00015586511159087886,   Weight
Decay:7.043702202643775e-08

Best-9(Val   acc:0.17) | lr:0.0007435964767573899,   Weight
Decay:9.167748886188489e-07

Best-10(Val   acc:0.17) | lr:0.0008287544500109695,   Weight
Decay:6.359356530918152e-05

Best-11(Val   acc:0.17) | lr:0.0013695313308560103,   Weight
Decay:2.7540392937106014e-05

Best-12(Val   acc:0.16) | lr:2.372087553699945e-05,   Weight
Decay:5.660841805612989e-08

Best-13(Val   acc:0.15) | lr:0.00017328999189673172,   Weight
Decay:5.117875055327933e-06

Best-14(Val   acc:0.13) | lr:8.061486833582763e-06,   Weight
Decay:2.5108789847720697e-08

Best-15(Val   acc:0.12) | lr:0.00011043530941174671,   Weight
Decay:2.7632630786251085e-05

Best-16(Val   acc:0.12) | lr:0.00016031845957595767,   Weight
Decay:2.280776479970992e-08

Best-17(Val   acc:0.11) | lr:3.7768423363180743e-06,   Weight
Decay:3.3797509175981876e-08

Best-18(Val   acc:0.08) | lr:4.447591256301315e-06,   Weight
Decay:1.1376847832677669e-07

Best-19(Val   acc:0.08) | lr:0.00012149426326512106,   Weight
Decay:6.311926588586751e-05

Best-20(Val   acc:0.08) | lr:1.8769270807604037e-06,   Weight
Decay:4.117270215426685e-06

Here, we can observe that learning progressed effectively, where the learn rate was 0.001 to 0.01 and the weight decay was 10−8 to 10−6. As a result, a limited range of values is seen for hyperparameters in which training can be successful. In the restricted range, you may repeat the same method. Therefore, you may restrict the range and choose the final hyperparameters at a given stage, if applicable.

Conclusion

This section described several major strategies that can be used for training of neural networks. How parameters may be updated, weight values can be specified, batch normalization and dropout are the key approaches for contemporary neural networks. Often in modern deep learning, the approaches mentioned here are employed. We learnt the following in this chapter:

- Four well-known parameter update methods: AdaGrad, Momentum, Adam and SGD.

- How to set the weight values that are extremely crucial if we want to train properly.

- The Xavier Initializer and the He Initializer are the initial weight values.

- Batch normalization accelerates training and gives the initial weight values resilience.

- Weight decay and dropout are approaches of regularization that reduce overfitting.

- To find good hyperparameters, gradually narrowing down your range where acceptable values are available is an effective method.

CHAPTER 7
CNN

This section discusses **convolutional neural networks (CNNs)**. CNNs, including image recognition and speech recognition, are utilized extensively in **artificial intelligence (AI)**. This chapter describes the CNN mechanisms and how they may be implemented in Python.

Structure

- CNN architecture
- The convolution layer
    - Issues with the fully connected layer
- Convolution operations
    - Padding
    - Stride
    - Performing a convolution operation on three-dimensional data
- Thinking in blocks
- Batch processing
- The pooling layer

- o Characteristics of a pooling layer
- Implementing the convolution and pooling layers
  - o Four-dimensional arrays
  - o Expansion by im2col
  - o Implementing a convolution layer
  - o Implementing a pooling layer
- Implementing the CNN
- Visualizing a CNN
  - o Visualizing the weight of the first layer
  - o Using a hierarchical information extraction structure
- Typical CNNs
  - o LeNet
  - o AlexNet

Objective

You will have a good knowledge of CNNs, image recognition, and speech recognition.

Architecture

Let us first look at the architecture of CNNs. Much like the neural networks we have seen up until now, you can build a CNN by merging layers. But CNNs also contain other layers: a convolution layer and a pooling layer. In the succeeding sections we will examine the specifics of the convolution and pooling layers. This section outlines the combination of the layers into a CNN.

All neurons in neighbouring layers are linked in the neural networks we have to yet observe. We have built these layers in affine layers as fully connected layers. For instance, as illustrated in *figure 7.1* you can utilize affine layers to construct a neural network of five fully connected layers.

As shown in *figure 7.1*, a fully connected neural network follows the ReLU layer (or sigmoid layer) for the activation function of the Affine layer. Here comes the affine layer, which is the fifth, following four pairs of Affine – ReLU layers. And lastly, the softmax layer produces the final outcome (likely):

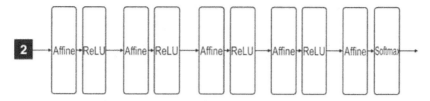

Figure 7.1: Sample network consisting of fully connected layers (Affine layers)

So, what is the architecture of a CNN? The *figure 7.2* shows a sample of a CNN:

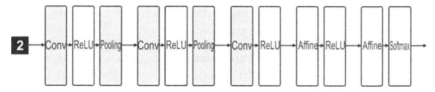

Figure 7.2: *Sample CNN – convolution and pooling layers are added (they are shown as gray rectangles)*

As illustrated in the figure, CNN contains extra convolution and pooling layers. In the CNN, layers in Convolution – ReLU – (Pooling) are coupled (a pooling layer is sometimes omitted). The preceding Affine – ReLU connection may be seen as substituted by Pooling – Convolution.

In the CNN in *figure 7.2*, observe that the layers close to output are the prior Affine-ReLU pairs, whereas the previous Affine-Softmax pairs are the final output layers. This is the structure commonly observed in the average convolutional neural network.

The convolution layer

Some words like *"padding"* and *"stride"* are CNN-specific. Unlike in previous fully connected networks, the data which passes through each layer in the CNN are data with shape (for example, three-dimensional data). So, when you hear about them for the first time, you may believe that CNNs are difficult to understand. The convolution layer method that is utilized in CNNs is examined here.

Demerits with the Affine

The fully connected neural networks employed by fully connected layers (Affine layers). All neurons in the adjacent layer are connected in a completely connected layer, which can arbitrarily decide the number of outputs.

The problem is that the shape of the data is neglected with a fully connected layer. For instance, if the input data is an image, it generally has a three-dimensional design, which is specified by the dimension of height, breadth and channel. However, if the data is supplied to a fully connected layer, it must be transformed into flat one-dimensional data. The shape of the input images that we used for the MNIST data in the previous examples were 1, 28, 28 (1 channel, 28 pixels in height and 28 pixels in width), but the elements were organized in a single line, and 784 pieces of data were submitted for the first affine layer.

Let us assume a three-dimensional image has some crucial spatial information. Essential patterns to recognize the information lie in three-dimensional shapes. The pixels are comparable in space, RBG channels are strongly connected to each other, and distant pixels are not linked. However, a fully connected layer does not take into account the shape, and considers all input data as neurons with the same number of dimensions; therefore it cannot utilize the information on shape.

On the other hand, the shape is maintained via a convolution layer. For images, the input data is given as three-dimensional data and three-dimensional data is provided to the next layer. CNNs can therefore effectively comprehend shaped data, such as pictures.

In a CNN, a feature map is the input/output data for a convolution layer. The input data for a convolution layer is known as an input feature map whereas the output data for a convolution layer is known as an output feature map. This book uses "*input/output data*" and "*feature map*" interchangeably.

Processing

The processing in a convolution layer is termed as "convolution operation" and is equivalent to the filtering operation of image processing. To understand a convolution operation, consider the following example (*figure 7.3*):

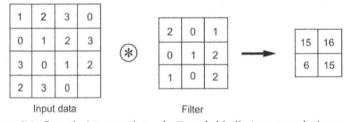

Figure 7.3: *Convolution operation – the ⊛ symbol indicates a convolution operation*

As seen in *figure 7.3*, the convolution operation adds a filter to the input data. The shape of the input data in this example has height and width and so does the filter shape. In this example, the input size (4, 4), the filter size (3, 3) and the output size (2, 2) are given when we express the shape of the data and filter as (height, width). Certain publications use the word "*kernel*" for "*filter*".

Let us break down the calculation made in the convolution operation in *figure 7.3*. The calculation is shown in *figure 7.4*:

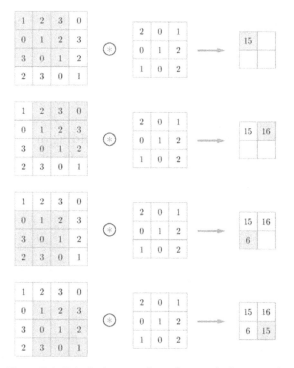

Figure 7.4: *Calculation procedure of a convolution operation*

The input data are converted while the filter window is moved at a predetermined interval. The window indicates the grey 3x3 area, as seen in *figure 7.4*. As illustrated in *figure 7.4*, the filter element and the matching input element are multiplied and summarized in each place (this calculation is sometimes called a multiply-accumulate operation). The result is saved at the appropriate location of the output. By performing this procedure at all locations, the output of the convolution operation may be achieved.

A fully connected neural network has biases and weight parameters. The parameters of a filter in a CNN are the same as the preceding weights. It also has biases. The *figure 7.3* indicated the stage when a filter is applied. The processing flow of a convolution operation is shown in *figure 7.5*:

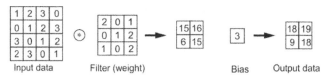

Figure 7.5: *Bias in a convolution operation – a fixed value (bias) is added to the element after the filter is applied*

In *figure 7.5*, a bias term is introduced to the data following the application of the filter. Here, there is just one (1x1) bias where there is one bias exists for four pieces of data after the application of the filter. After the filter is applied, this value is appended to all items.

Padding

Fixed values (for example, 0) are occasionally inserted around the input data before the convolution layer is processed. This is called padding and is usually utilized in a convolution operation. For example, in *figure 7.6*, padding of 1 is applied in the input data (4, 4). The padding of 1 implies that zeros with a width of one pixel are filled in the surroundings:

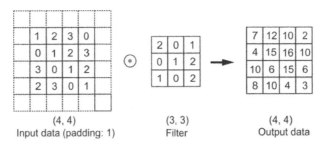

(4, 4)   (3, 3)   (4, 4)
Input data (padding: 1)   Filter   Output data

Figure 7.6: *Adding zeroes around the input data during a convolution process (padding is shown by dashed lines here, and the zeros are omitted)*

Padding turns input data (4, 4) into data (6, 6), as seen in *figure 7.6*. The output data is then created after the (3, 3) filter is applied. In this case, a padding of 1 was used. The padding value can be used for any number, like 2 or 3. When the padding value is 2, the input data size will be (8, 8). The size would be 3 if the padding is (10, 10).

> **Padding is generally used for adjusting the size of the output. For example, if a filter (3, 3) for a (4, 4) input data is applied, the output size is (2, 2). The output size smaller than the input size by two elements. In deep networks, where convolution operations are repeated several times, this presents problems. If every convolution operation spatially decreases in size, then at a particular point, the output size reaches 1 and there will be no more convolution operations. You may use padding to prevent such a scenario. In the example above, if padding width is 1, the output size (4, 4) remains the same as the input size (4, 4). Consequently, following a convolution operation, you may transfer the data of the same spatial size to the next layer.**

Stride

The interval of the filter position is known as a stride. The stride was 1 in all previous examples. If the stride is 2, for example, the window interval to apply a filter is two items, as shown in *figure 7.7*.

A filter with a stride of 2 on the input data (7, 7) is applied in *figure 7.7*. If the stride is 2, the output is set to (3, 3). Stride thus determines the filter interval:

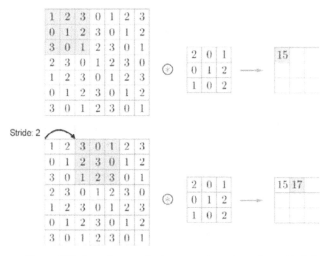

Figure 7.7: *Sample convolution operation where the stride is 2*

The bigger the stride, the smaller the output size; the larger the padding, the larger the output size. How can such relations in equations be represented? Let us examine how padding and stride are used to calculate the output size.

In the following equation, this input size is (H, W), the filter size is (FH, FW, OH, OW), padding is P, and stride is S. The size of the output is (OH, OW). The output size may be calculated with the following equation (7.1):

$$OH = \frac{H + 2P - FH}{S} + 1$$

$$OW = \frac{W + 2P - FW}{S} + 1$$

Equation 7.1

Now, let's use this equation to do some calculations:

Example 1 (Example is shown in *figure 7.6*)

Input size: (4, 4); padding: 1; stride: 1; filter size: (3, 3)

$$OH = \frac{4 + 2 \cdot 1 - 3}{1} + 1 = 4$$

$$OW = \frac{4 + 2 \cdot 1 - 3}{1} + 1 = 4$$

Example 2 (Example is shown in *figure 7.7*)

Input size: $(7, 7)$; padding: 0; stride: 2; filter size: $(3, 3)$

$$OH = \frac{7 + 2 \cdot 0 - 3}{2} + 1 = 3$$

$$OW = \frac{7 + 2 \cdot 0 - 3}{2} + 1 = 3$$

Example 3

Input size: $(28, 31)$; padding: 2; stride: 3; filter size: $(5, 5)$

$$OH = \frac{28 + 2 \cdot 2 - 5}{3} + 1 = 10$$

$$OW = \frac{31 + 2 \cdot 2 - 5}{3} + 1 = 11$$

As these examples show, you can calculate the output size by assigning values to equation (*7.1*). You can only obtain the output size by assignment, but note that you must assign values so that $\frac{W+2P-FW}{S}$ and $\frac{H+2P-FH}{S}$ in equation (*7.1*) are divisible. If the size of the output is not divisible (that is, a decimal result), you have to deal with it by making an error. Some deep learning systems advance this process without error; for example, when it's not divisible, they round the number to the nearest integer.

Performing a convolution operation on three-dimensional data

So far, we have examined examples of two-dimensional shapes with height and width. For images, we have to handle three-dimensional data with dimensions of channel, height and breadth. Here we will look at an example of a convolution operation on three-dimensional data that uses the same approach used in earlier examples.

A convolution example is shown in *figure 7.8*, while the calculation process is shown in *figure 7.9*. In *figure 7.8*, the results of a convolution operation for three-dimensional data can be seen. Compared to the two-dimensional data (example given in *figure 7.3*), the feature maps are enhanced in depth (channel dimension). If the channel dimension contains several feature maps, the input and filter convolution operations for each channel are done, and the results are combined to get a single output:

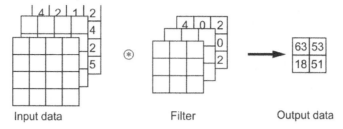

Figure 7.8: *Convolution operation for three-dimensional data*

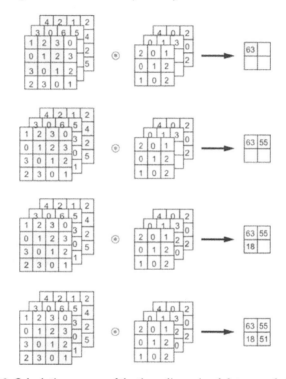

Figure 7.9: *Calculation process of the three-dimensional data convolution operation*

As in this example, in a three-dimensional convolution operation, the input data and the filter must be the same with respect to the number of channels. In this example, there are three channels in the data input and the filter. The filter size may be changed to whichever one you choose. The filter size in this case is (3, 3). It can be adjusted to any size, for example (2, 2), (1, 1), or (5,5). However, the number of channels should be the same as that of the input data, as indicated above. Three must be included in this example.

Thinking in blocks

You may view the data and filters in a three-dimensional convolution operation as rectangular blocks. A three-dimensional cuboid is a block, as shown in *figure 7.10* shows. A multidimensional array in the order channel, height, width represents three-dimensional data. When the number of channels is C, the height is H, and the width is W for shape, it is shown as (C, H, W). A filter of the same order is shown so that when the number of channels is C, the height of a filter is FH, and the width is FW; it is written as (C, FH, FW):

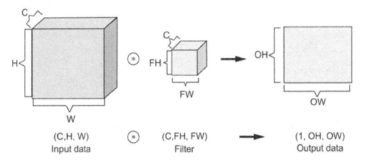

Figure 7.10: *Using blocks to consider a convolution operation*

The output of the data is a feature map in this case. One feature map means the size of the output channel is one. So how can we deliver several outputs of convolution operations in the channel dimension? We utilize several filters (weights) to achieve this. This is seen in *figure 7.11*:

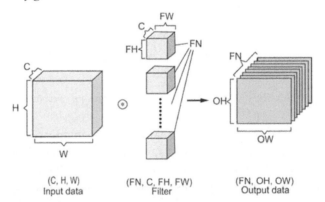

Figure 7.11: *Sample convolution operation with multiple filters*

The number of output maps produced is *FN* when the number of filters used is *FN*, as illustrated in *figure 7.11*. You may construct a block of the shape (*FN, OH, OW*) by joining *FN* maps. The process passed to the next layer by this finished block is a CNN.

The number of filters in a convolution operation must also be taken into account. We will use four-dimensional data (output channel, input channel, height, width) to create the filter weight data. For example, if there are 20 filters with three chains with a dimension of 5 x 5, it is represented as (20, 3, 5, 5).

There are biases in a convolution (like a fully connected layer). The *figure 7.12* shows the example given in *figure 7.11* when you add biases.

As you can see, there is just one bias data in each channel. The bias data here is (*FN, 1, 1*), whereas the filter output is of the shape (*FN, OH, OW*). The addition of two blocks in the filter output adds the same bias value to each channel (*FN, OH, OW*). The broadcast of NumPy creates blocks of various shapes (see the section *Broadcasting* in *Chapter 1: Python Introduction*):

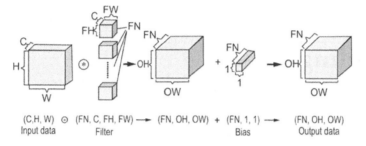

Figure 7.12: *Conversion process (the bias term is also added)*

Batch processing

Data input in the neural network process is processed in batches. The implementations that we have been looking at so far have enabled batch processing for fully connected neural network, which enables more efficient processing and facilitates mini-batch training.

In a convolution operation, we may additionally allow batch processing by storing data that flows as four-dimensional data across each level. Specifically the data is saved in the order (**batch_num, channel, height, width**). For example, if the processing of N data is performed in batches (as seen in *figure 7.12*), the shape of data is as follows.

As illustrated earlier, the dimensions for the batches are added at the beginning of each piece of data flow for batch processing. The data is therefore sent as four-dimensional data for each layer. Please note that four-dimensional information flowing across the network means that N data are converted; that is to say, N operations are done simultaneously:

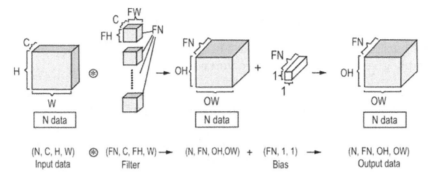

$$(N, C, H, W) \quad \circledast \quad (FN, C, FH, W) \longrightarrow \quad (N, FN, OH, OW) \quad + \quad (FN, 1, 1) \longrightarrow \quad (N, FN, OH, OW)$$

Input data   Filter   Bias   Output data

Figure 7.13: *Process flow of the transformation (batch processing)*

The pooling layer

The space of the height and breadth is reduced by a pooling operation. It transforms a 2×2 space into a single element for space reduction (*figure 7.14*):

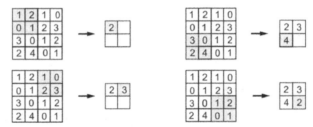

Figure 7.14: *Procedure of max pooling*

This example demonstrates this method when 2 x 2 max-pooling is carried out with a stride of 2. Max-pooling takes the maximum value of an area, while the size of the target region is indicated by "2 x 2". The largest element in a 2 x 2 area, as we can see, is taken. The stride in this example is 2 such that two components move the 2 x 2 window at once. The same number is usually used for the size and stride of the pooling window. For example, stride 3 for a window of 3×3, stride 4 for a window of 4×4.

> Average-pooling can also be utilized in addition to max-pooling. Max-pooling in the target area takes the maximum value whereas average-pooling in the target area averages the values. Max-pooling is mostly used for image recognition. A pooling layer in this book therefore represents max-pooling.

Characteristics of a pooling layer

There are different properties to a pooling layer:

No parameters to learned

Unlike a convolution layer, a pooling layer has no parameters to learn as it takes just the maximum value (or the average values) in the target region.

No change in the number of channels

In pooling, the number of channels in the input data and output data is the same. This calculation is done for each channel, as illustrated in *figure 7.15*:

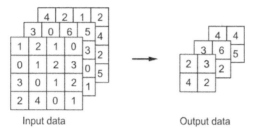

Input data   Output data

Figure 7.15: Pooling does not change the number of channels

It is resilient to a small change in position

Pooling gives the same output, even if the input data has significantly moved. This means that it is resilient to a little change in the input data. Pooling absorbs the shift of the input data, for example in 3×3 pools, as illustrated in *figure 7.16*:

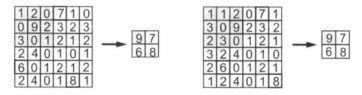

Figure 7.16: Even though one element shifts the input data in width, the result is the same (it may not be the same, depending on the data)

Implementing the convolution and pooling layers

We have learnt about convolution and pooling layers in detail. These two layers are implemented in Python in this section. The class to be deployed here also has forward and backward propagation (as shown in *Chapter 5: Backpropogation*), so that it may be used as a module.

You may feel it is difficult to implement convolution and pooling layers; however if you apply a specific trick, you can implement them quickly. This section discusses this trick and simplifies the work. Then a layer of convolution will be implemented.

Four-dimensional arrays

The four-dimensional data flows in each CNN layer, as stated before. It shows that there are ten pieces of data (height **38**, width **58**, and channel **5**) when the shape of the data is (**20, 5, 38, 58**). In Python, the following can be implemented:

```
>>> a = np.random.rand(20, 5, 38, 58) # Generate data randomly
>>> a.shape
(20, 5, 38, 58)
```

You can write **a[0]** to enter the initial piece of data (the index begins at 0 in Python). Likewise, to access the second piece of data you may type **a[1]**:

```
>>> a[0].shape # (5, 38, 58)
>>> a[1].shape # (5, 38, 58)
```

You may write the following to get the spatial data on the first channel:

```
>>> a[0, 0] # or a[0][0]
```

In this way, you may use a CNN to handle four-dimensional data. It can thus be hard to execute a convolution operation. But a trick called **im2col** makes the task easy.

Expansion by im2col

You typically need to nest **for** statements multiple times to carry out a convolution operation. This is a little difficult to implement and **for** statements slow down the processing speed in NumPy (in NumPy, it is desirable that you do not use any **for** statements to access elements). No statements are to be used here. Rather, we will utilize a basic **im2col** operation for easy implementation.

The **im2col** operation easily extends the data for a filter (weight). The *figure 7.17* shows that **im2col** transforms three-dimensional input data into a two-dimensional matrix (to be exact, it converts four-dimensional data, including the number of batches, into two-dimensional data).

The **im2col** operation easily extends the filter input data (weight). In particular, the region to which a filter is used in the input data (the three-dimensional block) is extended into a line, as illustrated in *figure 7.18*. The **im2col** operation extends to all filter positions.

In *figure 7.18*, a large stride is used so that filter areas do not overlap. It's done for purposes of visibility. When convolution operations really take place, the filter areas are usually overlapped. After expansion with **im2col**, the number of elements is higher than in the original block. An implementation using **im2col** thus has the drawback that more memory is consumed than normal. However, it is useful to place data in a large matrix to do computer calculations. Complex computation libraries, for example, highly optimize matrix calculations to enable huge matrices to rapidly multiply. Thus, by transforming input data in a matrix, you may utilize a linear algebra library effectively:

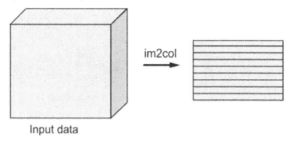

Figure 7.17: *Overview of im2col*

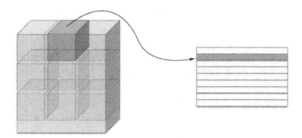

Figure 7.18: *Expand the target filter area from the start in a row*

The term **im2col** is an acronym of image to column, suggesting that images are converted into matrices. The **im2col** function for implementing a convolution-layer is provided with the deep learning frameworks like Caffe and Chainer.

All you have to do is expand the filter (weight) for the convolution layer to a row and multiply two matrices after using **im2col** to expand data (see *figure 7.19*). This method is virtually the same as a fully connected affine layer:

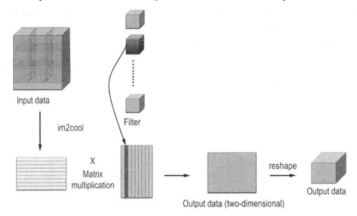

Figure 7.19: *Filtering details during a convolution – extend the filter into a column, then multiply the matrix by the im2col data. Finally, reshape the output data size result*

As illustrated in *figure 7.19*, the ouput of **im2col** is a two-dimensional matrix. Two-dimensional output data must be transformed into a proper shape because a CNN stores data as four-dimensional arrays.

Implementing a convolution layer

This book uses the **im2col** function, and we will use it as a black box without considering its implementation. The **im2col** implementation is located at **common/ util.py**. It is a simple function that is about ten lines in length. Please refer to it if you are interested.

The following is the interface for this **im2col** function:

im2col (input_data, filter_h, filter_w, stride=1, pad=0)

- **input_data**: Input data that consists of arrays of four dimensions (amount of data, channel, height, breadth).

- **filter_h**: Height of the filter.

- **filter_w**: Width of the filter.

- **stride**: Stride

- **pad**: Padding

In the **im2col** function, the filter size, stride, and padding are taken as follows:

```
import sys, os
```

```
import numpy as np
sys.path.append(os.pardir)
from common.util import im2col
a1 = np.random.rand(5, 9, 11, 11)
col1 = im2col(a1, 10, 10, stride=2, pad=1)
print(col1.shape) # (20, 900)
a2 = np.random.rand(30, 7, 9, 9)
col2 = im2col(a2, 10, 10, stride=2, pad=1)
print(col2.shape) # (30, 700)
```

Two examples are given in the previous code. The first uses 7x7 data with batch size of 1, with a channel number of 3. The second utilizes data with a batch size of 10 of the same shape. When using the *im2col* funtion, in both situations the number of elements is 75. This is the total number of filter elements (3 channels, size 5x5). The *im2col* output is 1 when the batch size is **(20, 900)**. The second example is **(30, 700)** since the batch size is 10. It can store as many data ten times.

Now we are implementing *im2col* as a class (**Convolution**) to implement a convolution layer:

```
class Convolution:
    def __init__(self, W, b, stride=1, pad=0):
        self.W = W
        self.b = b
        self.stride = stride
        self.pad = pad
    def forward(self, x):
        FN, C, FH, FW = self.W.shape
        N, C, H, W = x.shape
        out_h = int(1 + (H + 2*self.pad - FH) / self.stride)
        out_w = int(1 + (W + 2*self.pad - FW) / self.stride)
        col = im2col(x, FH, FW, self.stride, self.pad)
        col_W = self.W.reshape(FN, -1).T # Expand the filter
        out = np.dot(col, col_W) + self.b
        out = out.reshape(N, out_h, out_w, -1).transpose(0, 3, 1, 2)
        return out
```

The method of initialization of the convolution layer takes filter (weight), bias, stride, and padding as arguments. The filter is four-dimensional, (**FN, C, FH,** and **FW**). **FN** is the number of a filter, **C** the channel, **FH** the height of a filter, **FW** the width of a filter.

An essential part has been displayed in bold when using a convolution layer. Here, *im2col* serves to expand the input data, while reshape uses a two-dimensional array in order to extend the filter. There are several expanded matrices.

The code portion expanding the filter (the bold piece of the previous code) expands the filter block to one line, as seen in *figure 7.19*. Here, -1 is the reshape (**FN, -1**), given as one of the handy features of reshape. The number of elements is changed to match the number of elements in a multidimensional array if -1 is specified as reshape. For instance, a range in the form of (**10, 3, 5, 5**) contains a total of 750 elements. When **reshape(10, -1)** is given, it is transformed into a table in the shape of (**10, 75**).

At the end of the process, the forward function modifies the output. The transpose function of NumPy is utilized. In a multidimensional array the transpose function alters the order of the axes. The order of indices (numbers) starting at 0 can be specified to modify the axes order. This is illustrated in *figure 7.20*.

Thus, by using **im2col** operation for expansion, you may implement forward propagation of a convolution layer almost as well as a fully connected affine layer (see the section, *Implementing the affine and softmax layers* in *Chapter 5: Backpropogation*). Next, in the convolution layer, we'll implement backpropagation. Note that the reversal of **im2col** is due to backpropagation in the convolution layer. This is handled by **col2im** (found in **common/util.py**) that is included in this book. Unless **col2im**, backpropagation can be carried out in a convolution layer in the same way as the affine layer. Backpropagation in the convolution layer is found in **common/layer.py**.

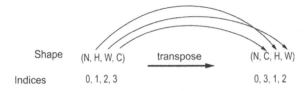

Shape   (N, H, W, C)   transpose   (N, C, H, W)

Indices   0, 1, 2, 3   0, 3, 1, 2

Figure 7.20: NumPy transpose to alter the axis order — provide the numbers to change the axis order

Implementing a pooling layer

When constructing a pooling layer, you may use **im2col** to expand the input data, like in a convolution layer. The difference is that unlike a convolution layer, pooling is independent of the channel dimension. The target pooling area is expanded individually for each channel, as illustrated in *figure 7.21*.

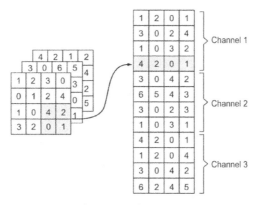

Figure 7.21: *Expansion of the input data target region (pooling of 2x2)*

Only the maximum value in each row of the expanded matrix has to be taken and the result transformed into an acceptable shape (*figure 7.22*).

This is how the forward propagation of a pooling layer is implemented. In Python, the following illustrates an example:

```python
class Pooling:
    def __init__(self, pool_h, pool_w, stride=1, pad=0):
        self.pool_h = pool_h
        self.pool_w = pool_w
        self.stride = stride
        self.pad = pad
    def forward(self, x):
        N, C, H, W = x.shape
        out_h = int(1 + (H - self.pool_h) / self.stride)
        out_w = int(1 + (W - self.pool_w) / self.stride)
        # Expansion (1)
        col = im2col(x, self.pool_h, self.pool_w, self.stride, self.pad)
        col = col.reshape(-1, self.pool_h*self.pool_w)
        # Maximum value (2)
        out = np.max(col, axis=1)
        # Reshape (3)
        out = out.reshape(N, out_h, out_w, C).transpose(0, 3, 1, 2)
            return out
```

In the implementation of a pooling layer there are three phases (illustrated in *figure 7.22*):

1. Expand input data

2. In each row, take the maximum value

3. Redesign the output appropriately

It is simple to execute each step and just takes one or two lines:

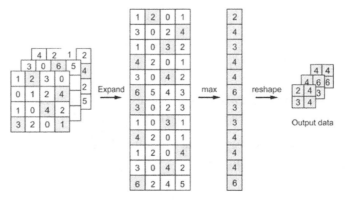

Figure 7.22: *Flow of pooling layer implementation –*
The maximum elements shown in grey are in the pooling area

The maximem value may be taken using NumPy's **np.max** function. You may take the maximum value along the given axis by setting the axis parameter in **np.max**. In each axis of the first dimension, for instance, **np.max(x, axis=1)** provides a maximum value of **X**.

This is all in a pooling layer for forward propagation. As seen below, implementation is relatively easy after expanding the input data into a shape appropriate for pooling.

More information is provided for backpropagation of **max** (used for reversing the ReLU layer in section *Backward propagation* in *Chapter 5: Backpropogation*). A pooling layer is implemented at **common/layer.py**.

Implementing a CNN

So far, we have seen the implementation of convolution and pooling layers. These layers will be combined to construct and deploy a CNN which recognizes handwritten digits, as seen in *figure 7.23*.

The Convolution – ReLU–Pooling – Affine – ReLU – Affine – Softmax layers is the network, as illustrated by *figure 7.23*. We shall implement this as a class called **SimpleConvNet**:

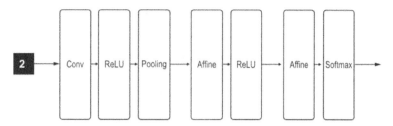

Figure 7.23: Network configuration of a simple CNN

Now, see how **SimpleConvNet(__init__)** is initialized. The following arguments are put forward:

- **input_dim**: Dimensions of the input data (channel, height, and width).

- **conv_param**: Hyperparameters of the convolution layer (dictionary). The following are the dictionary keys:

- **filter_num**: Number of filters

- **filter_size**: Size of the filter

- **stride**: Stride

- **pad**: Padding

- **hidden_size**: Number of neurons in the hidden layer (fully connected)

- **output_size**: Number of neurons in the output layer (fully connected)

- **weight_init_std**: Standard deviation of the weights at initialization

The convolution layer hyperparameters are presented here as a dictionary named **conv_param**. We suppose that the needed hyperparameter values are stored using the **filter_num:30** function, the **filter_size** value, **pad:0, stride:1**.

The implementation of the **SimpleConvNet** initialization is a bit long, thus it has been divided into three sections so that this is easier to follow. The following code shows the first part of the initialization process:

```
class SimpleConvNet:

    """Simple ConvNet


    conv - relu - pool - affine - relu - affine - softmax
    """

    def __init__(self, input_dim=(1, 28, 28),
                    conv_param={'filter_num':30, 'filter_size':5, 'pad':0,
'stride':1},
```

```
                  hidden_size=100, output_size=10, weight_init_std=0.01):
        filter_num = conv_param['filter_num']

        filter_size = conv_param['filter_size']

        filter_pad = conv_param['pad']

        filter_stride = conv_param['stride']

        input_size = input_dim[1]

            conv_output_size = (input_size - filter_size + 2*filter_pad) /
filter_stride + 1

        pool_output_size = int(filter_num * (conv_output_size/2) * (conv_
output_size/2))
```

Here, the hyperparameters of the convolution layer given by the initialization argument have been removed from the dictionary (so that we can use them later). The output size is then calculated for the convolution layer. Weight parameters are initialized with the following code:

```
        self.params = {}

        self.params['W1'] = weight_init_std * \
                np.random.randn(filter_num, input_dim[0], filter_size, filter_
size)

        self.params['X1'] = np.zeros(filter_num)

        self.params['W2'] = weight_init_std * \
                            np.random.randn(pool_output_size, hidden_size)

        self.params['X2'] = np.zeros(hidden_size)

        self.params['W3'] = weight_init_std * \
                            np.random.randn(hidden_size, output_size)

        self.params['X3'] = np.zeros(output_size)
```

The required parameters are the weight and bias of the first (convolution) layer and the other two fully connected layers. The instance dictionary variable stores the parameters. The **W1** key is utilized for the weight, whereas the **X1** key for the first (convolution) layer bias is employed. Similarly, the **W2** and **X2** keys are utilized for bias in the second (fully connected) layer, and the **W3** and **X3** keys are correspondingly used for weight and bias in the third (fully connected) layer. Finally, the necessary layers are implemented as follows:

```
        # Layer generation

        self.layers = OrderedDict()
```

```
            self.layers['Conv1'] = Convolution(self.params['W1'], self.
params['X1'],

                                        conv_param['stride'], conv_
param['pad'])
        self.layers['Relu1'] = Relu()
        self.layers['Pool1'] = Pooling(pool_h=2, pool_w=2, stride=2)
      self.layers['Affine1'] = Affine(self.params['W2'], self.params['X2'])
        self.layers['Relu2'] = Relu()
      self.layers['Affine2'] = Affine(self.params['W3'], self.params['X3'])
```

Layers are added in a suitable sequence to the ordered dictionary (**OrderedDict**). In another last-level variable, just the last-level is added, **SoftmaxWithLoss**.

This is the initialization of **SimpleConvNet**. After the initialization, the predict method and the loss method for computing the loss function value may be implemented:

```
def predict(self, x):
    for layer in self.layers.values():
        x = layer.forward(x)


    return x


def loss(self, x, t):
    y = self.predict(x)
    return self.last_layer.forward(y, t)
```

Here, an input data is the **x** argument, and the label is the **t** argument. The predict method only calls the additional layers from the top and moves the result to the next layer. In addition to the forward propagation in the *predict* method, **SoftmaxWithLoss** continues to process the loss method up to the last layer.

The gradients are obtained by backpropagation as follows:

```
def gradient(self, x, t):
    # forward
    self.loss(x, t)


    # backward
    dout = 1
```

```
        dout = self.last_layer.backward(dout)


        layers = list(self.layers.values())

        layers.reverse()

        for layer in layers:

            dout = layer.backward(dout)


        grads = {}
            grads['W1'], grads['X1'] = self.layers['Conv1'].dW, self.
layers['Conv1'].db

            grads['W2'], grads['X2'] = self.layers['Affine1'].dW, self.
layers['Affine1'].db

            grads['W3'], grads['X3'] = self.layers['Affine2'].dW, self.
layers['Affine2'].db


        return grads
```

Backpropagation is utilized to get the gradients of the parameters. This is done one-by-one, using forward propagation and backward propagation. Due to the perfect implementation of forward and backward propagation in each layer, we just have to call them in a suitable order. Finally, the **grads** dictionary records the gradient for each weight. This way, **SimpleConvNet** can be implemented.

Now, let us use the **MNIST** dataset to train the **SimpleConverNet** class. The training code is almost the same to that presented in the section, *Implementing a training algorithm* in *Chapter 4: Training Neural Network*. The code will not be displayed here (source code is located at **chapter07/TrainConvNet.py**).

When **SimpleConvNet** is used for the training of the **MNIST** dataset, the accuracy of training data is 99.82 percent and the accuracy of test data is 98.96 percent. (The recognition accuracies are slightly different from training to training.) 99 percent is a very high recognition accuracy for the test data of a relatively small network. In the next chapter, we will add layers for building a network that exceeds 99 percent recognition accuracy.

As we saw, convolution and pooling layers are essential modules in image recognition. A CNN can read the spatial features of images and achieve great accuracy in handwritten digit recognition.

Visualizing a CNN

What is the visual layer in a CNN for convolution? Here we will look at a convolution layer to see what's happening in a CNN.

Visualizing the weight of the first layer

Previously, using the **MNIST** dataset, we carried out simple CNN training. The shape of the weight of the first (convolution) layer was (30, 1, 5, 5). Their size was 5 x 5, their channel was 1 and their filters were 30. If the filter is 5 x 5 in size and contains 1 channel, it can be shown as a grey picture for a single channel. Let us now present the filters of the first layer of convolution as images. Before and after training, we will compare weights. The findings are presented in *figure 7.24* (source code at **chapter07/VisualizeFilter.py**):

Figure 7.24: *Weight before and after training for the first (convolution) layer. Weight components are actual integers; however, the pictures are standardized between 0 and 255 for black (0) and white (the greatest value) (255)*

As shown in *figure 7.24*, filters are initialized randomly. There is no pattern in the black-and-white hues. On the other hand, the filters (after training) are patterned images. Some filters feature white-to-black gradients, whereas some filters have little colored regions (called **blobs**), showing that the filters are patterned by training.

The filters with a pattern on the right-hand side "*see*" edges (color boundaries) and blobs (see *figure 7.24*). If a filter in the left-hand side is blank and the right-hand is black, for example, a vertical edge is reacted, as seen in *figure 7.25*.

The outcomes of the selection of two learned filters and convolution processing are shown in the input image in *figure 7.25*. **Filter 1** reacted to a vertical edge and Filter 2 reacted to the horizontal edge:

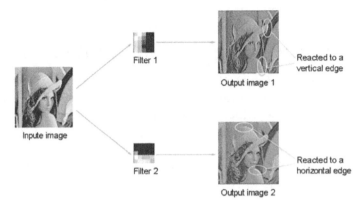

Figure 7.25: Horizontally and vertically responding filters. Filters. At the vertical border of image output, white pixels emerge1. Meanwhile, near the horizontal margin of output picture 2, several white pixels emerge.

You can see that the filters remove basic information, such as borders and the blobs, from a convolution layer. This basic information is transferred into successive layers from the previously constructed CNN.

Using a hierarchical information extraction structure

From the first (convolution) layer the previous result is. It retrieves information of low levels like edges and blobs. Thus, what kind of information is extracted from a multilayer CNN in each layer? Development research has shown that the deeper the layer, the more abstract the information retrieved (to be precise, neurons that react strongly).

Typical CNNs

So far, CNNs of various architectures have been suggested. Two major networks are discussed in this section. One is LeNet: grading-based learning, applied in document recognition. It was suggested in 2012 and highlighted deep learning.

LeNet

LeNet is a handwritten digit recognition network that was proposed in 1998. A convolution layer and a pooling layer (that is, a subsampling layer with just thins out elements) are repeated in the network and eventually the ouput is produced by a fully connected layer.

Discrepancies exist between the current CNN and LeNet. One is that the activation function is available. LeNet uses a sigmoid function, but ReLU is mostly utilized now. In the original LeNet, subsampling is utilized to minimize the size of intermediate data, while max-pooling is mainly employed today:

In this sense, LeNet differs from the current CNN, although these differences are not substantial. This is unexpected as we regard LeNet to be the first CNN proposed over twenty years ago.

AlexNet

After LeNet was proposed twenty years after LeNet. AlexNet's network architecture did not alter from LeNet, yet it generated a boom in deep learning. AlexNet stacks a convolution layer and a pooling layer and outputs the result through a fully connected layer. Its architecture does not change greatly from LeNet; however the following discrepencies exist:

- ReLU is the activation function
- A **Local Response Normalization (LRN)** layer is used to normalize local response.
- Dropout is utilized (see *Dropout* section in *Chapter 6: Neural Network Training Techniques*)

As for their network architectures, LeNet and AlexNet are not particularly different from each other. The surrounding environment and computing technology, however, have considerably evolved. Now, everyone may receive a large amount of data, and GPUs that enable enormous parallel processing allow for massive high-speed processes. The development of deep learning was spurred on by large data and GPUs.

In deep learning (a network with many layers), there are numerous parameters. Many calculations are necessary for training, and to satisfy these parameters, a vast number of data is required. These difficulties may be addressed by GPUs and by big data.

Conclusion

We learnt about CNNs in this chapter. In particular, to comprehend them at the technical level, we examined convolution layers and pooling layers (the core modules that form CNNs) with great detail. Most of the CNNs are used to view visual data. Before moving forward, please make sure you understand the material in this chapter.

We learnt the following in this chapter:

- In a CNN, convolution and pooling layers are added to the preceding network, which consists of fully connected layers.

- You can easily construct convolution and pooling layers by using **im2col** (a method for expanding images into arrays).

- Visualization of a CNN allows you to observe how the deeper layer collects complex information.

- LeNet and AlexNet are typical CNNs.

- GPUs and large data play an important role in deep learning research.

CHAPTER 8
Deep Learning

Deep learning is a machine learning process based on deep neural networks. By adding layers to the networks, we have described so far, you may construct a deep network. A deep network, however, presents difficulties. In this chapter, we discuss the features, challenges, and opportunities of deep learning, and give a review of recent deep learning techniques.

Structure

- Making a network deeper
  - Deeper networks
- Enhanced recognition accuracy
- Motivation for a deeper network
- A brief history of deep learning
  - ImageNet
  - VGG
  - GoogLeNet
  - ResNet

- Accelerating deep learning
  - o Overcoming challenges
  - o Acceleration by using GPUs
  - o Distributed training
- Reducing the arithmetic accuracy bit number
- Practical uses of deep learning
  - o Object detection
  - o Segmentation
  - o Image caption generation
- The future of deep learning
  - o Converting image styles
  - o Generating images
  - o Automated driving
  - o Deep Q-Nets (reinforcement learning)

Objective

You will get an understanding about deep learning with various examples.

Making a network deeper

Through this book, we have learnt a lot about neural networks, including different layers which comprise a network of neurons, effective training approaches, CNNs particularly suitable for the processing of images, and parameter optimization. All these are essential deep learning approaches. Hence, we will use the strategies we have learnt to build a deep network. Then we try to use the MNIST dataset for our handwritten digit recognition.

Deeper networks

First, a CNN with the network architecture depicted in *figure 8.1* will be created. It is based on the VGG network, explained in the following part of this network.

As illustrated in *figure 8.1*, the network is deeper than the network we have seen so far. There are tiny 3 x 3 filters in all of the convolution layers. Here, as the network deepens, the number of channels grows larger (as the number of channels in a convolution layer increases from 16 in the first layer to 16, 32, 32, 64, and 64). As you can see, pooling layers are included to gradually decrease the spatial size of mid-term data while dropout layers are used for the latter:

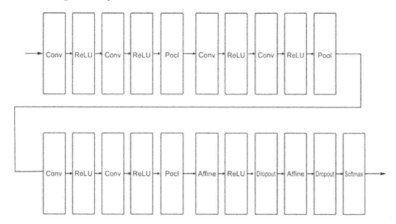

Figure 8.1: *Deep CNN for handwritten digit recognition*

The **He Initializer** is used in this network to initialize weight and Adam to update weight parameters, thereby creating the following characteristics:

- Layers with tiny 3x3 filters
- ReLU for activation function
- A dropout layer following a fully connected layer
- He Initializer optimizes the initial weight values

Thus, the network in Figure 8.1 employs a number of the neural networks techniques that we have studied so far. Let us now employ this for training.

The result reveals that the recognition accuracy is 99.38 percent (final recognition accuracies vary slightly, but this network will generally exceed 99 percent).

The source code for the network implemented in *figure 8.1* is at **chapter08/ DeepConvNetwork.py** while **chapter08/TrainDeepNetwork.py** contains the training code. You may recreate the training that is being carried out here by using this code. It takes time to train in a deep network (probably more than half a day). **chapter08/deep_convnet_params.pkl** in this book provides the trained weight parameters. A function for loading trained parameters is provided by the **DeepConvNetwork.py** source file. It can be used as required.

The error rate of the network in *figure 8.1* is just 0.62 percent. Here we may observe which images were wrongly identified. Examples of recognition errors are shown in *figure 8.2*:

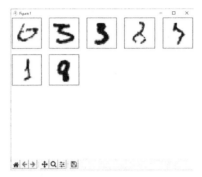

Figure 8.2: *Sample pictures improperly recognized — the top left side of every image shows a right label, while the bottom right side reveals the outcome of this network prediction.*

Even people find these pictures difficult to distinguish. The image on the upper-left corner looks like 0 (when the correct answer is 6) and the next image clearly appears to be 5 (the correct answer is 3). The differences between numbers 1 and 7, 0 and 6, and 3 and 5, are generally difficult. This explains why they were incorrectly identified.

Although this deep CNN is highly accurate, it wrongly recognizes images, just as people do. This demonstrates that a deep CNN has great potential.

Enhanced recognition accuracy

For the **MNIST** dataset, even if the network is not very deep, the highest accuracy may be reached instantly. The representation of the network doesn't have to be extremely high for a relatively easy issue, such as handwritten digit recognition. Thus, it is not very useful to add layers. Addition of layers substantially increases the recognition accuracy in the largescale general object recognition process since it is a complex problem.

We may uncover strategies and recommendations to further improve recognition accuracy via the examination of the specified high-class procedures. We can see, for example that the ensemble learning, learning rate decay and data augmentation help to improve recognition accuracy. The increase in data is a simple but very efficient way to improve recognition accuracy.

Data augmentation utilizes an algorithm to artificially expand images. As illustrated in *figure 8.3*, the images are added by changing a little the input images with rotation or vertical/horizontal movement. This is particularly useful if the data set contains only a minimal number of images:

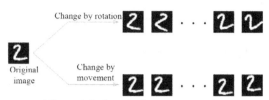

Figure 8.3: Sample data augmentation

For example, part of an image can be cropped out or an image can be reversed horizontally (called flipping, though this is only effective when the symmetry of the image does not need to be considered). Changing the look is also useful for regular images. For example, increasing brightness or scaling up or down. If you are able to utilize data augmentation to increase the quantity of images, you may apply deep learning to improve recognition accuracy. This might appear to be a simple approach, yet outcomes are good. Here we are not going to implement an data augmentation. Please try this for yourself if you are interested, because implementation is easy.

Motivation for a deeper network

Many things are still unknown regarding the importance of making a network deeper. Although theoretical discoveries are not adequate, certain things can be explained from prior study and experimentation (rather intuitively). This section gives some statistics and clarifications supporting the necessity of making a network deeper.

First of all, the outcomes of contests on large-scale image recognition like the **ImageNet Large Scale Visual Recognition Challenge (ILSVRC)** demonstrate the necessity of making the network deeper. They show that many of the current high-ranking techniques are built on deep learning and that the networks tend to be deeper. The deeper the network is, the better the recognition performance.

One of the advantages of this is that the number of parameters in the network can be reduced. When the network is deeper, a similar (or higher) representation with fewer parameters can be achieved. This is simple to grasp when you examine the filter size in a convolution operation. A convolution layer with a 5x5 filter is shown in *figure 8.4*.

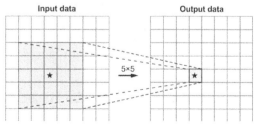

Figure 8.4: Example of a 5x5 convolution operation

Please note that the area of the input data where each node of the output data is calculated in. Of course, the area of the input data in the example illustrated in *figure 8.5* is used to support each node of the output data. Let us now consider a scenario in which operations with 3x3 convolution are twice repeated, as shown in *figure 8.6*. For each node of the output, intermediate data is based on a 3x3 area. So, what area is the 3x3 range of intermediate data of the preceding input data? You will notice that it is based on a five-fold area when you look attentively at *figure 8.5*. The output data of *figure 8.6* thus looks at the 5x5 area of input data for calculation:

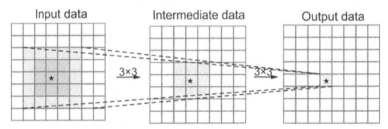

Figure 8.5: *Example where processes are performed twice in 3x3 convolution*

The area of one 5x5 convolution operation is the same as that of two 3x3 convolution operations. The first utilizes 25 parameters (5x5), the second parameter uses 18 parameters (2x3x3). Thus, the number of parameters is reduced by numerous convolution layers. The lower number of parameters is increased as the network becomes deeper. For example, when 3x3 convolution operations are performed three times, there are a total of 27 parameters. A 7x7 filter is required (meaning that up to 49 parameters is necessary) to "*look*" at the same area with a single convolution operation.

By using a tiny filter several times to make a network deeper, we can reduce the number of parameters and expand the receptive field (a local space area that changes neurons). When adding layers, an activation function, like ReLU, is set between convolution layers, which improves network representation. The activation function imparts to the network a "nonlinear" force. More complex formulations are possible through several nonlinear functions.

Efficiency in training is another benefit of a deeper network. A deeper network may quickly conduct training and reduce training data. Intuitive to this, you may remember the explanation presented in the section *Visualizing a CNN* in *Chapter 7: CNN*. You learnt in this section that the convolution layers hierarchically include information from the CNN extract. Neurons react to basic forms such as edges in the first convolution layer. The deeper a layer, the more hierarchically difficult neurons react to shapes, such textures and objects.

Consider the difficulty of recognizing a dog in view of such a hierarchical network structure. In order to resolve this challenge in a superficial grid, convolution layers must at once "understand" a dog's numerous features. There are different dogs and their appearance varies based on the setting in which the image has been taken. Therefore, it takes varying training data and a lot of time in training to grasp the properties of a dog.

However, by making a network deeper, you may split the problems by learning hierarchically. The problem then becomes easier for every layer to learn. The first layer may focus, for example, on learning edges. Therefore, with a minimal quantity of training data, the network can learn efficiently. This is because the quantity of images with edges is bigger than a dog's images, and the edge pattern is simpler than that of a dog.

It is also vital that you may hierarchically transmit information over a deeper network. For example, the layer next to the one which extracted edges can employ edge data, so that more sophisticated patterns can be learned effectively. This explains the significance of making the network deeper. Please note that new approaches and settings such as big data and computing power have given deeper networking in recent years, which allow for proper training in a deep network.

A brief history of deep learning

It has been stated that the **ImageNet Large Scale Visual Recognition Challenge (ILSRVC)**, which took place in 2012, began to attract much attention to deep learning in the competition of large-scale image recognition. In the competition, AlexNet won an overwhelming victory by overturning traditional image recognition techniques. It has always played the leading position in subsequent contests since deep learning began a counterattack in 2012. Here we are going to take a look at the current trend of deep learning surrounding ILSVRC.

ImageNet

ImageNet is a dataset with over 1 million pictures. It comprises of several types of images and each image is connected to a label (class name), as illustrated in *figure 8.6*. Every year, this enormous dataset is used to hold the **ILSVRC**:

The ILSVRC provides some test items, and one of them is *classification* (in the classification division, 1,000 classes are classified to compete in recognition accuracy). The *figure 8.8* shows the results of the winning teams for ILSVRC's classification division since 2010. Here, a classification is regarded as correct if the top 5 predictions contain the correct class. The following bar graph shows the error rates:

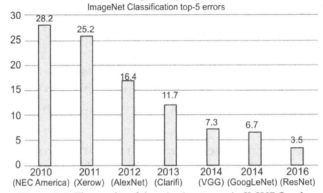

Figure 8.6: *The results of the winning teams in ILSVRC – the vertical axis shows error rates, while the horizontal axis shows years. Team names or technique names are shown in the parentheses on the horizontal axis.*

Please note from the preceding graph that deep learning techniques have always been on top since 2012. Actually, we can see that, in 2012, AlexNet significantly reduced the error rate. Since then, the accuracy of deep learning techniques has steadily improved. This was especially apparent with ResNet in 2015, which was a deep network with more than 150 layers and had reduced the error rate to 3.5 percent. It is even said that this result exceeded the recognition capability of ordinary humans.

VGG, GoogLeNet, and ResNet are some of the most famous deep learning networks that have achieved great results for the past several years. In different places relevant to deep learning, you will find them. We will look the three renowned networks in the next section.

VGG

VGG is a fundamental CNN made out of layers upon layers of pooling. As seen in *figure 8.7*, the weights (convolution layers and fully connected layers) of up to 16 (or 19) layers can be deep and are frequently referred to as "VGG16" or "VGG19", depending on the number of layers:

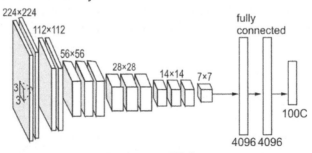

Figure 8.7: *VGG*

VGG has a tiny 3x3 filter, consisting of convolution layers. The two or four successive convolution layers and a pooling layer half the size, as seen in the previous figure, are repeated. The results are finally obtained through fully connected layers.

In the 2014 tournament, VGG received the second prize (GoogLeNet, which is described next, won in 2014). Its efficiency was not as excellent as a first-place network, but many engineers prefer to use a VGG network, as it is highly structurally simple and adaptable.

GoogLeNet

The network architecture of GoogleNet is shown in *figure 8.8*. The rectangles indicate the several layers of convolution and pooling:

Figure 8.8: GoogLeNet

The design of this network appears quite complex, but fundamentally it is the same as a CNN. What makes GoogLeNet special is that the network is not just deep vertically but also horizontally (spread).

GoogLeNet has a horizontal width. It is referred to as *inception architecture* and is based on the structure shown in *figure 8.9*:

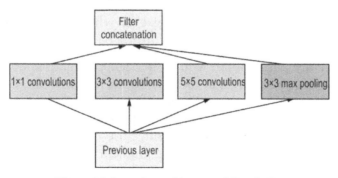

Figure 8.9: Inception architecture of GoogLeNet

As illustrated in *figure 8.11*, several filters of varying sizes (and pooling) are used in the inception architecture and the results combined. The fundamental feature of GoogLeNet is the use of this initial design as a construction piece (component).

GoogLeNet employs 1x1 filter convolution layers in several locations. In order to minimize the number of parameters and expedite the processing, this 1x1 converting procedure reduces the channel directions size.

ResNet

ResNet is a network created by a team at Microsoft. It is marked by a *mechanism* that can make the network deeper.

It is vital to make a network deeper to improve its performance. If the network becomes too deep, however, deep learning fails and the final results typically fail. ResNet proposed a "*skip architecture*" (also called shortcut or bypass) to tackle this problem. The use of this skip architecture can increase speed as the network deepens (though there is a limit to permissible depth).

In order to add the input data to the output, the skipp architecture slips through convolution layers into the data in *figure 8.10*:

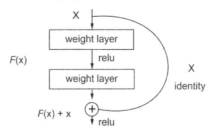

Figure 8.10: Components of ResNet – the "weight layer" here indicates a convolution layer

In *figure 8.12*, the input, x, is linked to the output using two successive layers of convolution. Originally, the output for the two convolution layers is $F(x)$, whereas the skip architecture changes it to $F(x) + x$.

This skip architecture enables quick learning, even when the network is deep. This is because the skip architecture sends signals during backpropagation without decay.

The skip architecture passes input as it is. In backpropagation, the gradients from the higher stream are transferred, as they are, to the lower stream without changing them. Thus you do not have to worry because the gradients with the skip architecture become tiny (or excessively great). You can expect the transmission of meaningful gradients to the front layers. The skip architecture can also be expected to ease a classic gradient problem which is vanishing gradients as the network deepens.

ResNet is built on the VGG network we previously defined, and uses the skip architecture to make the network deeper. The effect of this is seen in *figure 8.11*:

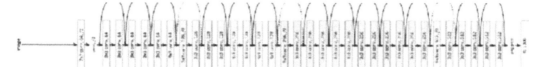

Figure 8.11: *ResNet - 3x3 convolution layers support blocks. The skip architecture that skips layers is its feature.*

As shown in *figure 8.13*, two convolution layers are skipped by ResNet to deepen the network. Even if the network comprises of 150 layers or more, experiments have shown that recognition accuracy continues to increase. At ILSVRC, an astounding 3.5 percent error rate result was attained (the percentage of correct classes that were not included in the top 5 predictions).

Weight data that is trained by the large ImageNet dataset are typically efficiently employed. This is called transfer learning. Part of the weights learnt will be replicated for fine tuning to another neural network. For instance, a network is supplied with the same structure as VGG.

Accelerating deep learning

Big data and big networks need enormous operations for deep learning. CPUs have been utilized till now, but CPUs alone are not enough to handle deep learning. In reality, many deep learning frameworks allow **Graphics Processing Units (GPUs)** to swiftly perform a huge number of operations. Recent frameworks facilitate distributed learning with the use of many GPUs or computers. This section covers accelerating deep learning calculations. Section 8.1 covered our implementation of deep learning. The acceleration (like GPU support) proposed here will not be implemented.

Overcoming challenges

Let us explore what processes require time to deeply learn before considering the acceleration of deep learning. The *figure 8.12* shows the amount of time spent in AlexNet's forward treatment for each class:

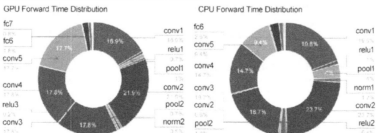

Figure 8.12: *The time each layer takes to execute AlexNet — the chart on the left indicates GPU time, the right displays CPU time.*

Here, **conv** refers to the convolution layer, **pool** refers to the pooling layer, **fc** refers to a fully connected layer, and **norm** refers to the normalization layer.

As you can see, AlexNet spends a good deal of time on convolution layers. In fact, the overall processing time in convolution layers is 95 percent GPU time and 89 percent CPU time! The primary difficulty of deep learning is therefore to execute quick and effective operations in convolution layers. The outcomes of the inference phase are shown in *figure 8.14*, but convolution layers also last a long period throughout the training stage.

In *Chapter 7: CNN*, operations in convolution layers are essentially *multiply-accumulate operations*, as explained in the section *Convolution operations*. Accelerating deep learning therefore depends upon the rapid and efficient calculation of huge multiply-accumulate operations.

Acceleration by using GPUs

Initially, GPUs were just utilized for graphics. They have recently been utilized both for general numerical and graphic computations. Since GPUs can swiftly perform parallel arithmetic operations, GPU computing exploits their enormous capacity for many applications.

Deep learning takes enormous multiply-accumulate operations (or products of large matrices). At such huge parallel processes, GPUs are good, whereas CPUs are good in continuous, complex calculations. In comparison to a single CPU, a GPU is surprisingly used to speed up deep learning processes. The time used by AlexNet to learn between a CPU and a GPU is compared in *figure 8.13*:

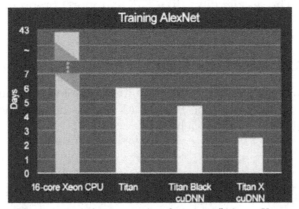

Figure 8.13: *A time comparison between a "16-core Xeon CPU" and a "Titan series" is made between AlexNet and Alex*

It takes almost 40 days for the CPU, and just 6 days for the GPU. We can also observe how the **cuDNN** library, which is optimized for deep learning, is used to speed up further training.

Two companies, NVIDIA and AMD, mostly supply GPUs. Although both their GPUs may be used for ordinary arithmetical calculations, the GPUs of NVIDIA are more familiar with deep learning. Many deep learning frameworks can actually only benefit from the GPUs of NVIDIA. CUDA is an integrated GPU computer development environment supplied by NVIDIA, because it is utilized in the context of deep learning. The **cuDNN**, as shown in *figure 8.15*, is a library running on CUDA in which deep learning functions are implemented optimally.

We utilized **im2col** to transform operations in a convolution layer into products of huge matrices. It is suitable for GPUs to implement this **im2col** technique. Instead of computing tiny batches one-by-one, GPUs are ideal for the calculation of a huge batch. With **im2col,** it is possible to show the true capability of a GPU to calculate the products of massive matrices.

Distributed training

You can speed up deep learning using a GPU, but a deep network has to be trained for several days or weeks. Deep learning, as we have seen so far, requires many trial and error. To establish a good network, you must attempt many trials. Of course, you wish to decrease as much as possible the time needed for training. Then it becomes necessary to scale deep learning or distributed training.

You may wish to distribute them over many GPUs or computers to speed up the calculations necessary for deep learning. Google developed TensorFlow, and the **Computational Network Toolkit of Microsoft (CNTK)**, among others focused on distributed training. Based on low retardation and high-performance networks in large data centers, distributed training through these frameworks has achieved unexpected results.

How much can deep learning be sped up by distributed training? The reply is that the larger the number of GPUs, the quicker the training speed. In reality, 100 GPUs (100 GPUs installed on several computers) is 56 times faster than one GPU.

This implies that, for example, a seven-day course is performed in just three hours and shows the unexpected effect of distributed training.

Contribution of calculations is a particularly tough topic in distributed training. There are several difficulties, such as communication and data syncing across devices that cannot be resolved easily. These tough challenges may be left to frameworks like TensorFlow. The details of the distributed training will not be discussed here.

Reducing the arithmetic accuracy bit number

Memory space and bus bandwidth, as well as computational complexity, can be constraints for deeper learning. A high number of weight and intermediate data parameters have to be stored in memory for memory space. A bottleneck arises when the data that travels over the GPU (or CPU) bus goes above the boundary for bus bandwidth. In these circumstances, you want the bit number of data travelling across the network to be as minimal as possible.

A computer utilizes floating points of 64- or 32-bit numbers to represent real numbers.

With the use of several bits to represent a number, the error effect is reduced, but processing and the consumption of the storage costs is increased, placing a load on the bus bandwidth.

From what we know about numerical accuracy (how many bits are utilized to represent a numerical value), it does not need extremely high accuracy. This is because of its resilience: one of the most significant features of a neural network. The resilience here indicates that the output results in a neural network, for example, do not alter even if there is little noise in the input images. Consider it a minor impact on the output result due to the resilience, even if the data that flows in a network is *deteriorated*.

A computer often employs 32-bit floating-point representations or 64-bit floating-point representations to represent a decimal. Experiments have shown that 16-bit half-precision floating-point representations (half float) are sufficient for deep learning. In fact, Pascal architecture used for NVIDIA GPUs enables the functioning of floating-point values with medium precision. Half-format is believed to be adopted in the future as standard.

NVIDIA's Maxwell generation of GPUs enabled storing of half-precision floating-point numbers (for data maintenance); however it did not perform 16-bit operations. The Pascal architecture of next generation also carries out 16-bit operations. We may assume that processing will only be accelerated by means of half-precision floating-point numbers for computations to around twice that of a pre-generation GPU.

In previous implementation of deep learning, we did not cover numerical precision. Python utilizes floating-point numbers of 64-bit in general. NumPy offers 16-bit half-precision floating-point data type (however, it is used only for storage, not for operations).

We can readily see that using NumPy's half-precise floating-point numbers do not decrease the recognition accuracy. See **chapter08/HalfFloatNetwork.py** if you are interested.

Some research has been undertaken to reduce the bit number in deep learning. In recent research, a technique dubbed a *binarized neural network* represents weight and intermediate data by 1 bit. Less bits are a matter we should keep an eye on, to speedup deep learning. This is particularly essential when considering the use of deep learning for built-in devices.

Practical uses of deep learning

As an illustration of employing deep learning, we mostly covered image classifications, such as handwritten digit recognition, termed as object recognition. However, we may apply deep learning in many more issues beyond object identification. Deep learning is good for various issues, such as image recognition, sound (speech recognition), and the processing of spoken language. This section explains what deep learning can achieve (its applications) in the realm of computer vision.

Object detection

Object detection identifies the positions of objects in images and classifies them. Object detection is harder than object recognition. Object recognition focusses on the full image, while object detection must identify positions of classes in the image (and there may be several objects).

Certain CNN-based methods for object detection have been proposed. They show great performance, showing deep learning is also efficient in object detection. A technique dubbed R-CNN is one of the CNN-based object detection approaches. The R-CNN process flow is shown in *figure 8.14*:

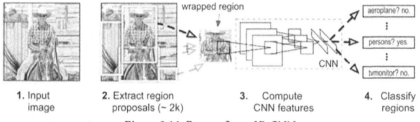

Figure 8.14: *Process flow of R-CNN*

Note "2. Extract region proposals" and "3. Compute CNN features" in *figure 8.16*. The former finds (in some method) those regions that appear to be objects, and then uses a CNN to classify the extracted areas. R-CNN transforms a square picture and utilizes classifying SVM support machines. Its operations are quite sophisticated, but include mostly the processes stated above: extraction of candidate areas and calculation of CNN characteristics.

The "*Extract region proposals*" phase of R-CNN detects applicants for objects and this is where different computer vision methods created may be applied.

Segmentation

In segmentation, images are classified pixel by pixel. It learns through using training data where objects are coloured on a pixel basis, and classifies every input image during inference. Our neural networks so far classify the whole image. So how can we classify it on a pixel basis?

A prediction for each pixel is the easiest way to perform segmentation with a neural network. For example, you may supply a network that categorizes a pixel in the middle of a rectangle region to predict all pixels.

As you can see, it takes as many processes as possible to complete the prediction of all pixels (the problem being that convolution operations re-calculate many areas uselessly). To eliminate such unnecessary calculations the **Fully Convolutional Network (FCN)** has been proposed.

A FCN is a network consisting just of convolution layers. Whilst the average CNN has fully connected layers, the FCN substitutes fully connected layers with convolution layers that perform a similar purpose. The space volume of the intermediate data is processed as nodes in a line in fully connected layers inside a network that is utilized in object recognition. On the other hand, the spacing volume can be maintained during processing till the final output in a network consisting just of convolution layers.

The fundamental feature of a FCN is that near the end, the space size is enlarged. This expansion can enlarge shrunken intermediate data to make it equal to the input image.

The output is linked to all inputs in a fully connected layer. In a convolution layer, you may also build a connection that is the same structure. For example, a fully connected layer with a 32x10x10 input layer (the channel count being 32x10, 10 in height, 10 in breadth) may be substituted by a convolution layer of 32x10x10 filter size. With 100 output nodes in its fully connected layer, 100 of the 32x10x10 filters are supplied to the whole convolution layer. A fully connected layer can therefore be substituted with a convolution layer that conducts equivalent processing.

Image caption generation

Interesting research is being carried out that blends natural language with computer vision. When an image is displayed, the text describing the image (image caption) is automatically produced.

For example, for a photograph of a motorcycle from a dirt bike race, one might insert the caption, "A person riding a motorbike on a dirt road" (this text is automatically generated from the image). The system even *understands* that it is on a dirt road that a person drives a motorbike.

A model known as **Neural Image Caption (NIC)** generates image captions for deep learning. NIC comprises of a deep CNN and a **recurrent neural network (RNN)** for dealing with natural language. RNNs have recursive links and are commonly used for sequential data such as natural language and data in time series.

NIC employs CNN in the extraction and transfer of image features to the RNN. The RNN leverages the features extracted by the CNN to produce a text recursively. The technical specifics here will not be discussed. The basic design of NIC is a simple one that combines two neural networks: a CNN and an RNN. It can produce remarkably accurate image captions.

Multi-modal processing is the processing of different information types, such as images and natural language. In recent years, multi-modal treatment has received much attention.

The R in RNN is *"recurrent"*, which refers to the recurring network architecture of a neural network. The RNN is influenced by information that is created before it. In other words, it recalls previous knowledge because of the recurring design. This is the key feature of an RNN. For instance, after generating the word *I*, it is influenced by the word and the following word *am* is generated. The words *I am* which were created before and which generate the term *sleep* are impacted. The RNN acts as if it recalls past information for continuous data like natural language and time series data.

The future of deep learning

Deep learning is increasingly being employed in several areas including traditional fields. This section explains the opportunities for deep learning and several studies to demonstrate the future of deep learning.

Converting image styles

Research is underway that uses deep learning to draw an image as an artist. In neural networks, a typical application is to build a new image based on two supplied images. One is called a content image, the other a style image. Based on these two images a new image is produced.

In an example, the style of the painting of *Van Gogh* may be specified as the style applied to the content image; a new picture is drawn by deep learning. The publication *A Neural Algorithm of Artistic Style* had this study published and it gained considerable attention throughout the globe as soon as it was released.

In general terms, intermediate data in the network are learned by the technique to approach the intermediate data of the content image. In this way the input image may be transformed to the content image in a comparable form. The notion of a matrix is presented in order to absorb a style from the style image. The input image may be approaching *Van Gogh's* style by training to reduce the gap in the style matrix.

Generating images

Two pictures are needed to produce a new image in the previous example of image style transmission. Some study, on the other hand, sought to produce new images without requiring photographs (the technique trains by using many images beforehand but needs no images to *draw* a new image.) For example, deep learning can be used to construct an image of a bedroom from scratch.

They could seem like actual photographs, but they were produced by a **deep convolutional generative adversarial network (DCGAN)**. The images generated by the DCGAN are images that nobody has ever seen (those that are not included in training data).

If a DCGAN generates genuine photos, it creates a model of the process in which the images were produced. By utilizing numerous images, the model learns (such as those of bedrooms). You may use the model to create new images after completing the training.

Deep learning is used by DCGANs. DCGAN's key aspect is that it employs two neural networks: a generator and a discriminator. The generator creates a true image, whereas the discriminator decides if it is real; that is, whether it was produced by the generator or it was actually photographed. Two networks are therefore taught to make them compete.

The generator learns a more comprehensive technique for producing fake images while the discriminator grows as a precise assessor capable of detecting fake images. Interestingly, both of them evolve through competition in a technology known as the **Generative Adversarial Network (GAN)**. Finally, via competition, the generator can generate images that appear genuine (or may grow even more).

The issues we have encountered so far are termed supervised learning problems. These problems utilize a dataset that comprises pairings of images and labels, for example in handwritten digit recognition. Here, no label data is supplied. There are just photos (sets of images). This is called **unsupervised learning**. Unsupervised learning has been studied for very a long time (deep belief networks and deep Boltzmann machines), but today, it seems, it is not very actively explored. As the use of deep learning techniques, such as DCGANs, is more attractive, unsupervised learning is likely to increase in the future.

Automated driving

Automated driving technology, in which a computer drives an automobile in place of a person, is expected soon to be achieved. In the field of autonomous driving, IT firms, universities, research organizations, and automakers are battling each other. This can only be achieved when different technologies, for example traffic plan technology, and sensor technology, like cameras and lasers, are combined.

It is believed that it is the most significant technology for correctly recognizing an environment. An environment that changes every minute of the day, as well as automobiles and people moving freely, might be very difficult to distinguish.

If the system can recognize the region robustly and reliably, even in different environment, automated driving can be realized in the very near future – a task for which deep learning should be beneficial.

Figure 8.15: *For example, a CNN based network named SegNet can properly detect the road surroundings.*

An example of how to segment a picture with deep learning is the recognition of roads, automobiles, buildings and sidewalks. For input imagery, as illustrated in *figure 8.15*, a segmentation (pixel level evaluation) is done. The result reveals a reasonably accurate distinction between roads, buildings, walkways, trees, automobiles, and motorbikes. In the not-too-distant future, automated driving can be used when deep learning enhances the accuracy and speed of these recognition systems.

Deep Q-Nets (reinforcement learning)

There is a branch of research called reinforcement learning, in which computers learn, for example, how to ride a bike independently through trial and error. This is different from supervised learning, which educates a *supervisor* face-to-face.

The fundamental foundation of reinforcement learning is that an agent picks actions according to the environmental condition and their actions alter the surroundings. The environment provides the agent a certain reward after taking an action. The goal of reinforcement learning is to define the agent's activity so that a higher reward may be obtained, as demonstrated here:

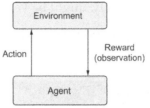

Figure 8.16: *The agent learns autonomously to get a better award – the fundamental foundation for strengthening learning*

Please note that the prize is not indicated as in supervised learning. For example, the exact amount of money you receive by moving Mario on your right is not necessarily obvious in the video game *Super Mario Brothers*. In such a scenario, unambiguous signs like game scores (coins, the enemy's defeat and so on) and game-over logic helps decide the prospective reward. Every activity may be properly assessed by the supervisor for supervised learning.

A **Deep Q-Network (DQN)** is a technique of reinforcement learning that uses deep learning. It is based on the algorithm of reinforcement learning called **Q-learning**. It determines a function termed the optimal action-value function to identify the ideal action. A DQN approximates the function by through deep learning (CNNs).

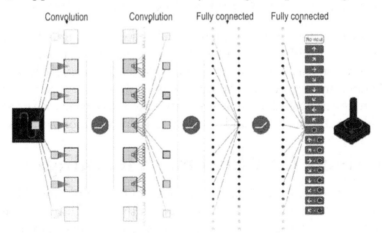

Figure 8.17: *The operations of a video game may be studied with a Deep Q-Network. The network gets the visuals of a video game and learns how to use the gaming controller (joystick).*

Some studies have demonstrated that DQNs can learn video games automatically to attain better success in playing than people. As illustrated in *figure 8.17*, the CNN, when employed in DQN, receives four frames of game images as input and outputs the *value* of a game control movement (the movement of the joystick and the button operation). Traditionally, the state of the game (for example the character placements) was generally extracted and provided by the network when a video game was learned by the network.

In the meanwhile, as illustrated in *figure 8.17*, DQN will only receive video game images as the input data. This is remarkable in a DQN and enhances its applicability greatly. This is because the parameters for every game need not be changed and game images just have to be provided for the DQN. Indeed, a number of DQNs have learned many games that have identical setups and produced greater outcomes than humans (for example, Pac-Man and Atari 2600).

The announcement that the AI named AlphaGo beat a Go champion attracted much attention. AlphaGo also used deep learning and reinforcement learning. It learned from thirty million professional game recordings and repeatedly played against itself to obtain enough information. Google's DeepMind has studied both AlphaGo and DQNs. We should to keep an eye on their work in the future.

Conclusion

In this chapter, we built a deep CNN and received outstanding recognition results of over 99 percent for handwritten digit recognition. The reason for making a network deeper, and the present trend towards deeper networks were also explored. We have also examined the trends and uses of deep learning and the studies on enhancing this technology in the future.

There is still a lot in the subject of deep learning that is unknown, and research is constantly being published. Researchers and engineers across the world continue to aggressively investigate and develop technology that we cannot yet fathom.

This chapter addressed the following points:

- Deepening the network will enhance efficiency for many issues of deep learning.

- Techniques utilizing deep learning are ranked high in image recognition competitions, and contemporary networks are deeper than their predecessors.

- VGG, GoogleNet, and ResNet are well-known networks.

- Deep learning can accelerate GPUs, distributed training, and decrease bit precision.

- For object detection, segmentation, and object recognition, deep learning (neural networks) may be utilized.

- Deep learning applications include generating image captions, generating images and accelerating learning.

Thank you for reading this book. We hope you now have a better grasp on deep learning and found it a fascinating journey.

Index

A

activation function
  defining 39, 40
activation function layer
  implementing 125
AdaGrad 154, 155
Adam technique 155, 156
addition layer
  implementing 123-125
affine layer
  about 130
  implementing 130-132
AlexNet 209
Anaconda distribution 4
AND gate 23, 24

B

backpropagation
  implementing 138
  neural network,
      implementing 139-142
  neural network training, overview 138
  presupposition 138
  used, for training neural network 144
backward propagation
  about 117
  chain rule 115, 116
  example 120, 121
  in addition node 117, 118
  in computational graph 115
  in multiplication node 119, 120
batch-based affine layer 133, 134

batch normalization
  about 166
  advantages 167
  algorithm 166-168
  evaluating 168, 169
batch norm layer 167
batch processing 69-72, 193, 194
bias 25, 26
blobs 207
blocks 192, 193
Boolean 8

C

chain rule 114, 116, 117
classes 10, 11
CNN architecture 184, 185
computational graph
  about 111, 114, 116, 117
  backward propagation, using 115
  need for 113, 114
  using, to solve problems 111, 112
Computational Network Toolkit
    of Microsoft (CNTK) 223
convolutional neural network (CNN)
  about 208
  AlexNet 209
  first layer, visualizing 207, 208
  hierarchical information extraction
      structure, using 208
  implementing 202-206
  LeNet 208, 209
  visualizing 207
convolution layer
  about 185
  implementing 195, 198-200
  with Affine 185, 186

convolution operation
  about 186
  performing, on three-dimensional
      data 190, 191
cross-entropy error 79, 80

D

data
  training 76, 77
data-driven 74-76
data learning 74
deep convolutional
      generative adversarial
      network (DCGAN) 228
deep learning
  accelerating 221
  acceleration, with GPU 222
  arithmetic accuracy bit number,
      reducing 223, 224
  challenges, overcoming 221, 222
  distributed training 223
  GoogleNet 219
  history 217
  ImageNet 217, 218
  ResNet 220, 221
  VGG 218
deep learning, future
  about 227
  automated driving 228, 229
  Deep Q-Nets 229-231
  images, generating 228
  image styles, converting 227
deep learning, usage
  about 225
  image caption generation 226, 227
  object detection 225
  segmentation 225, 226

deep network
  about 212-214
  building 212
  importance 215-217
Deep Q-Nets 229, 231
Deep Q-Network (DQN) 230
derivative 85-87
dictionaries 7
digit recognition 64
dropout 173-176

E
enhanced recognition accuracy 214, 215

F
for statement 9
four-dimensional array
  about 196
  by im2col 196-198
Fully Convolutional
    Network (FCN) 226
function 9

G
Generative Adversarial
    Network (GAN) 228
GoogleNet 219
gradient
  about 91, 92
  for neural network 96-98
gradient check 142, 143
gradient inspection 142
gradient method 93-96

H
He Initializer 213
HelloWorld.py file
  saving 10

hidden layers of activation
  distribution 159-163
hyperparameters
  optimization, implementing 178-180
  optimizing 177, 178
  validating 176
  validation data 176, 177

I
if statement 8, 9
ImageNet 217, 218
ImageNet Large Scale
    Visual Recognition
    Challenge (ILSVRC) 215, 217
initial weight values
  about 158
  for ReLU 164
  setting, to zero 158, 159

L
learning rate decay approach 154
LeNet 208, 209
linear 29
lists 6, 7
local calculation 112, 113
Local Response
    Normalization (LRN) 209
logic circuits
  about 23
  AND gate 23, 24
  bias 25, 26
  implementing, with bias 26, 27
  implementing, with weights 26, 27
  NAND gate 24
  OR gate 24
  perceptron, limitations 27
  weights 25, 26
  XOR gate 27, 28

loss function 74, 77

M

mathematical operations
  about 5
  data types 5
Matplotlib
  about 16
  graph, implementing 16, 17
  images, displaying 18, 19
  pyplot features 17
matrix multiplication 48-51
mini-batch learning 80-82
  cross-entropy
      error, implementing 82, 83
  loss function, configuring 83-85
mini-batch training
  implementing 103-105
MNIST 64
MNIST dataset
  about 64-67
  using, to compare
      update techniques 157, 158
  using, to compare
      weight initializers 165, 166
Momentum 152, 153
multidimensional array
  about 47, 48
  calculating 47
multilayer perceptron
  about 29
  computer, creating
      from NAND gate 32, 33
  gates, combination 30
  XOR gate, implementing 31, 32
multiplication layer
  implementing 121-123

N

NAND gate 24
Neural Image Caption (NIC) 226
neural network
  example 36, 37
  inference 67-69
neural network layers
  implementing 53
  signal transmission, in layer 54-57
  symbols, examining 53
neural network matrix multiplication 52
neural network propagation 64
neural system
  from perceptron 36
nonlinear 29
nonlinear function 45, 46
numerical differentiation
  about 85
  derivative 85-87
  examples 87-89
NumPy
  about 12
  array number, creating 12
  broadcasting 14
  elements, accessing 15, 16
  importing 12
  mathematical operations 12, 13
  N-dimensional array 13, 14

O

OR gate 24
output layer
  activation function 57-59
  design 59
overfitting 170-172

P

padding 188

parameters

  updating 148

partial derivative 89-91

perceptron

  about 22

  implementing 25

  limitations 27

  reviewing 37, 38

  to neural system 36

pooling layer

  about 194

  characteristics 195

  implementing 195, 200-202

processing 186, 187

Python

  about 2, 3

  external libraries 3

  setting up 3

  version 3

Python interpreter 4

Python script files 10

Q

Q-learning 230

R

Rectified Linear Unit (ReLU) 46

recurrent neural network (RNN) 226

regularization 170

ReLU function

  about 46, 47

  multidimensional array, calculating 47

ReLU layer 125-127

ResNet 220, 221

S

sigmoid function

  about 40, 41, 127

  implementing 43-45

  step function graph 42

  step function, implementing 41, 42

sigmoid layer 127-130

simple layer

  implementing 121

softmax identity feature

  about 59, 60

  characteristics 62-64

softmax identity function

  about 59, 60

  implementation issues 61, 62

softmax layer

  implementing 130-132

softmax loss layer 135-138

step function 40

stochastic descent gradient (SGD)

  about 148-150

  disadvantage 150-152

stride 188-190

T

test data

  training 76, 77

  using, for evaluation 105-108

three-dimensional data

  convolution

    operation, performing 190, 191

total squared errors 78, 79

training algorithm

  implementing 99

  presupposition 99

transfer learning 221

two-layer neural network
  as class 99-103

U
unsupervised learning 228

V
vanishing gradients 161
variables 6
VGG 218

W
weight decay 172, 173
weights 25, 26

X
XOR gate 27, 28

Made in United States
North Haven, CT
22 November 2021

11412799R00141